Indo-Nepalese Socio-Cultural Dimension

About the Author

K.K. Muktan, a retired bureaucrat turned author, was born and brought up in Assam, the North East Region of India in 1931. After graduating from St. Anthony's College, Shillong in 1953 he did his M.A. in Economics from the Allahabad University and joined Assam Civil Service (ACS) in 1960. On bifurcation of Meghalaya from Assam Mr. Muktan was absorbed in the Meghalaya Civil Service (MCS) in 1975. He acted in the capacity of District Sessions Judge and the Head of various development departments of the Government of Meghalaya and is now settled in Shillong after retirement.

Having been closely associated with the activities of social upliftment throughout his service life, Mr. Muktan is deeply interested in the dynamics of Indian society. As Advisor of the Meghalaya Pensioners' Association he has been serving the cause of retired pensioners and the aged people. Mr. Muktan has to his credit a number of books like—*The Legendary Gorkhas*, *Planning for Retirement*, *The Gorkhas in the Freedom Struggle of India* and many articles.

Indo-Nepalese Socio-Cultural Dimension

K.K. Muktan

CONCEPT PUBLISHING COMPANY PVT. LTD.
NEW DELHI-110059

ISBN-13: 978-93-86682-32-1

Edition : 2018

Published and Printed by

Concept Since 1974

Concept Publishing Company Pvt. Ltd.
A/15-16, Commercial Block, Mohan Garden
New Delhi-110059 (India)
T: 25351460, 25351794, *F*: 091-11-25357109
E: publishing@conceptpub.com, W: www.conceptpub.com

Cataloging in Publication Data—Courtesy: D.K. Agencies (P) Ltd. <docinfo@dkagencies.com>

Muktan, K.K., author.
Indo-Nepalese socio-cultural dimension / K.K. Muktan.
pages cm
Includes bibliographical references and index.
ISBN 9789386682321

1. Nepal—Relations—India. 2. India—Relations—Nepal. I. Title.

LCC DS494.8.I4M85 2018 DDC 303.4825496054 23

Dedicated

To

My Wife

in Her

Loving Memory

Foreword

I first met Mr. K.K. Muktan, former Administrator of the Assam/ Meghalaya State Civil Service Cadre, some two decades back at Shillong where I was teaching sociology in the local North Eastern Hill University (NEHU). He was an unassuming, mild and soft spoken gentleman and a father of three well groomed and talented children, who invariably came at the top in Masters degrees in their respective disciplines. His youngest daughter, who was a brilliant student of mine is now teaching sociology in the North Eastern Hill University. Mr. Muktan was working on a manuscript on the Gorkha soldiers in the Indian Army and their supreme sacrifice of lives in defending the Indian borders and their critical roles in keeping peace and order in the country. Very soon, he came out with a handsome publication—*The Legendary Gorkhas* in 2002. One after noon, he knocked at my office door and walked in, to present a copy of the book which I found quite interesting, a book with materials of considerable values on military history of India. Earlier on 20-22 March, 2001 the Department of Sociology, NEHU had organized an International seminar on "The Nepalis in North-East" which was attended by a group of eminent scholars from Nepal including many faculties from the Universities and Colleges of the North-East. Mr. Muktan was also invited to participate in it, which he did excellently by presenting a paper on "Gorkha's Contribution towards Internal and External Defence of India." All these brought me closer to Mr. Muktan and I came to know more about him. I learnt that his grand father had migrated to India from Nepal in 1892 and got settled in Sonitpur district of Assam. While studying in school, young Muktan was attracted to Indian freedom struggle and he actively participated during 1942 Freedom Movement. As a result of this he had to suffer break in his studies for some time. He graduated from Shillong, St. Anthony's College in 1952; then got Master's degree in Economics from the University of Allahabad and joined Assam State Civil Service in 1960. After his retirement from service he began, perhaps, a more constructive and fruitful role of a friend, philosopher, and guide to the superannuated Government personnel as the Secretary of the Meghalaya Pensioners Association. And for them too, he came out with a very useful book entitled, *Planning for Retirement: A Guide to Senior Citizens,* which was released in August, 2009 by the then Chief Secretary, Government of Meghalaya. I understand that Mr. Muktan is associated with various socio-cultural activities and keeps himself busy writing articles for magazines and newspapers, scripts for All India Radio and advising, guiding and helping the senior citizens and the pensioners.

He is well conversant with the socio-economic dynamics of the North-east and the identity problems of the Indian Nepalis living in India and is deeply interested for the welfare of the Nepali community. He appeared to me rather concerned on the indifference and ignorance of a large many Indians about the close commonality of history and culture between India and Nepal. That concern of his led him to pen down yet another book entitled—*Indo-Nepal Socio-cultural Dimension*, an interesting work on the socio-cultural fusion between India and Nepal. This book is a timely cautioning the people of both the countries not to fritter away their common culture and heritage through short-sightedness, selfish motives and sterile one-upmanship. Mr. Muktan's style of writing is lucid, easy, and straight to the point.

In this book Mr. Muktan has attempted to trace out the ethnographic history of Nepal beginning from the Kiratas, the earliest known tribe to settle in Nepal. The Kiratas who are variously called by historians as Paleo-Mongoloid, Proto-Mongoloid or Indo-Mongoloid were the people of North East India, who migrated to the hills of sub-Himalayan countries like Nepal, Sikkim, Bhutan etc. as the comparatively more powerful Aryans dispossessed their habitats. Diving deep into the antiquity and heritage of Nepal Mr. Muktan believes that Nepal was peopled since not less than ten thousand years ago. The Neolithic tools discovered by Archaeologists from Kathmandu valley reveal that

Nepal was inhabited by people at least nine thousand years before. Like India Nepal also received settlers of various racial affiliations from the north and the south in the dim past and continued to do so till the advent of fourteenth century AD. From the north came the people of Tibeto-Burman linguistic group while from the south entered more dominant races like the Kiratas, Lichchhavis, Thakuris and the Rajputs. These new comers from India who were advanced in knowledge, culture and religion vanquished the local tribal chiefs and established their sway over Nepal. They not only ruled over them, but also initiated them into Hindu religion, culture and Vedic social system. Over the centuries of continuous rule in Nepal by various Hindu dynasties the history of Nepal turned to be a spectacular account of inter-mixture and assimilation of multiple races, cultures, religions and languages which have close affinities with those of India in the minutest details. In this book Mr. Muktan has made a comprehensive re-appraisal of the socio-cultural unities and uniformities that exist between India and Nepal and has called upon the peoples of the two countries to know their antiquity, heritage and identity which would go a long way to bring them closer to each other more than ever before.

I have enjoyed reading this book and I recommend to anybody, who has interest in the welfare of the nation and wants to know about Nepalis' place in the Indian cultural commonwealth, to read this book in particular and author's other publications in general. The political leaders of India and Nepal would be especially benefited by this book to boost up their bi-lateral ties under the current global political scenario.

Vasant Kunj
New Delhi

Prof. A.C. Sinha
Formerly Dean, School of Social Science
North Eastern Hill University, Shillong

Preface

This book is an attempt at the critical appraisal of the origin and history of the peoples of the two ancient countries of India and Nepal and focussing on the socio-cultural and ethnic affinities between the two peoples. The two great rivers of India and Nepal, *viz.*, Ganga and the Gandaki rise from two different points of the same Himalayan ranges and merge with each other after traversing a great length through their respective countries symbolizing the merger of two great cultures and civilizations of India and Nepal that flourished side by side in the Gangetic valley of India and the Gandaki basin of Nepal. History bears testimony to the human civilizations that grew up and flourished around river basins in the dim past, such as, the Indus Valley Civilization of Harappa and Mahenjodaro, the Sumerian Civilization in the lower valley of Euphrates and Tigris, and the Nile Valley Civilization of Egypt. In the similar process, the fertile Gangetic valley, once happened to be a centre of Aryan civilization, historically known as the *Mahajanapada* where the Vedic culture developed to its highest glory. It was this holy land of *Mahajanapada* where the seeds of great religions like Jainism and Buddhism were first sown, grown up and propagated by Lord Mahavira and Gautama Buddha. It was on the banks of the river Ganga where the ancient *Rishis* composed the holy Vedas and chanted the Vedic hymns. It was again in this Gangetic basin that the indigenous knowledge of arts, science, medicine, architecture, astrology, astronomy etc. were born and developed by eminent scientists like Aryabhatta, Varahamihira, Brahmagupta, Charaka etc.

On the other hand, the river basin of Gandaki happened to be the earliest seat of Nepalese culture and civilization. In ancient time, the kingdom of Nepal was a small country confined within the territory between river Gandaki and Tambakosi while Kathmandu, the capital, was but a lake where the first whisper of human civilization began after its water was drained out along the river Bagmati by a Saint named Manjushri (legend). During 7th century AD when Hiuen Tsang visited Nepal her size was approximately 800 miles in circumference which means that the area was smaller by two-thirds of present area. According to the map of Nepal projected by D.R. Regmi, the boundary of Nepal during eighth century was confined between the river Burhi Gandaki in the west and the Tambakosi in the east.[1] Therefore, the river Gandaki with its seven tributaries collectively known as the *Sapta-Gandaki* was the lifeline of the ancient people of Nepal where the first Nepalese civilization had begun, grown-up and sustained.

The bracing climate and somewhat flat topographic condition of the place gradually attracted other settlers from the north and the south ever since and before the Christian era. From the north came the Mongolians of Tibeto-Burman linguistic group while from the south migrated the Kiratas and the more dominant and culturally advanced Aryans, Dravidians and Indo-Mongoloid races. For centuries continuous batches of people from the north and the south were finding their ways into Nepal settling down side by side meeting and mixing together for generations, at times fighting each other, at another, living peacefully and mixing their cultures and languages that paved the way for building up of a new Nepali nation. The Kiratas who are variously called by historians as Indo-Mongoloids, Palaeo-Mongoloids or Proto-Mongoloids were the first historically known people to enter Nepal from the north-eastern frontiers of India. It is possible, said D.R. Regmi, that at the very earliest time the Kathmandu valley was the settlement of the people closely resembling the Astro-Asiatics and the Kol, Bhils.[2] A few centuries thereafter, the Kiratas were followed by many other more advanced Hinduised people from India called the Lichchavis, Thakuris, Mallas and Shahas one after another. They vanquished

1. D.R. Regmi, *Ancient Nepal,* Calcutta, 1969.
2. *Ibid.*, p. 35.

or subdued the ruling chieftains, established and extended their own dominions over various parts of Nepal and ruled there. Jayadeva, the first king of the Lichchavis left his kingdom at Vaisali (Present Patna) and entered Nepal with his troups in the third quarter of the second century having been forced by the Kushan Emperor. The Thakuris represent the Kshatriyas from Rajputana, of India. Amsuvarma the king of the Thakuris is believed to have been crowned as Regent in Nepal in 606 A.D. The Harigaon inscription recorded by Amsuvarma gives details about his reign. The kings belonging to various dynasties brought with them Hindu religion and initiated the local people into their religion and culture and propagated the Vedic social system in Nepal. The geographical proximity too helped Indian missionaries to reach out to Nepal with their culture and religion. The advent of Hindu Rajputs in Nepal during 14th century A.D. and the rise in power of the Shah dynasty finally heralded an era of consolidation and perpetuation of Brahminism in Nepal. The unification of greater Nepal by the Gorkha king Prithvinarayan Shah in 1769 A.D. and thereafter, the continuous regime of the Rana dynasty for more than one and a half centuries put Nepal on the solid foundation of "only Hindu kingdom in the world". The original religion of Buddhism continued to co-exist, though as minority. With the assimilation of the Nepalese people with Indian immigrants, Nepal came to be like a miniature India with common history, culture, religion, language and even ethnic composition.

While that was the real history commonly shared by India and Nepal in the past and present, unfortunately today, the people of the two countries are, blissfully unaware of the historical fact that they were the descendants of the same ancestors. They seem to have totally forgotten the past, nor there is any effort to impart this knowledge to their school children. We find that the map of Nepal is invariably superimposed on the top of India's map as though it is a part of India, but the Indian geography does not speak a word about Nepal. A host of Nepal's rivers like the Kosi, Gandaki, Kali and Bagmati are the lifelines of the people of Uttar Pradesh and Bihar but Indian geography does not mention a word about these rivers. The history of India and Nepal are so closely interlinked with each other, but our Indian history does not make even a fleeting reference to Nepalese history and its people. Of late, some Indian universities like the North Bengal University, Jawaharlal Nehru University, North Eastern Hill University etc. have begun to evince interest in Himalayan Studies, nevertheless much remains to be focussed in this direction, especially in the domain of the close unity and uniformity between the two countries in respect of their culture, religion, language, literature, art and architecture and of course about the history.

Intentionally, this book is aimed at generating interest among the scholars as well as general readers about the history, origin and development of Nepalese ethnicity, language and culture and their close relations with those of Indians. The purpose is to trace out the ethnographic history of Nepal and to make a comprehensive re-appraisal of the socio-cultural affinities between the two neighbouring peoples of India and Nepal in respect of their language, literature, art, culture and religion, and thereby to bring the two peoples closer to each other. Jawaharlal Nehru said that "a close understanding of life and culture of two countries always yield a positive results and produce harmony, balance and richness in life". It will be my greatest pleasure if this work succeeds a wee bit in creating an awareness of the deep commonality of life and culture between the two peoples and can "produce harmony, balance and richness" between them for their common good.

Shillong (Meghalaya) **K.K. Muktan**
10th December, 2016

Acknowledgements

During the course of writing and publishing this book I had the privilege of receiving material, intellectual and moral feedbacks from a number of notaries, academics, friends and relatives and now I feel it my pleasant duty to express my gratitude to them.

I am deeply grateful to Prof. A.C. Sinha (Retd.), Department of Sociology, North Eastern Hill University who was so generous to go through this manuscript and write the Foreword of this book. He has always been a source of inspiration and guidance to me and whenever I approached him for any help he ungrudgingly shared his valuable views and suggestions. He obliged me greatly with his matured guidance.

I owe an enormous debt to Prof. Tanka B. Subba, Reader and Head of the Department of Anthropology, North Eastern Hill University, Shillong, with whom I had the liberty of meeting and interacting on wide parameters of topics. His deep perceptions into subjects matters and erudite opinions have definitely added up significant weight to my present book.

No less obliged do I feel to my *Gurudev*, late B.L. Upadhyaya, Ex-M.L.A. of Tezpur who evinced keen interest on my work and was never tired of inspiring and counselling me when he was still alive. As the President of the Assam Gorkha Sammelan, he provided me with important materials concerning activities of the Gorkha Sammelon, which greatly enriched my present book. It really meant so much to me that the amount of indebtedness I owe to him will never be repaid.

As I write this note of acknowledgement, I miss deeply my dear wife whose watchful company and timely help when occasioned, accounted so much for me that now I believe, the process of writing of this book would not have been so smooth and easy had she not been by my side during the past five years of writing this book. May her soul rest in peace.

I want to thank my daughter, Dr. Rekha Muktan Shangpliang, Assistant Professor, Department of Sociology, North Eastern Hill University who helped me with library books and relevant materials for this book. She also helped me a lot in taking care of many other necessities of my daily life at home.

I would also like to thank many other friends and relatives who were directly or indirectly involved at various stages of getting this book done, whose names cannot be mentioned here individually for want of space. I thank them collectively.

Last but not least, I express my deep gratitude to Mr. Ashok Kumar Mittal, Managing Director of Concept Publishing Company Pvt. Ltd., New Delhi, who readily agreed to take-up the work of printing and publishing of this work, without which this book would not have seen the light of the day.

Shillong (Meghalaya) **K.K. Muktan**
10th December, 2016

Contents

Introduction

India and Nepal are two ancient countries with common history and ethno-cultural heritage. Both the countries are characterized by natural and geographical diversities, multiplicity of races, religions and languages, and marked by political vicissitudes. India is a largest democracy in the world with 1.2 billion population and an area bigger than France, Italy and Spain put together. Pitted with this enormous size of India, Nepal compares a tiny mound that accounts for less than one-twentieth fraction of India's total geographical area. Far more remarkable than its geographical vastness are the enigmatic natural features with diverse altitude, rainfall, climate, soil condition and flora and fauna. The map of Indian sub-continent invariably contains, on its top, the map of Nepal in bold dotted lines which looks like an insignia tucked on the shoulder flap of a soldier.

In India despite the bewildering heterogeneity of ethnicity, culture, religion and the geophysical conditions mentioned above, there exists a deep underlying unity which has kept the Indian people together as one nation over the ages. This unity in diversity may escape the notice of common man but certainly not of the scholars like Herbert Risley, G.A. Grierson, Brian Hodgson and other Ethno-historians who have deeper insight into the Indian civilization, antiquity and history. Herbert Risley wrote—"Beneath the manifold diversity of physical and social type, language, custom and religion which strike the observer in India, there can still be discerned a certain underlying uniformity of life from the Himalayas to Cap Comorin". This unity in diversity has for ever endured in the great country of India inspiring a feeling of Indianness, a sense of oneness and vastness synonymous with the vast surface of the ocean.

Coming to Nepal, we can see similar diversities in a wide parameters of ethnicity, culture, language and religion, despite the country being small in size. Its antiquity and heritage are as old as the human civilization itself. Archaeological evidences show that Nepal was peopled since more than ten thousand years ago. Dr. Anotoly Shetenko, Russian Archaeologist who carried out archaeological studies in Nepal, in his book *Dynasty of Nepal* mentioned that the stone weapons, artifacts etc. that date back to Stone-age (30,000 BC) found in Kathmandu were the same as those found in Gobi of Mangolia, Asia and America. The Neolithic tools found in Kathmandu reveal that the Himalayan region was inhabited by people at least nine thousand years ago. The earliest record about Nepal can be traced from the *Arthashastra* of Kautilya written as back as third century B.C. The *Skanda Purana* speaks highly of the temples and shrines of Nepal and their sanctity and holiness. Nepal's ancient art and architecture are still visible in the temples, shrines and buildings around Kathmandu, Bhatgoan and Lalitpur which are incredibly glorious.

Like India, Nepal also received foreign settlers of various racial affiliations from the north and the south ever since the dim past and till the advent of 14th century AD. From the north came the people of Tibeto-Burman linguistic group who crossed over the high Himalayas through mountain passes called Kuti, Hatia, Kerong, Mustang, etc.; while from the south entered more dominant races like the Kiratas, Lichchavis, Thakurs, Mallas, Shahs and Rajputs. Historians believe that long before these people migrated to Nepal from the north and the south there were aboriginal tribes residing in the country who belonged to Mongolian race. Describing about these aborigines, Brian Hodgson writes—"The physiognomy exhibits generally and normally the Scythic or Mongolian type of humankind, but the type is often much softened and modified and even frequently passes into a near approach to the full Caucasian dignity of head and face."[1]

Finding these aborigines of Nepal "broken and depressed" and easily tractable, and the country of Nepal beautiful with bracing climate, hordes of alien people came to Nepal batch by batch consistently over a period of time stretching several centuries. These newcomers from northern India who were advanced in knowledge, culture and religion, easily vanquished the ruling chiefs in Nepal and founded their new kingdoms. They not only ruled over the people of the new found country, but also gradually initiated them into their own religion. They brought them under the fold of Hinduism and the elaborate Vedic social system. The proximity to Nepal and its 800 km. long open border helped Hindu priests and preachers of India to enter Nepal freely and preach Hinduism and Indian culture. Nepalese history tells us that during the reign of king Rudradeva (635-656 AD) one Sankaracharya, a bigoted Hindu preacher, visited Nepal under whose instigation the king of Nepal persecuted the Buddhist monks, destroyed Buddhist monasteries and burned down Buddhist libraries.[2] Under the royal patronage of the ruling Hindu dynasties, Indian art, culture, religion and architecture continually found their ways into the Sub-Himalayan country, which in course of centuries developed into a typical orthodox Hindu kingdom. The history of Nepal is, essentially an account of the assimilation of two peoples who lived side-by-side meeting and mixing-up their cultures, traditions and languages for centuries. India and Nepal, thus share a common history and heritage which are so intricately woven-up each other that it is difficult to comprehend the one without understanding the other.

Looking from this angle Nepal may be perceived as a miniature India with its wonderful blend of variegated ethno-cultural traits, legends and faiths with those of India. If India is, as stated by Radha Kumud Mookerjee, "a museum of cults and customs, creeds and cultures, faith and tongue, racial types and social systems", then Nepal is verily the confluence of them all. Both India and Nepal have inherited from the past common system and forms of art, culture, literature, philosophy, metaphysics, astronomy, astrology and medicine. The people of both the countries have been influenced by the same *Vedas*, *Upanishads* and *Puranas* which have permeated deep down into their socio-religious psyche. The great Epics of *Ramayana* and *Mahabharata* are held in highest esteem in both the countries. Great Prophets like Buddha and Mahavira, and the mighty kings like Ashoka and Vikramaditya belong to Nepal as much as to India. This being the kind of relationship between India and Nepal from the ancient times till to day, it is imperative for every citizen of India and Nepal to know the history of one another's country.

This book is an attempt at tracing out the chain of unities and uniformities underlying between the two countries, in respect of their ethnicity, language, customs, faith and traditions and to underscore the need of understanding this unique bond by the peoples of both the countries for a better relationship between the two countries in the days to come. This book is written to unravel the greatest truth that the peoples living in India and Nepal are no other than the descendants of the same ancestors who belonged to different human races, anthropological stocks and linguistic groups.

Chapter 1 of this book endeavours to focus on how India and Nepal, ever since time immemorial, have been sharing a common history, culture and tradition. This relationship between the two countries is so close that the course of history of one country is profoundly influenced by that of the other and that both of them trail behind them an heritage so intimately interlinked with each other that it is well nigh impossible to comprehend one without understanding the other.

Nepal, like India, is a land of unity in diversity. She is a multi-ethnic, multi-lingual and multi-cultural country. She has, more or less, sixty different ethnic groups with distinct dialects of their own. Racially the people of Nepal can be divided into two broad divisions, *viz.*, the Caucasoids and the Mongoloids. Linguistically the Caucasoids speak Indo-Aryan language or the Nepali, while the Mongoloids are the speakers of Tibeto-Burman group of tongue that comprise a great many of dialects not intelligible to each other. The Caucasoid, for that matter the Indo-Aryans people, profess Hinduism and they are governed by the Vedic system of orthodox social order with elaborate and rigid caste system. The Mongoloid group of people, on the other hand, are by and large Buddhists, socially more egalitarian and do not recognize caste hierarchy.

According to a Census report, there are thirty odd languages spoken in Nepal of which fourteen are Indo-Aryan, fourteen Tibeto-Burman and one each of Munda and Dravidian origin. Apart from this bewildering diversities of ethnicity, language, religion and culture, Nepal is also unique in its geographical varieties like, climate, topography, soil, vegetation, flora and fauna etc. As regards the surface elevation, her northern frontiers as demarcated by the Himalayan ranges stretching from east to west, is in a sharp contrast with the low lying Terai areas which form the southern boundary of Nepal. Corresponding to this difference in topography and altitude there is a marked variance in the climatic conditions between the Himalayan region and the plains region below. These geographical variations have greatly influenced the entire system of economy, production, industry, animal husbandry and the ways of living of the people of Nepal. Despite the wide dissimilarity of ethnicity, culture, language and the people's ways of livelihood, there exists a deep underlying unity in Nepal which has served as an endearing factor and kept the people of the country together, as one body, one nation and one country. They speak one Nepali language, bear allegiance to one constitution and feel proud of the country's sovereignty.

Chapter 2 of this book introduces to the readers two important rivers of India and Nepal, *viz*. the Ganga and the Gandaki, which represent the two ancient civilizations of the two great countries. Over the centuries they have watered and nurtured the two cultures side by side and helped them prosper to the highest glory and eventually, mixed-up each other's water into one great river, symbolizing the merger together of two cultures. The Ganga and Gandaki, two major rivers of India and Nepal, take their rise from the same Himalayan ranges like two sisters of same mother, traverse a long way through their respective countries and eventually merge into each other near a place called Bhagalpur of Bihar. Natural rivers like the water courses play a significant role in the growth and development of trade and commerce between countries and influence the life and culture of people. History bears testimony to a great many of human civilizations which grew-up and flourished around the river valleys in the past. The Indus Valley civilization of Harappa, the Sumerian civilization of Mesopotamia, and the Nile valley civilization of Egypt were all situated on the banks of rivers. The fertile Gangetic valley of the north-east India, like the historic Tigris and Euphrates basins of the Middle east flourished to the highest glory in ancient times by the name of *Mahajanapada*. The *Mahajanapada* included sixteen independent and powerful kingdoms which covered the whole territory of the north-India comprising the present Uttar Pradesh, Jharkhand, Bihar, Madhya Pradesh, part of Orissa, and northern Bengal. The Gangetic valley was the centre of Aryan civilization where the Vedic culture had developed together with art, science and literature. It was on the bank of river Ganga where the famous capital of Emperor Chandragupta Maurya known as Pataliputra was situated. It was again in this Gangetic basin that the indigenous knowledge of arts, science, architecture, astronomy, astrology, and medicine were born, cultured and developed by Indian scientists like Aryabhatta, Varahamihira, Brahmagupta, Charaka etc. In ancient times Indian art, literature, religion and Vedic culture developed and flourished not only within the country, but they travelled all the way to south east Asia, Ceylon and Nepal and greatly influenced them.

The Ganga is considered by the Hindus as a sacred river, and its water as the purifier of all sins. According to mythological account, the river Ganga was created by Brahma by collecting the sweat from the feet of God Visnu. The Epic of *Ramayana* contains an interesting story about the origin and significance of the river Ganga which has been described in detail in this Chapter.

While on the other hand, the river Gandaki of Nepal, ever since ancient times, had been the life-line of Nepalese people whose civilization grew up around the basin of Gandaki. The river Gandaki with its seven tributaries takes the name of *Sapta-Gandaki* and like the famous *Sapta-Sindhu* civilization of India, it washes the broad hilly basin of Nepal immensely contributing to the prosperity of the people living around it. In ancient times the kingdom of Nepal was a small country confined within the territory between river Gandaki in the west and river Tambakosi in the east and Kathmandu, its capital, was but a lake where the first Nepalese civilization sprang up after its water was drained out by a Buddhist Saint named Manjushri.[3]

The Indo-Gangetic civilization developed along the banks of Ganga ever since the Epic age when the Aryan expansion and colonization shifted from Punjab to the land lying between the river Saraswati and the Ganga. The rivers contribute immensely to the growth and development of the life and culture of people. The rivers flow down and traverse through one country to another they help meeting and mixing of different peoples and their cultures. In the Gangetic valley there established as many as sixteen independent kingdoms known as *Mahajanapadas* of which the most powerful were Avanti, Kosala, Vatsya and Magadha. These *Mahajanapadas* roughly covered the whole landmass of present north India comprising Uttar Pradesh, Jharkhand, Bihar, Madhya Pradesh, part of Orissa and northern Bengal. The Gangetic valley was the centre of Aryan culture and civilization where the Rishis (seers) composed *Vedas* and the great religious movements like Jainism and Buddhism were propagated by Mahavira and Gautama Buddha. All the ancient and medieval Hindu temples which still exist as important centers of pilgrimage like the Viswanath temple of Benaras, Baidyanath temple of Deoghar, the Sun temple of Konark, Orissa, Badrinarayan temple and Kedarnath temple of Uttarakhand etc. are located within the Gangetic basin. It was again this Gangetic valley where indigenous knowledge of arts, science, astronomy, astrology, medicine were born, and developed by eminent Indian scientists like Aryabhatta, Varahamihira, Brahmagupta, Charaka etc.

India had a long cultural and commercial intercourse with western Asia ever since the invasion of Darius in 510 B.C. who annexed the Indus valley and made it the twentieth province of Persian Empire. The Persian rule in north-western India which lasted for nearly two centuries, made a profound impact upon the life and culture of Indian people. Similarly, the Greek settlement in Indian frontiers around 300 B.C. greatly accelerated Indo-Greek trade and commerce which heralded a direct and visible influence on Indian art of Gandhara. The Iranians had a lasting influence on Indian culture. Right from the advent of the Afghans and the Moghuls in India till the beginning of the British rule Persian language continued to occupy the place of Court language of India.

Chapter 3 discusses at length how the Indian culture travelled from Gangetic valley of India to the Gandaki basin of Nepal during the past couple of millennia. As early as the 5th century B.C. when Indian culture and religion had begun to influence, the Asiatic countries like Indo-China, Malaya, Indonesia, Shri Lanka, Burma, etc. Nepal, a close neighbour of India, could hardly remain unaffected by the wind of change. Herds of invaders from India found their ways into Nepal at different points of time who subdued small ruling chiefs of Nepal and established their kingdoms. They carried with them more advanced culture, language, religion, and introduced them in Nepal. The change that came to Nepal in the process was not merely of religious dimension, but was of a broad civilizing and humanizing influence."It brought to them intellectual awakening, social consciousness and material prosperity".[4] The history of both India and Nepal, thus turned out to be a spectacular account of intermixture and assimilation of multiple races, religions and languages that crystallized into two unique pluralistic nations. Hinduism entered Nepal together with its elaborate caste system and spread throughout the length and breadth of the country under the royal patronage of various successive Hindu dynasties. However, in spite of the supremacy of Hinduism, throughout the centuries, it did not supplant Buddhism from the soil of Nepal. Buddhism in Nepal continued to hold its own against all adversaries even to this day.

In respect of social institutions we find that the Nepalese social system, like India, is predominantly based on the Vedic traditions, except for a section of non-Hindu population. The Nepalese population is composed of multiple races, and ethnic groups, each having distinct dialects not understandable to each other and separate social customs of their own. The caste distinction is the benchmark of Hinduism and the same came in its entirety when Hinduism entered into Nepal. Socio-culturally the Nepalese population can be divided into two broad divisions, *viz*., Tagadharis and the Matawalis. The former group include the Brahmins, Thakuris and the Chetris who ritually wear sacred thread around the shoulder and occupy the highest place in the social order. The latter group comprises the rest of the larger half of the population who belong to the middle and the lowest ranks of social hierarchy. The group falling in the middle rank of social hierarchy include, by and large, the indigenous communities like the Newars, Magars, Gurungs, Rais, Limbus, Tamangs, Thakalis, Sunuwars, Lepchas etc. who profess Buddhism, and those in the lowest rank group fall communities like Kami, Damai, Sarki etc. and they belong to

Hinduism. The Tagadharis are chest Hindus and are strictly governed by Vedic system of social order while the Matawalis are ritually liberal in their religious pursuits.

As in India, Nepal also has the patriarchal form of society. The father is the head of the family who exercises authority over the family affairs while mother occupies the next subordinate position. Marriage is fixed by negotiation and polygamy is permissible in society, though not in much practice. Women are, by and large, respected in society and are free to move about without veil or *purdah*. They can also take-up any profession or do any work the male member does without social bar. Nepal is free from the scourge of *dawry* system (tradition of giving valuable gifts to bridegroom by the parents of the bride), but there are other social evils which still plague the Nepalese society like child marriage, forced labour, illiteracy, superstition, practice of shamanism etc.

Chapter 4 highlights on the ethnographic history of Nepal. We find that long before the first whisper of human tradition in Nepal there came streams of people of various racial stocks and ethnicity from different places and started their early settlement in the lap of the sacred Himalayas. One of them were the Mongolians, who in search of warm valleys left their home in the snow-covered plateau of Tibet, crossed over the mighty Himalayas into the fertile valleys of Nepal. Finding here a cool and bracing climate and fertile soil they settled down in Nepal. We find them today inhabited in the northern part of Nepal by the names like Lepchas, Bhutias, Sherpas, Thakalis etc. They came mostly as peaceful settlers with their flocks of sheep and yak, in several batches and settled down there. Then came the Kiratas, the first ever known tribe of Nepal, in seventh century B.C. from the south, i.e. India. The Kiratas were the people of the north-east India around Pragjyotispura who were pushed into the mountainous regions of Nepal by the Aryans as they advanced from the Gangetic plains. Dr. S.K. Chatterjee observed that the "Sino-Tibetans known as Kiratas originally belonged to the Brahmaputra valley of Assam." According to E.A. Gait, Ghataka, one of the Kirati king ruled in Kamrup, the ancient Assam who was defeated and slain by Naraka Asura. The ancient records seem to indicate that long before the Kiratas came to settle in Nepal there must have been some unknown tribe living in that land. Dr. Regmi echoes the same view and states that this tribe had a close affinity with the Munda, Kol, Bhil tribes of Chotanagpur.

History tells us that herds of invaders from India found their ways into Nepal at different points of time who subdued the small ruling chiefs and established their kingdoms at various places in Nepal. These rulers belonged to various races like Indo-Mongoloid, the Aryans and the Dravidians who hailed from different parts of India. According to Hindu and Buddhist traditions, the valley of Nepal, in the early days, was a lake which was converted into a fertile habitat by cutting a canal to flow out the water to river Bagmati, by Manjusri, a Buddhist saint from China. He installed Dharmakara as the king of Nepal who having no issue appointed one Dharmapala as his successor.

Jayadeva, the Lichchavi prince, fled to Nepal after the fall of his kingdom at Vaisali[5], present (Bihar). He defeated the Kirati king of Nepal and ruled over the country for a considerably long period of time. *Jataka* stories tell us that Vaishali, the original capital of Lichchvis in Bihar, was a beautiful city. Although most of the Lichchavi kings were devout Hindus, they did not impose Brahmanic social codes or values on their non-Hindu subjects. Manadeva, like other Lichchavi kings, had a liberal view about religion. Although he himself believed in the worship of Vishnu, his wife set-up Siva Lingas, the pillars representing the phallus near Visnumati river in 474.[6] Buddhism existed side-by-side with Vaisnavism, Shaivism and the *Sakta* cult. Sivadeva II another Lichchavi king was a devout Hindu king and he saw to it that the duties of Mahayana Buddhism were not neglected and that Buddhists were properly looked after.[7] But the Thakuri kings who replaced the Lichchavis were not liberal in matters of religion like the Lichchavis. They were conservative Hindus and did not like other religion to exist in Nepal. The Thakuri dynasty was started by Amsuvarman and this dynasty had eighteen kings.

After the Thakuris reigned for 225 years, Harisingh Deva, king of Simraun, of Mithila (now Tirhut) India, founded Ayodhya dynasty in Nepal. After the death of Shyamasingh Deva, the fourth and the last king of Ayodhya dynasty, the throne passed on to Malla dynasty by matrimonial relations. Joyasthiti Malla, the famous king of this dynasty is accredited to have introduced a true and precise

Hinduism in Nepal and laid the foundation of a Brahminical order of society. His descendants under the title of Malla dynasty ruled over Nepal till their defeat by the Gorkhas. In 1303 A.D. Allauddin Khiliji attacked Chittor when freedom loving Rajputs, on their defeat, refused to remain in slavery and moved towards the Himalayan hills. They settled down in Palpa and gradually carved out their little principality around a place called Gorkha. Prithvinarayan Shah, the famous king of Gorkha dynasty conquered all the principalities and petty kingdoms including Kirtipur, Lalitpur and Bhaktapur of the Mallas and unified a greater Nepal in 1767-68.

Thus, Nepal is a country originally inhabited and ruled by peoples coming from two different directions—one from the north, being the Mongolian of the Tibeto-Burman linguistic group and the other from the south as Kiratas, Aryans and Dravidians. Thus, the peoples of different racial stock and ethnicity meeting and mixing together for generations, at times fighting each other, at another living peacefully and mixing their cultures and languages paved the way for building-up a nation which is now called the Nepalese. Ethnographically, the Nepalese belong to many racial stocks, sub-tribes, cultures, religion and linguistic groups. Barring a small population of Tibetan origin, the larger section of Nepalese are the descendants of the Lichchavis, Thakuris, Mallas, Shahs and the Rajputs from India whom we may call the Indian descendants.

Chapter 5 deals with the matters of faith and religion in which there exists a close uniformity between India and Nepal. Both the countries are deeply religious. As in India, Hinduism is widely professed while in Nepal, Buddhism is followed by the indigenous people belonging to the Tibeto-Burman linguistic group. The existence of numerous Hindu and Budhist temples and shrines in the Valley of Kathmandu and the thousands of fluttering Buddhist prayer flags around the hills and valleys of Nepal speak loudly how deeply and extensively have the two religions influenced the lives of the Nepalese people. Nepal is the only country in the world where Hinduism is the State religion (Nepalese constitution 2015 has abolished Hinduism as state religion and adopted secularism). Despite this, the Nepalese are strictly secular minded. Hinduism and Buddhism have co-existed in Nepal side-by-side over the centuries and at no point of time have they come to clash each other. There are a large number of Buddhist people in Nepal who are allowed freely to profess their religion and to perform Buddhist rituals publicly without any hindrance. The Hindus visit the Swayambhunath temple of Lord Buddha while the Buddhists freely worship at the Pashupatinath temple at Kathmandu. The temple of Pashupatinath occupies a unique place in the history of Indo-Nepal cultural relations. Every year on the *Sivaratri* day it draws large number of pilgrims from different parts of India. In the similar vein, great number of Nepalese pilgrims visit Indian temples like Haridwar, Kedarnath, Rameswaram, Prayaga etc. round the year. The Kamakhya temple of Guwahati, Assam is a shrine of special attraction for the people of Nepal. The king of Nepal was a life patron of Kamakhya and many Indian temples such as Jagannath temple, Puri and Rameswaram temples. Thus, ever since time immemorial, there exists an exceptional religio-cultural relations and spiritual co-sharing between the peoples of India and Nepal.

Chapter 6 focuses on the linguistic affinities that exist between India and Nepal. Both India and Nepal come under Indo-Aryan linguistic zone being the off-shoots of Sanskrit. Nepali language is the *lingua-franca* of Nepal and is spoken by all of the multi-ethnic groups although many of them have their own separate dialects. Nepali is also spoken by over five million Indians of Nepalese origin residing in India. Nepali is a State language of Sikkim, a State in India where two-thirds of its population speak Nepali as their mother tongue. The Government of West Bengal has recognized Nepali as one of the official languages of the State. Nepali and Hindi are both Indo-Aryan languages and both are written in Devnagri script which is derived from Brahmi script. Sanskrit is the mother language of both Hindi and Nepali and therefore, there is a very close similarity between the two. Apart from Hindi and Nepali, many other major Indian languages are originated from Sanskrit. Scholars claim that even some foreign languages like Pashto of Afghanistan, Urdu of Pakistan, Singhalese of Sri Lanka and Bangla of Bangladesh are derived from Sanskrit language. Today, Nepali is one of the richest literary languages not only in Nepal, but also in India where it has been recognized as one of the major languages under eighth schedule of the Constitution of India. By dint of its being an off-shoot from Sanskrit language and also written in Devnagri script Nepali is easily understood by people all-over India and, so also the case in respect of Hindi in Nepal. Hindi films from India are as popular in Nepal as they are in India; Hindi newspapers from India are also widely read in Nepal. Thus, language has played a very significant role in mutual understanding between the two countries and in bringing the two peoples closer to each other.

Chapter 7: The art and architecture are the hand-maids of religion. As Buddhism and Hinduism entered Nepal from India at different points of time they invariably brought with them their hand-maids of art and architecture to glorify and perpetuate them. The traces of ancient art and architecture are extant to this day. The ancient temples, shrines and stupas are there all-over India and Nepal enduring the wear-and-tear of time to tell their glorious annals. The history of Indian sculpture and architecture begins from the Mauryan period particularly during the reign of Ashoka. "The Ashokan stupas, caves and pillars constructed by Ashoka at various places of India and Nepal which can be seen even today are the glaring examples of high engineering and artistic skills of those days." The imposing pillars of Sarnath with majestic figures of lions, horses and deers and the wheel of "*Dharmachakra*" forcefully announce the grandeur and beauty of Mauryan art and sculpture. The art forms and architectural styles of Gupta period have definitely influenced the art and architecture of Nepal. For example the Garuda pillars of Changu in Nepal betrays the Garuda of Guptas in its entirety. There are great many numbers of stupas constructed by Ashoka in India, Nepal and Afghanistan which bear the style and art forms of Gupta period. The Swayambhu and Bodhnath shrines of Nepal are the fine examples of Sanchi style of stupa construction.

During Hindu period the *shikhara* design of temple construction that prevailed in India with lotus, *kolos* or *trisul* on the top of domes greatly influenced the Nepalese temple designs. This kind of temples are everywhere to be seen in India and Nepal. The Krishna temple of Patan constructed by Malla kings is a typical example of this design.

Nepalese art and architecture can be broadly classified into three structural designs—the *pagoda* design, the *stupa* design and the *shikhara* design. The *pagoda* design is the indigenous style of Nepal herself while the other two are borrowed from India. The *pagoda* design consists of multi-roofed structure with wide eaves supported by carved wooden struts. The *Kasthamandapa* built by Malla king, and the Basantapur palace built by Prithvinarayan are the typical examples of this design.

Chapter 8: Politically both India and Nepal have a long border and peoples of both countries constantly crossing into each others' territory to find means of livelihood, importing and exporting commercial goods etc. Sometimes political fugitive entering the other country for seeking political asylum, or some desperate criminals sneaking into the border country with an intent to evade legal punishment. The treaty of peace and friendship,1950 provided a solid foundation to a lasting bond between India and Nepal which enables the citizens of one country to migrate, stay and carry out any economic pursuit in the other country without any passport or visa.

Politically both India and Nepal suffered prolonged subjugation under foreign and autocratic rulers. India came under British rule since 1857 while Nepal was ruled by the Rana family under the titular king of Shah dynasty both being of Indian origin. India and Nepal both had to struggle hard for their political emancipation and make supreme sacrifices of life and property for over a century. India became independent in 1947 and this was closely followed by an overthrow of the autocratic Rana rule by the civic revolt in Nepal in 1950. India played a significant role in the struggle of the Nepalese insurgents in bringing down the 104 years old Rana rule. The history of freedom struggle of India and Nepal is essentially a story of long and sustained goodwill and co-operation between the peoples of both the countries.

It was the Indian political leaders who first ignited the fire of nationalism in the hearts of Nepalese young men who came in close contact with them in early 20th century.

As early as 1920s when Mahatma Gandhi launched the Civil Disobedience movement in India, a group of Nepalese young men including B.P. Koirala, Matrika Prasad Koirala, D.R. Regmi, S.P.

Upadhyaya and Krishna Prasad Bhatarai joined the movement from their base at Patna. Another enlightened Nepali gentleman, Tulshi Mehr, being greatly inspired by Mahatma Gandhi's philosophy of life started *Khadi* and Village industry movement in Nepal. He established "*Charakha-Guthi*,"an institution for imparting training to the women folk of Nepal in spinning and weaving *khadi* clothes. This was viewed by the Rana rulers as an attempt in spreading *swadeshi* movement in Nepal. It was considered as a serious offence in Nepal for which Tulshi Mehr, a staunch follower of Mahatma Gandhi in Nepal, was awarded life imprisonment. Inspired by Mahatma Gandhi's 'use *swadeshi* garment' movement Tulshi Mehr founded *Charakha-Guthi*, an institution for the propagation of *khadi* and village industries in Nepal.[8]

Similarly, we have instances of galore of political leaders of India supporting the cause of Nepal's political emancipation from the tyrannical rule of the Ranas of Nepal. The Indian freedom movement in which the Nepalese young leaders actively participated, proved to be an opportunity for them to learn how to launch similar movements against the autocratic rule in Nepal. The anti-Rana movement in Nepal got a new momentum for a final thrust that came in 1950 when the Nepali Congress launched an open liberation movement with the secret connivance of the King Tribhuvan Vir Vikram Shah. On the 6th November,1950, the king exiled himself with his family members and took refuge in the Indian Embassy at Kathmandu who were later on brought to Delhi by special plane. This followed an armed confrontation between the Rana Government and the insurgents of the liberation force called "Mukti Sena" which captured the Governor and other officials of Birganj. The Government of India actively helped the Nepali insurgents in toppling the autocratic Rana Government.

Chapter 9: Economically Nepal, a land-locked country, is dependent on India in the matters of import and export of essential goods through Indian ports. By the Treaty of Trades and Commerce, 1950, India recognized Nepal's right to import/export commodities from any country across India. Article II of the Treaty of Trade and Transit, 1960 specifically allows goods originated in either country and intended for consumption in the territory of the other, to cross the border free of customs duties and other equivalent charges. India has contributed significantly to Nepal's economic development like construction of Tribhuvan Air Port at Kathmandu, Tribhuvan Rajpath connecting Kathmandu and Birganj, construction of major irrigation projects such as Kosi and Gandaki barrage etc.

In 1950 when the last of the Rana ruler was vanquished from Nepal, the country was bereft of roads and communication, schools and hospitals, infrastructural development, job opportunities and even from the basic amenities of life. More than a half of the population were denied of drinking water, health care facilities, education for children and even not enough food for at least 30 per cent of population. Nepal's economy was at complete disarray with her GDP at the lowest and her people in the backwardness as if in medieval period, with only two per cent literacy rate. The construction of major irrigation projects such as Kosi and Gandaki barrages, construction of Hydro-electric projects etc. are other important development schemes by India. The longest National Highway of Nepal connecting the East to the West Nepal which was named as Mahendra Rajmarg (1024 km) was also constructed by India. This road also includes 22 numbers of bridges and innumerable culverts with its long span.

One of the major projects that India will undertake consists of construction of a 680 km long highway in Terai region of Nepal at the cost of ₹ 810 crore. The proposed road will run from the east to the west of Nepal across the Terai areas and provide connectivity within the regions as well as provide a better linkage between India and Nepal. This east-west highway when completed will also, to a great extent, remove Nepal's longstanding constraint of being a land-locked country. As Dr. Jagadish Pokhreal, former Vice-Chairman of National Planning Commission puts it, "we suffer from a tremendous inferiority complex", Nepal has got to shed her psyche of being squeezed between two rocks and should look beyond her political boundaries, if she really wants to prosper in trade and commerce. With better road connectivity "Nepal would be closer to Delhi than are the Indian cities of Kanpur, Lucknow and Allahabad. The markets of north-east India can more easily be serviced by the Nepal border towns of Birganj, Jogbani or Kakarvita in the east than they would be by the geographically more distant northern Indian States".[9]

Under power sector, both sides agreed that five villages of Nepal will be electrified at the cost of ₹ 6.3 crore. India is already providing 20 MW of power out of the existing power projects and further agreed to provide another 20 MW power to meet the increasing demand of Nepal. Another agreement between Nepal Stock Exchange Limited and Central Depository Services Limited of India was also signed under which India will assist Nepal in setting up a Central Depository and clearing and settlement system at the cost of ₹ 5.75 crore. Apart from this, the two sides also signed an MoU for establishment of Nepal-Bharat Maitri Science Learning Centre in Khumaltar, Lalitpur at the cost of ₹ 15.5 crore.

Chapter 10: The supply of military man-power to India is one of the oldest and largest contribution of Nepal to India which continues till today. Ever since the British Government of India began recruiting Gorkhas in Indian Army in 1816, the flow of man-power from the Himalayan kingdom has never ceased. The Gorkhas served the British well while after independence they contributed magnificently to India by sacrificing their lives. The Gorkhas figured conspicuously in all the theatres of war, such as Kashmir, Arunachal Pradesh, Bangladesh etc. where they left their deads.[10] In Kargil war of 1999 as many as twenty-two young Gorkhas laid down their precious lives. Today they are more than a lakh in number serving in India, guarding steadfastly the borders stretching from Siachen of Kashmir to the Tawang of Arunachal Pradesh and maintaining internal peace and order of India. Our Indian borders are assuredly safe in the hands of redoubtable Gorkhas.

In Chapter 11 we have discussed about the matrimonial relations with India and Nepal that has been continuing till today ever since the Epic age. India and Napal have a very long tradition of matrimonial alliances. History of Nepal and India are replete with interesting accounts of matrimonial connections between the princes and rulers of the two countries ever since prehistoric times. The great Epic of *Ramayana* describes about the king of Janakpur of Nepal having given his beautiful daughter Sita on marriage to Shri Ramchandra, the prince of Ayodhya in India. Today Janakpur, the ancient capital of king Janaka is an important city of Tarai

Nepal. Here stands a magnificent Janaki temple said to have been constructed by an Indian prince about one hundred years ago at an expenditure of Rs. nine lakh. Nearly 2200 years ago emperor Ashoka visited Nepal to glorify Lord Buddha. During these days emperor Ashoka's daughter Charumati and Nepali prince Devpal had tied a nuptial knot in this beautiful city of Kathmandu. This significant event of Nepalese history leads one to believe that the sub-Himalayan kingdom of Nepal, in those days, must have been a prosperous and powerful country to match the high dignity and honour of the prince of the great Mauryan empire of India.

The king Harshavardhana, is said to have given his daughter Rajyamati in marriage to Jayadeva II, the king of Nepal.[11] It is to be noted that Nepal was a country with its name and fame well known to all parts of India during ancient period of history. Later in the 16th century A.D., the Koch dynasty rose in power in the north-east India under the leadership of Viswa Singha, the founder of the Koch dynasty. It is recorded in the *Raj-Vamsavali* that Viswa Singha, the Koch king had eighteen wives from different countries like Gova, Kashmir, Tippera etc. and one of them was Ratnakanti, a princess from Nepal. Ratnakanti Devi was the daughter of Malla king of Kantipur. It is stated that Viswa Singha's son Naranarayan, the greatest king of the Koch dynasty was born out of Ratnakanti's womb, the Nepalese princess (D. Nath).

The process of matrimonial relations between the royal families of Nepal and the Indian kings has continued from the pre-historic period down to the contemporary times despite the vast changes that have taken place in the political arena as well as in their royal status. After India's independence, the numerous native states of India merged with Indian dominion and the native kings lost their royal status, while in Nepal the Rana rule ended in 1950 yielding place to democratic pattern of government in the name of the king of Nepal as the titular head. However, the royal families of Nepal are still maintaining the matrimonial alliances with the erstwhile princely States of India like, Gwalior, Kapurthala, Mayurbhanj, Jodhpur, Kashipur etc. To give a few instances, Shri Pasupati Shamsher Rana, the former Minister of Nepal married Usharaji Scindia, the daughter of late Vijairaji Scindia, the mother of late Madhav Rao Scindia, former Union Minister of India. Madhav

Rao Scindia himself married a daughter of Rana family. Mention may be made here that Miss Devyani Scindia whom the Crown Prince of Nepal, late Dwipendra Vir Vikram Shah wanted to marry and failing which he had to take the extreme and ghastly steps to kill his father King Birendra Vir Vikram Shah, his mother, Queen Aisharya Rajya Lakshmi and six other members of the royal family on the 1st June, 2001,was none other than the daughter of Usharaji Scindia and the niece of late Madhav Rao Scindia. Dr. Karan Singh, the former Union Minister of India married Yasho Rajyalakshmi, the grand daughter of General Mohan Shamsher Jangbahadur Rana, the Prime Minister of Nepal. Yasho Rajyalakshmi is also the cousin sister of Pasupati Shamsher Rana of Nepal. The king,Tribhuvan Vir Vikram Shah of Nepal had two wives and both were the daughters of the king of Kashipur State. All the three sisters of the king Mahendra Vir Vikram Shah were married to the princes of Indian native States like Poonch, Sikar and Mayurbhanj. Late king Birendra Vir Vikram Shah of Nepal was directly related to the Maharaja of Jodhpur and also the Maharaja of Mayurbhanj. Further, Hemlata, the wife of Maharaja Gaja Singh of Jodhpur and the Rajkumari of Poonch are the nieces of king Mahendra Vir Vikram Shah and the aunties of late king Birendra Vir Vikram Shah of Nepal. Besides all these matrimonial relations the royal families of Nepal have many other blood relations with their counterparts in India.

Chapter 12 deals with the diaspora of India and Nepal. Migration of people from one country to another is a global phenomenon and history is replete with stories of human movements all-over the world from ancient times till date. India has a very long history of migration across different countries of the world. It starts before the beginning of the Christian era, or even earlier than that, when the Indian saints and seers went out to far reaching countries like Shri Lanka, Indonesia and Nepal to spread the message of Lord Buddha.

The diasporic relations between India and Nepal is very old which is bolstered by common language, tradition, history and culture and facilitated by geographical proximity. The open border policy followed by both countries and also the privileges offered to the nationals of one country to settle down and carry out trade, commerce and other economic activities in other's country, under Article seven of the Indo-Nepal Peace and Friendship Treaty, 1950 have immensely contributed to the diasporic movement into each other's country. According to an estimate nearly four million people of Indian origin are residing in Nepal, while on the other hand, approximately six million people of Nepalese origin are presently settled in various parts of India. In other words, at least 16.7 per cent of the total population of Nepal is composed of the people of Indian origin, whereas, 0.75 per cent of India's population consists of the people of Nepalese origin. Speaking in terms of ratio, Nepal has one Indian for every six Nepalese, while India has one Nepali for every 200 Indians. The vast majority of the immigrants are permanently settled down in their respective countries of domicile for generations as citizens by swearing allegiance to the constitutions of each other's country.

There are currently about four to five million Nepalese of Indian origin living in Nepal. They are settled mostly in the Terai region of Nepal. The immigration of Indian people started since nineteenth century and it continues till recent times. The Government of Nepal encouraged the Indians living in Bihar to settle down and do cultivation in the Terai region of Nepal where Nepalese from the hills dare not to come down due to fear of malaria and hot climate of the place. The Indian immigrants who moved into Terai were mostly landless tenants from the Indian State of Bihar. They were primarily agriculturists and also do animal husbandry and other minor occupations. They settled down in Terai in large number and turned the fertile land into a granary of Nepal. They are mostly Hindus and Muslims. The Government of Nepal passed the Citizenship Bill in 2006 and converted more than four million stateless Bihari immigrants into Nepalese citizens by virtue of naturalization. The Government of India welcomed the reformed citizenship Act while certain section of Nepalese leaders expressed deep concern.

Chapter 13 deals with the devastating earthquake that struck Nepal on April 25, 2015 and India's help in rescue and relief of the victims. With the magnitude of 7.8 Richter Scale this earthquake was said to be the worst of its kind since the great earthquake of 1934. It killed 8669 people, destroyed lakhs of dwelling houses and rendered millions of people homeless. This chapter also gives an account of the immediate help offered by India with men and material for quick relief and rehabilitation of the victims of the earthquake.

In Nepal, the intensity was so great and extensive that it levelled down entire villages in both the upper mountain areas on the north and the Terai regions on the south. At Barpak village which was the epicenter of the quake all the1200 houses were totally erased by the quake. In Kathmandu regions hundreds of historical buildings, monuments and heritage sites were turned into rubbles. It looked as if the very clock of Nepalese civilization was pushed back to more than a couple of centuries. The age old pagoda temples in the Darbar Square of the Malla Kings with all their grandeur and exquisite artistic workmanship were left in ruins by the unprecedented tremors. Gone was the renowned wooden temple of Kasthmandapa that gave Kathmandu its name. The Hanuman Dhoka Darbar Square at Kathmandu, the temple palaces in Patan and Bhaktapur were all raged down to earth making them completely untraceable.

India came out of its way to Nepal's rescue. Narendra Modi, the Prime Minister of India, ordered immediate rushing of NDRF (National Disaster Relief Force) teams to Nepal with food, medicine and all necessary relief materials. He tweeted—"Nepal's pain is our pain", India is ready to "wipe out the tears of every Nepali—and hold their hands and stand with them". The 'Operation Maitri' got under way—Indian army personnel swung into action. Within a matter of four hours they landed in Kathmandu with helicopters loaded with food, medicine and other relief materials and started rescue operation. Some one from India cracked a joke—Sushil Koirala, Prime Minister of Nepal came to know of the earthquake only from Narendra Modi. The Indian Embassy in Kathmandu too buzzed into action—"Within 7 hours of the earthquake", the Embassy spoke to media, "7000 officers of the NDRF were despatched to Nepal to rescue the earthquake victims". There were also medical teams with doctors and medicine deputed to Nepal who reached the affected areas in time. They started rescue and relief operation in tandem with local voluntary organizations like—Clubs and civil volunteers of Nepal.

Notes

1. Eden Vansittart (1915), *Gurkha*, Calcutta: Government Press.
2. *Ibid.*
3. D.R. Regmi (1969), *Ancient Nepal,* Calcutta: Rupbani Press.
4. B.N. Luniya (1998), *Evolution of Indian Culture,* Agra: Lakshminarayan Agarwal.
5. Some historians including K.P. Jayaswal maintain that towards the 200 A.D. Nepal was under the suzerainty of the Lichchhavis who had their capital at Vaisali, D.R. Regmi thinks that there is ample ground to believe that a major part of the north Bihar which passes through obscurity all these centuries might have been a part of Nepal.
6. Rishikesh Shaha, *Ancient and Medieval Nepal*, p. 156.
7. *Ibid.*, p. 164.
8. Shriman Narayan (1971), *India and Nepal*, Orient Paperback, p. 29.
9. Sujeev Shakya (2009), *Unleashing Nepal*, p. 236.
10. K.K. Muktan (2002), *The Legendary Gorkhas*, Guwahati: Spectrum Publication.
11. E.A. Gait (1967), *History of Assam.*

1
India and Nepal

India and Nepal are two ancient countries. The relations between them can be traced back to the epic age. Its references are found in *Mahabharata* and *Arthashastra* of Kautilya and many other ancient scriptures. Ever since then the relationship has sustained on the firm ground of common culture, faith and trust. The geographical vicinity, common history and ethnological identities of the two peoples have been the cornerstones of this long standing relation. Politically both India and Nepal passed under alien rule for more than a century and they joined hands together to fight against the foreign rulers for their liberation. During freedom struggle of India, young Nepali political leaders came to India and took active part in the freedom movement and suffered imprisonment. India too played a significant role in helping Nepal out of the yoke of autocratic Rana rule during peoples revolution in Nepal in nineteen hundred fifties. This reciprocal bond of friendship and co-operation has ever continued and in the recent past after the establishment of popular Government in Nepal the political ties between the two countries have become even deeper and broader through wide range of bilateral agreements in the domains of economic, political, trade and cultural affairs.

India and Nepal's relations have two dimensions—political and cultural. The first, political dimension, is a relationship based on mutual agreement for each others benefit concluded by two Governments from time to time; the second, cultural dimension, is a relationship between the two peoples that arise out of the social virtues they have inherited from the past. The former is a temporary adjustment of convenience between two Governments which usually exists between many countries, while the latter is an enduring bond of culture, language and faith rarely seen among other countries of the world. The former is a relationship between two governments while the letter is a relationship between two nations. Thus, India and Nepal enjoy a kind of relationship which is ever sustaining and endearing and needs no agreement or adjustment. It is a knowledge and understanding of past history, traditions, legends and myths of each other, rather than a matter of mutual convenience that binds the two countries together. The commonality of ethnic origin, tradition, belief system, language and literature obtaining between the two peoples over the centuries, have moulded their mindset in such a way that they are identical to each other in every detail. Their worldview had been influenced by the same set of religious books and scriptures and inspired by the same prophets and saints. In the words of Sriman Narayan, former Indian Ambassador to Nepal—"The relationship is, therefore, not between the two Governments but between the two peoples: for the Governments have changed in India and also in Nepal but our friendship has sustained as ever before. This is a unique bond which, perhaps, no other country in the world. possess."[1]

The Treaty of Peace and Friendship of 1950 provides a solid foundation for a unique and ever lasting tie between the two nations which makes them feel as if they live in the same country. This is a unique treaty which has no parallel in any other country in the world. The citizens of one country can migrate, stay and carry out economic pursuits in the other country, no passport or visa is necessary; only a convincing proof of citizenship is enough for travelling from one country to another. Under the treaty, each Government agreed to acknowledge and respect each others sovereignty, territorial integrity and independence; to continue diplomatic relations and on matters pertaining to industrial and economic development to grant rights equal to those of its own citizens to the nationals of the other residing in its territory. In accordance with the Treaty of Peace and Friendship, 1950, the Government of Nepal passed Citizenship Act, 1952 which allowed Indian nationals to migrate into Nepal and acquire Nepalese citizenship with ease. In recent past, there has been some controversy over the Article 7 of the Peace and Friendship Treaty of 1950 which grants, on reciprocal basis, to the nationals of one country in the territories of the other, the same privileges in the matter of residence, ownership of properties, participation in trade and commerce, movement and other privileges of similar nature. The issue arising out of free movement of peoples between the two countries for seeking economic pursuits granted by the above treaty, became a matter of concern for both the peoples resulting in ethnic violations in some areas especially in the North Eastern part of India. Considering the socio-political conflict emerging out of the treaty leading to ethnic violence and the serious concerns expressed by some political leaders and NGOs, it is considered necessary that the two countries may examine the feasibility of bringing suitable changes in the said provision.

Politically, Nepal occupies a very strategic position from the point of view of India because of its geographical location on the border with China. With India it shares a border of over 850 km in the east, south and west with five Indian States—Sikkim, West Bengal, Bihar, Uttar Pradesh and Uttarakhand. In the north there is Tibet Autonomous region of the People's Republic of China. Nepal has an area of 1,47,181 sq km and a population of 29 million. Nepal being a small land-locked country lying between two Asian giants, she has to be always careful in handling her foreign policy. She has thus chosen to be at equal distance keeping a friendly relationship with both India and China. On the other hand, India has to be equally watchful to ensure that the Chinese Government do not take undue advantage which may result in a threat to the security of India. It must be noted that India's relationship with Nepal should be based on positive and constructive co-operation and not on animosity towards China or, for that matter, towards any other neighbouring country. Nepal, on her part, ought to be aware of the fact that there can be no genuine friendship between democracy and commumism. The construction of the Kathmandu-Kodari road by the Chinese to provide a road link between Nepal and Tibet, which was beneficial for Nepal, had been an issue of concern for New Delhi. For that matter, any growth of Chinese influence in Nepal would pose a direct threat to India's security and therefore, India must maintain a cordial ties with Nepal and at the same time keep an eye that the other side does not take upper hand. This was what the Government of India wanted from the very beginning and more emphatically after the Chinese aggression of 1962. Prime Minister, Jawaharlal Nehru in his address in 1959 stated—"It is not necessary for us to have a military alliance with Nepal but the fact remains that we cannot tolerate any foreign invasion from any foreign country in any part of the sub-continent. Any possible invasion of Nepal would inevitably involve the safety of India". As far as the security issues are concerned both India and Nepal must acknowledge each others sensitivity and keep the closest possible ties between each other.

Jawaharlal Nehru, Prime Minister of India had, of necessity, maintained a very close political and economic ties with Nepal. After the death of Nehru, Shri Lal Bahadur Shastri's efforts to improve the relations did generate a positive response from Nepal. His personal visit to Nepal created congenial atmosphere although the process could not be advanced further due to his tragic demise in Tashkent. Indira Gandhi and Rajiv Gandh, in their turn, tried to maintain close relationship through frequent visits and talks at their own levels and effecting further improvements in the trade and transit facilities between India and Nepal. Prime Minister Chandra Shekhar's support to the movement for democracy of Nepal earned a lot of goodwill between the two countries. Chandra Shekhar's visit to Nepal and constitution of a Joint Commission to finalise the proposals for various bilateral treaties formed the basis of negotiations between Prime Minister Koirala of Nepal and Shri P.V. Narasingha Rao, the Prime Minister of India in later years.

In recent times, especially after 2008, the political situation in Nepal is drifting towards a direction not very favourable to India. The Nepali Congress Party and other democratic parties of Nepal which were closely allied to India are gradually losing their grounds to Communist and diehard leftist parties which have a natural leaning towards China by virtue of their basic party principles. The CPN (Marxist) Maoist Party which had been fighting a civil war in Nepal since 1996 under the leadership of Baburam Bhattarai and Puspa Kamal Dahal (Prachanda) succeeded in capturing the highest number of seats in the Nepalese Constituent Assembly in the general election held on April 10, 2008. After that, two consecutive Governments were formed, once by Shri Puspa Kamal Dahal (Prachanda), Maoist on August 15, 2008 and by Shri Jhala Nath Khanal, CPN (UML) with the support of the Maoist on 6th February, 2011. Taking this advantage, the Chinese Government is increasing its involvement in the affairs of Nepal's economic activities by advancing financial grants and soft loans for hydro-projects and infrastructure development. In such situation, the Government of India needs to take all possible measures to renew its old ties with Nepal through improvement of both political and cultural relations. The Maoist Supremo, Prachanda, during his visit to India in April, 2008, gave assurance that he will maintain equal distance from the two giant neighbours India and China. He said, "Nepal has a historical relationship with India and shares open borders. It is very important to have good relations with India". India looked forward for a good relationship. The political history of Nepal, however took a 'U' turn as the coalition Government led by Maoist leader Shri Puspa Kamal Dahal did not continue for long. The Government of Nepal came to a dramatic end in May 2009, with the sudden resignation by the Maoist Prime Minister, Puspa Kamal Dahal, pushing Nepal once again into a state of political chaos and uncertainty.

Geographical Uniformity

Nepal, a land-locked country, is situated on the southern slopes of the mid-Himalayas. It is bounded on the north by Tibet; on the east by Sikkim and the river Michi; on the south by Uttar Pradesh, Bihar and West Bengal and on the west by Uttarakhand and the river Kali. It has 800 km long border with India on the south, east and the west. The pre-historic traditions and ancient texts seem to indicate no territorial demarcation between India and Nepal. According to Buddhist tradition, India and Nepal were included within the landmass called "*Jambu-Dwipa*" a territory referred to during the third century throughout which the lordship and the prowess of the great imperial dynasty of Maurya were made themselves manifested.[2] In other words, ancient territory of *Jambu-Dwipa* included both Nepal and India which constituted the empire of the Mauryan dynasty. The Indian epics and *Puranas* also defined India's boundary as—

Uttaram yatsamudrasya
Himadre haiva dakshinam
Varsham tad Bharatam nama
Bharati yatra santatih.

(*Vishnu Purana,* 11.31).

Meaning : The country that lies to the north from the ocean and to the south from the snowy mountains is called Bharata; for there dwell the descendants of Bharata.

Here the snowy mountain means the Himalaya, to the south of which is located Nepal and the Indian boundary lines begin from the Himalaya in the north and to the ocean in the south.

Geographically, Nepal can be broadly divided into three natural divisions are: (1) The **Himalayan region,** or Northern zone in the extreme north comprising an alpine formation with an altitude between 16,000 to 29,000 feet above sea level. The mountain ranges remain perpetually covered with snow and glaciers all the year round and are broken-up at places by passes which are open to travellers during warmer months. It is in this region that the highest mountain peak in the world, *viz.* the Mount Everest (29,002 ft.) is located flanked by five other high mountains like the Kanchenjungha (28,156 ft.), Gosainthan (26,305 ft.), Dhaulagiri (26,826 ft.), Gaurisankar (23,457 ft.) and Nandadevi (25,700 ft.). (2) The **Mountain region**, or Central zone in the middle, is formed by smaller hill ranges that rise-up to the level of about 16,000 feet with dunes or valleys at their bases, generally at about 2,500 feet above sea level. This is the major land mass of Nepal which is watered by three main river systems, Kosi, Gandaki and Karnali and populated by the Nepalese people. It is the hub of Nepalese civilization, their culture and tradition. (3) Lastly, the **Terai region** or the Southern zone in the extreme south bordering Indian Gangetic valley, is a plain belt of Nepal stretching 10 to 30 miles breadth and skirting India from Sarda to Michi rivers. This Terai region comprises only seventeen per cent of the total geographical area of Nepal while it is populated by almost half of the Nepalese population.

The geographical conditions of a country, its climate, mountains, rivers etc. have always influenced the course of its political, social and economic history. They go a long way in determining the livelihood and character of the people. The formidable Himalayan ranges, the natural wonders of the world, have played a significant role in the socio-economic life of both the people of India and Nepal. The great barrier of lofty mountain ranges along the northern frontier has served as a wind-breaker to induce plenty of monsoon rains to Indian plains during summer season for forest and agricultural growth of India.

The great Himalaya is often metaphorically called the "Water Tower" of the world, because it contains the largest store of water on earth in the form of snows. Geo-physically, it is referred as the "Third Pole of the World", because it comprises the third biggest fresh water reservoir of the world after the North and the South Poles. The water of the Himalaya is reserved mostly in the form of snow and glaciers which melts by the heat of the sun and form into numerous rivers, waterfalls and streams that flow down to the valleys. As many as seven major river systems originate from the southern Himalaya which flow down the Indian subcontinent and sustain the lives of over one-sixth of the total humanity of this planet. The direct beneficiaries are mostly the people of India and Nepal who receive life giving water from the rivers like Sindhu, Ganga, Jamuna, Brahmaputra in India and the Kosi, Gandaki and Kali in Nepal. These rivers take their rise in the high Himalayan region, some of them in Tibetan territories, cut across rocky mountains covered with snow and glaciers, flow down to the plains of India and Nepal and finally drain themselves into the Bay of Bengal and the Arabian Sea. This explains why the great Gangetic valley happened to be the centre of the Aryan civilization and simultaneously the Gandaki basin sustained the early Nepalese settlement in the past. The Himalaya is, thus a common spiritual repository, and the rivers Ganga and Gandaki are the common heritage of both India and Nepal. Today, the Himalaya stands out as the prime source of religious, spiritual, and cultural unification between India and Nepal, besides playing the strategic role of political and economic relations between them.

For the Hindus, the great Himalaya holds a deep religious significance that conjures up a profound reverence and awe in their minds. Man has always seen in nature and in her beauteous forms, a truth, beauty and purpose in life—*satyam, shivam, sundaram*. The Greeks found the Olympus mountain as the abode of their Gods, so also the Indians found in the wilderness of Himalayas, their gods and goddesses. Both the Greeks and the Indians developed out of them, a maze of mythology and legends and linked them up with their cultural history in a manner difficult to separate the one from the other. The Himalaya is a holy place, an abode of Gods and Goddesses and at the same time, a sacred land of meditation and spiritual attainment for Indian saints and sages. The *Skanda Purana* writes—"He who thinks of Himalaya, though he should not behold him, is greater than he who performs all worship in Kasi. In a hundred ages of Gods, I could not tell thee of the glories of Himalaya. As the dew is dried up by the morning sun, so are the sins of mankind by the sight of Himalayas". Himalaya, a Sanskrit word meaning 'abode of snow'—"the very utterance of the word carries with it some inexplicable thrills—the thrills that pass from the mind to some deeper plane of consciousness."[3] For a poet, it is an object of high soaring imagination. Kalidas, the great classical poet, compared Himalayas with the great beam of a weighing balance that is meant for weighing the globe. The Nepalese call the Mount Everest, the highest peak in the world—the *Sagarmatha,* which means the pinnacle of the sky, and they look at it as a symbol of pride and unity of their country.

The great Himalayan ranges stretching from east to west and covering a distance of 1500 miles, girdle India and Nepal as an impregnable natural wall and the lofty snow-clad peaks, lined-up as they are, from the Everest in the east to the Dhaulagiri and the Annapurna in the west, adorn mother India with a silvery crown that glitters in the morning sun. Nepal, once a world famous Hindu kingdom (now a Democratic Republican State), nestles eternally in the lap of the bewildering maze of the descending mountain ridges like the daughter of Parvati, the mythological queen of the Himalaya which can be resembled with the veritable *Tapovan* (abode of meditation) of Lord Siva himself. The country of Nepal, an elongated rectangle, stretching 520 miles in length and some 90 miles in breadth, looks like a glittering necklace of jade across the snowy neck of mother India. The geophysical consanguinity between India and Nepal is such that the bearing of the one can only be comprehended with the localization of the other; if one is taken away the other fades away like a shadow. The Himalayas, the abode of snows, as the name signifies, can better be termed as the 'Abode of eternity' from the point of view of Indian mythology, which is the source of ancient history of India and Nepal. The Himalaya has been described as "the most magnificent scenery in the world", by Landon.[4]

From the point of view of natural beauty, the Himalaya offers a most spectacular panoramic view of mountains ranges, each overlapping the other till they culminate into eternal snow under the wide canopy of blue sky. No wonder, the Indian *Rishis* and *Munis* found them veritable abode of numerous deities that exuded deeper spiritual sentiment in them than the Greeks had ever found in their pantheons in the natural forces. The very utterance of the name of great Himalaya conjures up a notion of spiritual sanctity in the mind of every Hindu irrespective of whether he is an Indian or a Nepalese.

The great rivers of north India, such as the Brahmaputra, Sindhu, Sutlej, Ganga,Yamuna all take their rise from the bosom of the Himalaya and cutting across the snowy ridges they flow down to Indian plains. These rivers have ever been the lifelines of Indian people who made their country, the "land of milk and honey". Around names of these rivers and their tributaries, that the Indian people's dreams were made. It was also with the holy waters of these rivers that a plethora of mythological history were cooked up which are intricately woven up with Indian culture, religion and tradition. It was in the basins of these legendary rivers that the great *Vedas* were written. Each of these rivers has been personified in names of some god or goddess and glorified in the epics of *Ramayana* and *Mahabharata* for its particular spiritual powers and attributes. Their sources of origin such as, the Kailash mountain, the Mansarovar, the Gangotri and Yamunotri have been described to be the places of great religious significance to Hindus of both India and Nepal. Prayaga of Allahabad, the holy place of confluence of three sacred rivers *viz.*, the Ganga, Yamuna and the Saraswati (as an underground/invisible river), is considered a place of deep religious importance. Hindus from both India and Nepal perform special rites at this *Sangam* for the salvation and eternal peace of the souls of their immediate dead progenitors. Great number of Hindus from Nepal come to Prayag in order to immerse the relics of their dead parents at the holy waters of *Sangam*. Kashi (Benaras), the Macca of the Hindus stands on the bank of Ganga, which is the greatest pilgrimage of the Hindus. From the snow-clad mountains emerge a number of glaciers and spring-fed rivers of Nepal like the Koshi, Gandaki, Karnali, Baghmati, Mechi and Kali which wash the soil of Nepal and flow down to the Indian rivers and merge with the Indian ocean. The Koshi river system of the eastern Nepal consists of Tamur, Arun, Dudhkoshi, Tamakoshi, Sunkoshi, Likhu and Indrawati, seven in numbers. They are collectively known as the *Sapta-Koshi*, as they meet together and flow down to India to merge in the river Ganga. The Gandaki river system of the Central Nepal has seven tributaries, *viz.*, Kali-Gandaki, Budhi-Gandaki, Trisuli, Seti, Marsyangdi, Madi and Daraundi, collectively called the *Sapta-Gandaki*. They too meet each other on their journey and ultimately flow their waters into the Indian ocean. The Kali-Gandaki originates in Mustang and converges with Trisuli at Devghat and takes the name of Narayani and falls in Ganga, while Arun and Sun-Koshi, the two principal tributaries of Koshi, originate in Tibet.

How great and enigmatic is the nature's plan that provide us with breath-taking examples of a grand geophisical harmony in its umpteen diversity. The third major river system of Nepal is Karnali in the western region of Nepal which consists of Humla-Karnali, Mugu-Karnali, Seti and Bheri. It is the longest river system of Nepal. The Humla-Karnali originates from Tibet and after entering India, it takes the name of Gogra and flows into Ganga. All these rivers are perennially fed with melted waters of glacier and snow as they cut their ways through the lofty crags and deep gorges in Tibet and Nepal. As they enter Indian plain regions they meander and broaden into wider expanses, carry heavy sediments and debris and leave the alluvial silt enriching the fertility of soil.

Thus, the geography of India and Nepal and their myriad natural features of mountains, rivers and valleys have all forged an alliance to make a single and wider geo-physical entity that any political boundary between them would appear to be a misnomer.

Because of this bizarre uniformities that exist in the nature and human culture between India and Nepal, the peoples of both the countries fondly cherish in their hearts a deep sense of unity and solidarity.

Unity in Diversity

India is a land of varieties. Its geographical vastness, natural diversities and racial plurality have combined together to designate it as "The epitome of the world." India is a largest democracy in the world with a geographical area bigger than France, Italy and Spain put together, and its population as the second largest in the world. But more remarkable than all these, are her enigmatic physical features with extreme varieties of altitude, topography, rainfall, climate, soil conditions and the vegetative growths. Its physical aspects, the lofty sub-Himalayan mountains in the north eternally covered with snow are in sharp contrast with the vast stretch of flat landmass spread out in the south up to the coastal areas of India that submerge in the Bay of Bengal and the Arabian Sea. Indian climate too varies in its intensity from the extreme cold in the States of Jammu & Kashmir and Arunachal Pradesh in the north, to the sweltering heat in the southern peninsular. The north-eastern part of India comprises one of the wettest eco-zones in the Pacific region with Cherrapunjee (Meghalaya) receiving the highest rainfall in the world, while in stark contrast to this, the western region of India comprising Gujarat and Rajasthan desert represent an extreme hot, dry, and arid zone of India.

Corresponding to the above variation in the climate and rainfall, India offers a wide range of flora and fauna. The north-eastern States adjoining Myanmar (Burma) are covered with dense sub-tropical rain forests which contain valuable evergreen trees like *sal*, *segun*, *teak*, *pinus khasia* etc. that grow to enormous height. The hill States of Meghalaya, Sikkim and Arunachal Pradesh are the homes to rich varieties of fruits, orchids, medicinal plants and many other rare species of herbs. Khasi and Jaintia Hills alone are endowed with seventy-five orchid genera, representing 265 species. This region has been described as one of the Asia's richest botanical habitats more than a century ago by the British scholars. The

Kaziranga National Game Century in Assam is one of the largest habitats of wild animals and birds in India. The one horned rhino of Kaziranga is an animal exclusive to Assam as much as the wild horse of the Rann-of-Kutch to Gujarat, which are rarely found in other places.

Demographically, India is a country of multiple races, religions and languages. Vincent Smith, the historian, rightly called India as "an ethnological museum". The huge conglomeration of Indian population broadly made up of three principal races viz., the Aryans, Dravidians and the Mongolians living side-by-side over the centuries closely mixed-up their cultures and languages. They also came in contact with a host of foreign peoples like the Greeks, Persians, Shakas, Hunas, Arabs and Turks who profoundly influenced Indian culture. Each one of them contributed its own share to the common storehouse of Indian culture and civilization. The Indians today identify themselves in as many as twenty-two different ethnic groups, with their own languages as recognized and incorporated in the Eighth Schedule of the Constitution of India. Besides the above major ethnic groups, there exists a host of minor tribes and communities scattered all-over the north-east, Chhattisgarh, Jharkhand, Orissa, Rajasthan, Gujarat, Tamil Nadu and Andaman & Nicobar, who have their distinct and colourful culture, religion, faith and costumes. Thus, India is a melting pot of diverse cultures, religions, costumes and languages.

Despite the bewildering diversities in race, religion, language and culture, mentioned in the preceding paragraphs, there exists a deep underlying unity which has kept the people of India as one nation. The close affinities in their languages, faith and religion, history and the strong cultural ethos and values have united the 1.23 billion population into a second largest nation in the world. This unity in diversity may escape the notice of a casual observer, but certainly not of the people who have deeper knowledge about Indian civilization, antiquity and history. Herbert Risley wrote, "Beneath the manifold diversity of physical and social type, language, custom and religion which strike the observer in India, there can still be discerned a certain underlying uniformity of life from the Himalayas to Cap Comorin. It is a unity of thoughts, of ideals, of spirit, born of general acceptance of Hindu principles of religion, culture and tradition."[5] This unity in diversity has for centuries sustained the feeling of oneness in the hearts of Indian people which is their common heritage.

Nepal Compared to India

Nepal, compared to India, is a very small country which comes to less than one-twentieth of India's total geographical area. But its physical features, climate, topography, soil, vegetations and demographic composition etc. are as varied and distinguished as those of India. From this point of view, Nepal is very much identical with India. Like India, the northern boundary of Nepal is defined by long ranges of great Himalaya stretching from the east to the west in an unbroken line, forming a natural barrier. These mountain ranges remain covered with snow and glacier throughout the year which form the fountain heads of numerous rivers and streams that water the soil of Nepal and India. At irregular intervals these mountains have raised their heads in the form of snowy peaks of enormous height to be known as Gaurishankar, Dhaulagiri, Gosaithan, Nandadevi, Kanchenjungha and, of course, the famous Mt. Everest. Major rivers of Nepal like Kosi, Gandaki, Kali, Bagmati, etc. flow down to India by different names and pour out their waters into the river Ganga.

Nepal, like India, is an ancient country with a varied cultural heritage and a long chequered political history. Archaeological evidences show that Nepal was peopled since more than ten thousand years ago. The Neolithic tools found in Kathmandu valley reveals that the Himalayan region was inhabited by people at least before nine thousand years. But the actual historical data that could be gleaned so far, goes back only up to about five thousand years from now. The earliest records about Nepal can be traced from the *Arthashastra* of Kautilya written as back as third century B.C. Kathmandu, the capital of Nepal, has a history of more than two thousand years which is incredibly glorious. The *Nepal Mahatmya*, incorporated in the *Skanda Purana* speaks highly about the temples and shrines of Nepal. Its ancient art and architecture are still visible in temples, monuments and buildings.[6] Hiuen Tsang, the Chinese traveller, who visited the north-east frontiers of India during seventh century A.D. calls Nepal as Ni-po-lo and states that it is situated at a distance of 1,400 li (i.e. about 280 miles) north-west of a ruined city. Nevertheless, recent archaeological discovery of ancient stone tools and implements pushes the history of Nepal back to the Neolithic age.

The history of both India and Nepal is a spectacular account of inter-mixture and assimilation of multiple races, religions and languages that resulted into two unique pluralistic nations. Since the remote past till the advent of the fourteenth century, India received foreign invaders like the Aryans, Persians, Scythians, Turks, Tartars and the Mughals through the openings of the great Himalayan mountain walls known as Khyber, Gomel, Balam, Kurem etc. In the similar way, Nepal, as a land-locked country sandwitched between the great Himalaya in the north and the vast Gangetic plains of India in the south, received settlers of various racial and linguistic affiliations from both north and the south. From the north came the people of Tibeto-Burman linguistic races across the Himalayan passes known as Kuti, Hatia, Kerong, Mastang etc., while from the southern frontiers of Indo-Gangetic regions, entered more dominant tribes like the Kiratas, Lichchhavis, Thakurs, Mallas, Shahs and the Rajputs. A peep into the early history of Nepal gives us an interesting insight into the historical process that came to play in moulding the racial character of the early dwellers of the Sub-Himalayan country. Historians think that Nepal was originally inhabited by Mongolians who came to settle down there, perhaps, during the great Mongolian conquest of Asia. According to D.R. Regmi, the earliest settlers in the Nepal valley were of the same stock as the Mundas, Kols and Bhils of Chhotanagpur of India, but no archaeological evidence has yet been traced about their settlement in Nepal.[7] The Kiratas who speak the language of Tibeto-Burman origin are said to have settled in Nepal long before the religion of Buddhism came to the region. Originally, the Kiratas were the people of the north-east India around Pragjyotishpura who were pushed into the mountainous regions of Nepal by the Aryan settlers as they advanced from the Gangetic plains. Dr. S.K. Chatterji observed that probably the people with Mongoloid features entered the confines of India through Assam at some time before 1000 B.C. and that they might have been pushed along the Himalayan slopes as far as the hills of eastern Punjab.[8] The epic of *Mahabharata* provides us with ample attestations to the fact that the Sino-Tibetans known as Kiratas belonged to the Brahmaputra valley of Assam. To cite an example out of many, in *Sabha Parva* there is specific reference to the Kiratas living on both sides of the Lohitya (Upper Brahmaputra) who appeared with their tributes at the *Rajasuya Yajna* performed by Yudhishthira. We also find mention of Kiratas as forming an essential part of the army of the Pragjyotisha king Bhagadatta who took part in the battle of Kurukshetra on behalf of Durjyodhana. Speaking about the Kiratas, Grierson writes—The Tibeto-Burman speaking Mongoloids with yellow complexion came to be known among the Vedic Aryan as Kiratas. According to E.A. Gait, "Ghataka, one of the Kirata kings ruled in Kamrup, the ancient Assam who was defeated and slain by Naraka Asura."[9] In the chronicles of Tippera Kings, it is recorded that the ancient name of their country was Kirata and the word still survives as the designation of the tract in the sub-Himalaya between Dudh Kosi and Arun rivers.[10] Nepalese tradition and chronicles or *Vamshavali* also indicate that they were an offshoot of the tribes now living in that part of the country called *Kiratadesha*.[11] The ancient literature of India like the *Vedas*, *Puranas* and the epics all seem to use a blanket term Kirata to designate the heterogeneous tribes of present days who inhabited the southern slopes of Himalaya, and the States of Bhutan, Nepal, Sikkim and the north-eastern region of India. In Nepal, the land mass stretching from Sunkosi river in the west to the Arun river in the east was known as *Kiratadesha* which constitutes eastern Nepal today. According to Brian Hodgson, an authority in Nepalese ethnology, the aboriginal tribes of Nepal are the Magars, Gurung, Newars, Limbus,Tamangs, Rais and Lepchas who are of Mongolian race and speakers of Tibeto-Burman language. The Kiratas who settled down in the valley of Nepal in ancient times, probably in the pre-Christian era, are identified with the present day Kiratas, i.e., Kulung, Thulung and Yelung.[12] The Newars who happened to be one of the oldest inhabitants of Nepal valley are also identified with Kiratas. They are supposed to have lived between Gandaki and Sunkosi.[13] Hodgson found that the sub-Himalayan races named above are all closely affiliated to each other by their vocabularies, physical attributes as well as creeds, customs and legends. According to Dr. Suniti Kumar Chatterjee,

"Rai, Limbu, Tamang, Gurung, Lepcha, Mogar and Sherpa all belong to Kirata group."[14] The Tharus or Thadus, who live in the Terai region of Nepal and eastern Rohilkhanda along the frontier of Oudh and Gorakhpur are also supposed to be identical with the Kiratas.[15] Most of the Kiratas of Nepal live in the eastern part of Nepal which is geographically not very far from Assam and similarly, Assam too has a large number of Kiratas like the Boros, Kacharis, Garos, Ravas, Mismis etc. They are very similar to each other in their physical appearance, languages, customs and legends. Thus, if one ignores the political boundary between Nepal and north-eastern India the entire region will constitute a Kirata culture zone. Actually, Mithila, Nepal, Kamrup and Bengal constituted one cultural zone both historically and geographically.[16] A careful and dispassionate study of the ancient Indian historical traditions and the classical records that the non-Aryan tribes such as the Kiratas, Mlechchhas, Dasas, etc. were the inhabitants of India long before the Aryans came to settle in India. Unfortunately, they have no history apart from the Vedic or Brahmanical traditions. For ages their relics have been turning to dust in caves and cromlechs or lying buried beneath the shapeless mounds.[17] All that we know about them today is by gleaning scant references lying scattered in the Vedic scriptures and Hindu classical records.

From the ancient records it can be perceived that Nepal was originally inhabited and ruled by peoples coming from two different directions—one from the north being Tibeto-Burman race and the other from the south as people of Indian origin. Thus ever since before and after the Christian era, continuous batches of peoples were finding their ways into Nepal and settling down side-by-side meeting and mixing together for generations, at times fighting each other, at others living peacefully and mixing their blood in legitimate marriages, paved the way to the inevitable historical process of emerging out a new nation in Nepal with one *lingua-franca* called Gorkhali or Nepali language and yet speaking their own dialects and preserving own cultures to some extent. The assimilation of cultures, thus, remained confined to the areas where the two races lived in close proximity. In the areas of extreme northern Nepal where the Indian culture did not reach the aboriginal people, culture and language remained more or less as before. The geography too played its role in the ethnic distribution of population in Nepal which can be perceived as an assimilative factor even today. As the entry of Aryans into Nepal started from the south-west and that of the Mongolians from the north-east, we find the population in the south-western region of Nepal are more or less similar with the Indians in their appearance, customs and religion; and as we go further to the north-east the stronger becomes the Mongolian strain in their features, customs and manners. Thus, we find in Nepal, people of different ethnic groups wearing different costumes and ornaments, speaking their own tribal dialects and following different cultures, religions, rites and rituals. Nevertheless, they call themselves Nepalese and speak Nepali language and feel themselves as one nation.

Ever since time immemorial India and Nepal have been sharing a common history, culture and tradition. The relationship between the two countries is such that the course of history of one country is profoundly influenced by that of the other and that both of them trail an heritage so intimately interlinked with each other that it is well nigh impossible to comprehend one without understanding the other. History tells us that since the remotest past till the advent of the fourteenth century the valley of Nepal received hoards of outside settlers most of whom migrated from India. They subdued the original dwellers of Nepal and ruled over them for several centuries. The newcomers from the southern plains, who were Hindus brought with them Brahmins and priests and with their superior knowledge and civilization they gained ascendancy over the highlander tribes and turned situation to their advantage. Gradually, the hill communities adapted the language and culture of their rulers as their own and many of them accepted Hinduism and felt themselves advanced and elevated in social status.

It is interesting to note that both the countries possess unique features of unity in the midst of diversity—diversity of races, languages, customs, dresses, and yet a marked unity as one nation, one broad culture and heritage and one country. Way back in the nineteenth century, the British historian, Vincent Smith rightly called India an "Ethnological Museum". Looking from this angle Nepal may be perceived as a miniature India with its wonderful blend of variegated ethno-cultural traits. If India is, as stated by Radha Kumud Mookerjee, "a museum of cults and customs, creeds and cultures, faith and tongue, racial types and social system", then Nepal is verily the confluence of all these elements into one whole. Both India and Nepal have inherited from the past common form and style of art, culture, literature, philosophy, metaphysics, astronomy, astrology and medicine. The people of both the countries have been influenced by the same *Vedas*, *Upanishads* and *Puranas* which have deeply embedded into their socio-religious psyche. The great epics of *Ramayana* and *Mahabharata* are held in highest esteem by both the countries. Great prophets like Buddha, Mahavira, and mighty kings like Ashoka and Vikramaditya belong to Nepal as much as to India in so far as they have played their unique roles in shaping the history of Nepal no less than that of India. Both the nations feel equally proud of them. Even to this day, the memory of great emperor Ashoka vividly lingers in the hearts of the people of India through the emblem of *Dharmachakra* (wheel of virtues) superimposed in their National flag, and in the same way, the *Stupas* erected by Ashoka around Kathmandu eternally proclaim his abiding presence with the people of Nepal.

Vikramaditya, the legendary emperor of Gupta dynasty left behind his legacy of Vikram Era to the people of Nepal as national calendar that begins from 58 B.C. which is still in vogue in Nepal by the name of Vikram Samvat. The origin of the Vikram era is traditionally assigned to King Vikramaditya (Chadragupta II) of Ujjain.[18] The devotional movements launched in India by great saints like Sankaracharya, Ramanuja, Kabir, Ramananda, Mira, Tulsidas etc. created the same spiritual waves in Nepal as in India. The Bhakti movement propounded by these saints was grounded on the belief that the real religion consisted in understanding the tenet that teaches about the basic unity of all religions and not in merely adhering to its form and rituals of external practices. It also believed in the universal equality of all human beings and that the distinction of birth and castes was unreal and therefore abominable.

All these factors go to indicate that there exists an inexplicable unity and underlying uniformity in the life and ethos between the people of India and Nepal. Perhaps there are no two countries in the world so closely identical to each other as India and Nepal are. They look like one people and one nation, in every respect of their lives. They suffer same kind of social discrimination, as the Indian *dalits*, the oppressed and the people living below poverty line do. Like India Nepal too has multi-ethnic groups comprising nearly sixty communities whose destinies are dependent on a few advanced classes, like the Brahmins,Thakuris, Chhetries and Newars while the larger segment of the population are left in abject poverty, hunger and disease. It is sad to say that more than fifty years of independence from the autocratic Rana rule and the advent of popular Government in Nepal have miserably failed to bring about a semblance of socio-economic upliftment of the down-trodden rural mass of Nepal. The Nepalese society had been historically oppressed by the higher and ruling class for the last more than a couple of centuries and they continue to be marginalized and deprived of social justice, equalities and basic human rights and even to this day.

Notes

1. Sriman Narayan (1971), *India and Nepal,* Delhi: Hind Pocket Books.
2. R.C. Majumdar and H.C. Roychoudhury *et al.*, *Advanced History of India*, p. 4.
3. K.C. Bhanja (1948), *The Himalayan Wonders.*
4. Percival Landon, *Nepal* (1928), Vol. II, Delhi: Cosmo Publication.
5. K.L. Mukerjee, *History of India*, Calcutta, p. 3.
6. D.R. Regmi (1969), *Ancient Nepal*, Calcutta: Rupbani Press.
7. *Ibid.*
8. S.K. Chatterjee (1969), *Kirata-Jana-Kriti,* 2nd Edition, Asiatic Society.
9. E.A. Gait (1926), *History of Assam*, Calcutta.
10. *Ibid.*
11. D.R. Regmi, *Ancient Nepal*, pp. 55-56.
12. *Ibid.*, pp. 55-56; N.B. Thapa, *A Short History of Nepal,* pp. 8-9.
13. *Ibid.*
14. S.K. Chatterji (1947), *Kirata-Janakriti*, Asiatic Society.
15. P. Carnegy, *Notes on the Races, Tribes, and Castes Inhabiting the Province of Avadh*, p. 1; Regmi, D.R., *Ancient Nepal*, p. 24.
16. G.P. Singh (1947), *The Kiratas in Ancient India*, New Delhi: Gian Publishing House.
17. *Ibid.*
18. K.L. Mukerjee (1995), *History of India*, Calcutta, p. 249.

2

Rivers and Human Cultures

The Ganga and the Gandaki are the two major rivers of two neighbouring countries of India and Nepal. They rise from two different points of the same Himalayan ranges and merge with each other after traversing a great length through their respective countries symbolizing the merger of two great cultures and civilizations of India and Nepal. The two great civilizations flourished side by side in the Gangetic valley of India and the Gandaki basin of Nepal. The Gangetic valley was the cradle of Indo-Aryan civilization while Gandaki basin, the ancient habitat of the Nepalese people. The former was known as *Aryavarta* while the latter was called *Sapta-Gandaki*. These two historic rivers originated from the same lofty snow-clad Himalaya, flowed down the valleys of India and Nepal and eventually met each other to make one great river, symbolizing the confluence of two cultures and traditions of India and Nepal.

The Ganga, a legendary river of India, takes its rise from Gangotri, a glacier at Uttarakhand in the Central Himalayas and after traversing a distance of 2510 km across Uttarakhand, Uttar Pradesh, Bihar and West Bengal, it drains itself into the Bay of Bengal making a delta in the Sundarbans. It has the largest drainage area of about one million sq. km that support the world's highest density of human population.

On the other hand, Gandaki is one of the principal river systems of Nepal which contribute immensely to the socio-economic and cultural well-being of the people of Nepal. These rivers constitute three major river basins of Nepal known as the Koshi, Gandaki and the Karnali. The Koshi river system consists of seven tributaries collectively known as the *Sapta-Koshi*, they are—Dudh-Koshi, Tama-Koshi, Sun-Koshi, Tamur, Arun, Likhu and Indrawati, all of which drain the eastern region of Nepal. The Gandaki river system comprises another group of seven tributaries called—Kali-Gandaki, Budhi-Gandaki, Marsyangdi, Trisuli, Seti, Madi and Darandi which drain the central region of Nepal by the name the *Sapta-Gandaki*. Lastly, the Karnali river system has four major tributaries, viz., Humla-Karnali, Mugu-Karnali, Seti and Bheri and they form the western river drainage system of the country of Nepal. All the above mentioned eighteen hilly riverines originate in the high Himalayan mountains, cut across Nepalese territory and flow down to the Gangetic plains and after traversing considerable length finally pour out their waters into the Ganga either individually or jointly by taking various names. The river Arun and Sun-Koshi, the tributaries of Koshi river, originate in Tibet, while the Kali-Gandaki,the tributary of Gandaki, originates in Mustang and as it flows down the valley of Nepal it converges with river Trisuli at Devghat where it takes the name of Narayani and falls into Ganga. Again the Humla-Karnali, the branch of the river Karnali originates in western Tibet and after cutting through the snowy mountains of Nepal it flows down to Ganga by the name Gogra. Thus, all the rivers coming down from Nepal, at one point or the other become the tributaries of Ganga, joining her from the northern direction while Yamuna and Sone rivers join the Ganga from the south.

Topographically, the country of Nepal is divided into three large natural divisions by the lofty and massive ridges which are branched out respectively from four high peaks of Himalaya, namely, Nandadevi (25,700 ft.), Dhaulagiri (26,826 ft.), Gosainthan (26,305 ft.) and Kanchanjanga (28,156 ft.). These four enormous ridges stand out at right angles to the central axis of the Himalayas and slope down gradually as they advance towards the south running almost parallel to each other. The three major river systems of Nepal mentioned above flow between these lofty ridges in a systematic way down to the south cutting across the country of Nepal into three slices so as to form three different large river basins which are locally known as the Kosi basin or *Sapta-Kosi*, the Gandaki basin or *Sapta-Gandaki* and the Karnali basin. Each of these three river basins is watered by a numerous small tributaries which take their rise in the surrounding Himalayan ridges and enter into Nepal through the mountain passes known as Takla Khar Pass, Mastang Pass, Kerong pass and Hatia pass etc. They traverse a long way through thickly populated areas, cultivated fields and small towns and semi-urban areas and ultimately merge with their respective sister rivers.

In India, the river Ganga is considered by the Hindus as a sacred river that trails a great religious significance. According to mythological account, the river Ganga was created by Brahma by collecting the sweat from the feet of God Visnu. The legend alluded to in *Ramayana* is a long story about the origin of the Ganga. It recounts that Sagara, the King of Ayodhya, had two wives, Kesini and Sumati, but had no son for a long time. He went to Himalaya and performed *puja* to the sage Bhrigu who being pleased with the king granted one son to Kesini and sixty thousand sons to Sumati. Soon, Kesini gave birth to one son named Asamanjas while the other queen Sumati gave birth to a fissiparous mass which divided out into sixty thousand babies. In course of time they all grew-up to manhood and handsome princes. Asamanjas, however, turned out to be a cruel and mentally imbalanced prince who oppressed the subjects by all sorts of wicked deeds. Years rolled by, Asamanjas married and got a son named Amsuman who turned out to be a brave, virtuous and amiable prince.

King Sagara being happy at the prosperity and well-being of his descendants performed a great Horse sacrifice, a symbol of victory, and placed the sacrificial horse under the charge of his grand son Amsuman. God Indra had a strong objection to this desperate act of king Sagara, which amounted, in the eye of god, to throwing up a mortal challenge to Gods in Heaven by a mere human being of the earth. So, he took the guise of a *Rakshasa* and kidnapped the sacrificial horse. King Sagara was greatly perturbed at this unauspicious event and he sent out his army of sixty thousand sons to search the horse all-over the earth even not sparing the under world (*patala*). The princes having failed to locate the horse anywhere on the earth went down to the *patala* where they saw the animal grazing near the *Ashrama* of sage Kapila who was engaged in meditation nearby. The princes instantly jumped upon the sage thinking that he was a thief pretending to be a *jogi*. Sage

Kapila being greatly disturbed opened his fiery eyes by which the sixty thousand princes were burned down and reduced to a heap of ashes. The mission of Horse Sacrifice was defeated and the tricks played by God Indra became a success.

The king Sagara, tired of waiting for the return of his sixty thousand princes with the missing horse, called his grandson, Amsuman and said, "Go immediately to *Patala* and find out what has happened to my brave sons. Amsuman, at once set out for the search and reaching *Patala* he found the sacrificial horse grazing at the corner of a green field and nearby he saw a heap of ashes. As he was looking at the heap of ashes in utter surprise a Garuda, bird-king, happened to pass by that way who told the prince that the heap of ashes was all that is left of the sixty thousand sons of king Sagara. He also advised him that the souls of the sixty thousand dead princes could attain salvation only if the heap of ashes were immersed in the water of Ganga brought down from the land of Devas. Amsuman not knowing what to do, took the sacrificial horse and returned home to report to his grand-father the plight of his sixty thousand uncles. King Sagara died grieving at the fate of his dear sons.

Thousands of years passed away but no one could perform the feat of bringing down the Ganga from heaven to earth and then to the under-world (*patala*). Bhagiratha, a descendant of king Sagara, determined to bring salvation to his unfortunate sixty thousand forefathers, went through a severe austerity through worship to Lord Siva, who, at last, became pleased at the *tapas* and caused Ganga to descend on his matted bunch of hair and then to flow down on earth. The Ganga merrily flowed down the hills and as she did so, unknowingly damaged with flood the holy alter of Rishi Jahnu who was in meditation. He became furious and scooped-up the entire flow of water into his palm and sipped it off. To the great surprise and dismay of Bhagiratha, the water of Ganga suddenly disappeared. Seeing the consternation of Bhagiratha, the Devas felt pity on him and begged Jahnu to forgive Ganga and allow her to flow again so that the righteous aspiration of Bhagiratha could be fulfilled. The sage relented and let the Ganga come out through his right ear. So, Ganga got the name *Jahnavi*, Jahnu's daughter, as she came out of the body of the Rishi. From now onward there was no more obstruction. Ganga reached underworld (*patala*) and with her holy waters Bhagiratha performed funeral rites of his sixty thousand ancestors and secured their entry into heaven."

This being the story behind the origin of the river Ganga as narrated in the great epic *Ramayana*, the Indians attribute a great religious significance to Ganga. She is regarded as the mother, *Ganga Mai* and her water a purifier of all sins. Every Hindu likes to take a holy dip into the river Ganga for the ablution of his body, mind and soul. Many temples and shrines are situated on the banks of river Ganga besides the famous Viswanath temple of Benaras and the Gangamata temple at Gangotri, the source of river Ganga. It is believed that the waters of three sacred rivers, namely the Ganga, Yamuna and Saraswati (an underground current, not to be seen by human eyes) converge at Prayag (present Allahabad) making the spot, *Sangam*, the most holy and sanctified. People from both India and Nepal bring ashes of their dead parents to Prayag and immerse them in the holy waters of *Sangam* for the salvation of their souls from earthly sins and bondages. It is believed that no performance of funeral rites is complete without immersion of the ashes of the dead into the holy waters of Ganga. This connotes the same religious significance that has been related above in connection with the ashes of sixty thousand sons of king Sagara who were burnt down by the fiery eyes of sage Kapila in the underworld, *patala*. *Kumbha mela* is held every six or twelve year at the bank of Ganga at a place called Prayag, perhaps, in order to commemorate the event of the salvation of the souls of sixty thousand sons of king Sagara with the touch of the holy Ganga waters. On completion of every twelve years, a *Purna Kumbha Mela* is held at the same place when Hindu pilgrims and *sadhus* from various parts of India and Nepal gather with a view to taking a dip into the Holy Ganga. The Hindus of both India and Nepal consider the Ganga as the most sacred river and the immersion of the ashes of their dead parents into the holy waters of Ganga as an essential part of religious rite.

The geographic conditions and natural features of a country or a place like the rivers, mountains, soil, climate etc. have always influenced the course of political, cultural and economic history of its people. The rivers and their tributaries, more than anything else, play a significant role in moulding and developing the life and culture of the people. History bears testimony to a great many of human civilizations which grew-up and flourished around the river valleys in the dim past. The graphic example of the early human civilizations can be found in the Indus Valley Civilization of Harappa and Mahenjo-Daro which flourished around the fertile basins of the seven tributaries of river Sindhu known as the '*Sapta-Sindhu*'. We also know about the Sumerian Civilization in the lower valley of Euphrates and Tigris rivers of Mesopotamia. The name Mesopotamia means a territory of land between two rivers that played a significant role in building-up the culture of the people. The southern part of Mesopotamia was known as Sumer and so the civilization is called the Sumerian Civilization. Another civilization that grew-up along the valley of river Nile about the same period of time is known as the Egyptian Civilization. All these early civilizations had their beginnings between 7000 to 6000 B.C.

The rivers flow down from one place to another, traverse from one country to another and meet different peoples and carry their cultures. They provide excellent means of transport, communication and trade facilities for the economic growth and prosperity of mankind. In olden times, the rivers were the principal means of trade and communication in India. The *Jatakas* tells us that great deal of river traffics and ships travelled from Benaras, Patna, Champa (present Bhagalpur) and many other places to the sea and thence to southern ports of Ceylon and Malaya. The Oxus river in central Asia formed a link in an important chain along which Indian goods were carried to Europe by way of the Caspian and Black sea. The rivers help industrial growth and open-up multiple avenues of livelihood for the people. They also carry, as they rush down the valleys, organic sediments, silts and alluvial deposits and enrich the soil and help agricultural production. The rivers may be called the supreme gifts of god to mankind, as they serve as lifeline of the people or a nation. Man needs water to live, the plants and animals and all living beings need water for their life. It is due to this reason that men have always preferred to settle down in the river valleys where big cities, and commercial centres have grown- up across the world. The great industrial cities around the banks of the river Thames, the Mississippie, Nile, Brahmaputra, Sindhu, Godavari etc. are some of the good examples of how rivers contribute to the growth of modern civilization.

Geographically, the great Himalaya standing like a gigantic wind-screen controls the climate and environmental conditions of the entire Indian sub-continent by causing monsoon rainfall every summer. Apart from this, they also play important role in political and international relations, trades and commerce, economic development, internal and external securities etc. Nepal, a land-locked country, with her lofty Himalaya ranges in the north stretching from east to west has, for ages, acted as an impregnable natural wall against foreign invasions to India and herself. The fact that the country of Tibet and the formidable China lie to the north of Nepal makes her geo-politically strategic for both India and China.

For the Hindus, the Himalaya holds a great religious significance. For them the Himalaya is a holy place, an abode of Gods and Goddesses and a sacred place of meditation and spiritual attainment for Indian saints and sages. The lofty snow-clad peaks of Mount Everest and Dhaulagiri that glitter in the morning sun shine look as if they are adorning mother India with a silvery crown upon her head. Nepal, the tiny Hindu kingdom, nestles eternally in the lap of bewildering maze of descending mountain ridges. Thus, the geographical consanguinity between India and Nepal is such that the bearing of the one can only be comprehended with the geo-location of the other. The Himalaya which means the abode of snows, can better be termed as the "Abode of eternity" as a prime source of Indian mythology and ancient lore on which are based much of the ancient history of India and Nepal.

The great rivers of north India, such as the Brahmaputra, Ganga, Jamuna all have taken their rise from the bosom of Himalaya. These rivers, being fed with the icy waters of melted snows and glaciers of Himalaya, cutting across the snowy crags and ridges, flow down the Indian plains watering vast areas of the northern India and contributing to the development of agriculture, forest, industry and the biosphere. They have virtually become the lifelines of the people of north India and helped them to boost-up their economy, life and culture for the last more than a couple of millenniums. That is the reason why, each of these rivers has been glorified by the Indian sages for its spiritual and temporal values in the epics of *Ramayana* and *Mahabharata*. How great and enigmatic is the nature's plan which makes the lives and culture of two peoples so interwoven and dependent to each other.

The fertile Gangetic basin of the north-east India, like the historic Tigris and Euphratis basins of the Middle-east, have always attracted peoples of different races and cultures to settle down around their fertile basin. In early about 1000 B.C. the Aryans, as they increased in population, moved from the Sind basin and settled down in the Gangetic valley which was inhabited by heterogeneous non-Aryan tribes. They drove them away and proudly called their new found land, '*Aryavarta*', the land of Aryans. According to Budhist and Jain texts there flourished as many as sixteen independent states or kingdoms known as '*Mahajanapadas*' of which the most powerful were, Avanti, Kosala, Vatsya and Magadha. These *Mahajanapadas* roughly covered the whole landmass of the north India comprising the present Uttar Pradesh, Jharkhand, Bihar, Madhya Pradesh, half part of Orissa and northern Bengal. In fact, the contemporary Gangetic valley, India's largest ever river basin, covers approximately twenty-five per cent of the total of riverine drainage area of India. Jawaharlal Nehru, in his monumental book, '*Discovery of India*', writes—"The story of Ganga from her source to the sea, from all time to now, is the story of India's civilization and culture, of the rise and fall of empires, of great and proud cities, of adventures of men".[1] This Gangetic valley was the centre of Aryan civilization and culture where the Vedic culture had developed to its highest glory and spread all over India. It was on the banks of river Ganga where the ancient *Rishis* had chanted the Vedic hymns and consecrated holy Ganga waters to their Gods and Goddesses. It was usual practice of the devout Brahmins, it is still in vogue among many, to rise from bed early morning before the first rays of the sun touches the mother earth and to take a holy dip in the nearest river after offering a handful of water as *arghyam*. It was this holy soil of *Aryavarta* where the seeds of great religious movements like Jainism and Buddhism were first sown and propagated by Lord Mahavira and

Gautama Buddha. The ancient capital of emperor Chandragupta Maurya known as Pataliputra, present city of Patna, was situated on the bank of river Ganga. Megasthenese, a Greek traveller, who came from Bactria (Turkistan) crossed over Ganga with a boat and walked into Pataliputra, the capital city in 322 B.C. He lived at the court of Chandragupta in royal hospitality for several years, took bath in the holy Ganga, as many Hindus did and wrote valuable accounts about India and her people.

The religious importance of the river Ganga can be very well understood from the fact that all the ancient and mediaeval Hindu temples like Viswanath temple of Benaras; Baidyanath temple of Deoghar, the Sun tenple of Konark, Orissa; Badrinarayan temple and Kedarnath temple of Uttarakhand etc. are situated along the bank of the Ganga. To the north of Ganga was the great kingdom of Koshala that was made fertile by the river Sarayu. Ayodhya was the capital of Kosala established by Manu, the famous ruler of Solar dynasty and ruled by Dasaratha, the father of Rama, the hero of the epic *Ramayana* during the seventh century B.C. Great kings like Chandragupta Maurya, Ashoka, Samudragupta and Vikramaditya were born in this Aryavarta who conquered far-flung countries and unified them into a great kingdom of *Bharat Varsha*. Great prophets like Buddha and Mahavira were born in this holy land and preached new religions of Buddhism and Jainism. They taught people a new way of life, the path of truth which only would lead to salvation. Buddha said, truth is noble and sweet; happy is he who has overcome all selfishness; happy is he who has attained peace and happy is he who has found the truth. Mahavira emphasized asceticism and self-mortification, the reference to which can be found in the *Vedas*, the *Aranyakas* and *Upanishads*. The centre of ancient learning was located at Nalanda, the famous Nalanda university, in Bihar where great scholars like Hieun-Tsang came to learn about Buddhism. Many other important Buddhist monasteries were developed at various places such as, Pataliputra, Valabhi, Ujjaiyini, Mathura, Ayodhya, Varanasi etc.

It was again in this Gangetic basin that the indigenous knowledge of arts, science, architecture, astronomy, astrology and medicine were born and developed by eminent scientists like Aryabhatta, Varahamihira, Brahmagupta, Charaka etc. The

Mauryan period was the landmark in the history of Indian art and architecture which grew-up around Indo-Gangetic basin. The Mauryan emperors were marvellous builders of magnificent buildings and other artistic stone monuments which have survived till today. Great progress was achieved in the field of scientific studies by famous mathematicians and astronomers like Aryabhatta, Varahamihira etc. who were credited to have formulated the theory of Zero in mathematics and used decimal system of calculations. Europe got the knowledge of arithmetic and Algebra from India. It first went to Arab country then it was taken to Europe. That is why Arabic numerals are still in use in Europe.[2] When we closely observe the shape and form of the English numerals and Hindi numerals from number one to ten, their stunning similarity strongly suggests us that the Europeans might have adapted their numerals from Hindi numerals. The following table shows as many as seven numbers of numerals of both the languages are almost identical to each other.

Table of Comparison between English and Hindi Numerals

Hindi numerals	१	२	३	४	५	६	७	८	९	१०
English numerals	1	2	3	4	5	6	7	8	9	10

The above table shows very close similarities in the forms and shapes of the numerals 2, 3, 5 and 7 and nearly similar in respect of 1, 6 and 10 numerals. Unless there is some kind of influence of one over the other there cannot be so close similarities between the two numerals.

Equally famous were the Indian physicians like Charaka and Sushruta who had the knowledge of Ayurveda, medicinal plants and herbs and medical surgery. In the field of literature and language, many astute Sanskrit scholars like Kalidasa, Bharavi, and Vatsabhatti lived in this Gangetic basin and produced works of great literary values. The Sanskrit dramas *viz.*, *Shakuntalam*, *Malavikagnimitram* and *Vikramorvashiyam* and the epic poems like *Ritusamhara* and *Meghaduta* of Kalidasa are the ageless works of literature. Visakhadatta, the author of famous *Mudrarakshasa* and the lexicographer Amarsingh, the author of *Amarkosha*, the noted Sanskrit dictionary also belonged to the Gangetic valley civilization. When we think of these great accomplishments attained by ancient India our hearts swell-up in joy and pride.

The rivers also act as catalysts to cultural contacts between nations and exchanges of human thoughts and ideas. As the rivers flow from one place to another and merge with another river or ocean, the human culture, language and religion too travel across the countries of the world through trade, transport and communication, meet with different cultures and languages and get merged into one another. Over the past millennia India has come in contact with numerous alien cultures and traditions which have influenced the course of life of the Indian people and left an indelible mark in their culture and history. India had a long cultural and commercial intercourse with western Asia ever since the invasion of Darius in 510 B.C. who annexed Indus valley and made it the twentieth province of the Persian empire. The Persian rule in north-western India for a period of nearly two centuries made a profound impact upon the life and culture of Indian people. The Kharoshti script, an off-shoot of Aramaic language, introduced by the Persian rulers in their official documents came to be used in the north-western frontiers for several centuries. There was a great development in Indo-Persian trade which had a tremendous impact on the art, architecture and domestic usages of household articles which changed the lifestyle of the people of both countries. According to B.N. Luniya, the Persian style of architecture influenced the art of the Mauryan architecture as reflected in the "lion capitals of the Ashokan pillars".[3] Similarly, the Greek settlement in Indian frontiers around 300 B.C. accelerated Indo-Greek trade and commerce which heralded a direct and visible influence on India's art and culture. The emergence of the Graeco-Buddhist art of Gandhara in India is an example of culture fusion, the traces of which are still to be seen in various caves and temples of India. The Greek rulers, whom the Hindus called Yavanas, not only brought their culture to India but also succumbed themselves to the fascination of Indian culture and embraced the religion of India. Menander, for example, the Greek ruler in India became a devout Buddhist under the noted Buddhist monk named Nagasena who is referred to as *Milindapanha* in popular Buddhist legend and regarded as a saint by the Buddhists. Heliodorus, the Greek ambassador of King Antialcidas embraced Hinduism, as a staunch believer in Vishnu.[4] The Shakas or Scythians who came to India from Central Asia established their supremacy over Indian people and ruled northern India, were influenced by Indian culture and religion and became converted into Buddhism and Hinduism. The Kushanas, after having pushed the Shakas towards South India, established their sway over the entire North India and ruled for a long time during which period they also became converted to Buddhism. The great king Kanishka of Kushana dynasty not only embraced Buddhism but also patronized Buddhism and held the first Buddhist Council in India. In the great Council Buddhism was divided into two sections—the Mahayana and the Hinayana. The university of Takshashila, near modern Peshawar became the centre of learning religion and culture where the scholars of various communities—the Scythians, the Turks, the Kushanas, the Chinese etc. flocked together. Thus, India not only hosted many alien tribes from outside, but also opened-up her doors of culture and religion to them and Indianised them all. India's mixing-up with peoples of other races not only affected their life and culture, but also equally influenced India too. The above facts make it clear that the Shakas, Pahlavas, Yavanas, and all those races who entered India were gradually integrated into the Indian society and they soon formed integral part of India. Many of them opted for Hindu names such as Dharmadeva, Manadeva, Amsuvarman etc.

The foreigners who had the longest and most persistent impact on Indian life and culture were the Iranians. Their relationship with India precedes even the beginnings of Indo-Aryan civilization, for it was out of some common stock that the Indo-Aryans and the ancient Iranians diverged and took their different ways.[5] The Persian language continued to occupy the place of court language in India right from the time of Afghan and Mughal periods and lasted till the advent of the British rule. During this long period of nearly 500, years the Persian language so deeply permeated into Indian literature that modern Hindi and many other languages are full of Persian words. The Mughal rulers brought scholars, architects and artists to their courts in India who wrote beautiful poems, and chronicles and built royal palaces, monuments and mausoleums, which had a lasting influence on Indian art and architecture.

Two very important religions, namely Christianity and Hebrew came to India long before the British missionaries entered India. According to Christian tradition, the Apostle Saint Thomas came to India after about thirty years of the crucifixion of Jesus Christ. They were followed by the Zoroastrians who came from Iran during the seventh century and thereafter came the religion of Islam with the Turkish, Afghan and Mughal invaders around eleventh century A.D. and thereafter. All these races came as invaders, but stayed back and settled in India and ultimately got absorbed with Indian people and became integrated into Indian life. The process of Indianization of these people was accelerated mostly during the reign of Akbar who was a man of very large heart and liberal mind. During his long reign of nearly fifty years he endeavoured to unite India into one nation one people. He made his enemy, the Rajput Maharajas his own friends through matrimonial alliance by marrying the Rajput princess from whom Jahangir, the Mughal crown prince was born. Akbar looked both Hindu and Moslem with equal eye and his court became a meeting place of men of all faiths. He even tried to evolve a new synthetic faith for the people of all religions. He said, there was good in every religion, and those who really loved God would find Him everywhere whether they went to the mosque or a Hindu temple or a church. But his great-grandson, the last of the "Great Mughals", Aurangzeb was a diehard Muslim bigot. As soon as he became the Emperor he followed a divide and rule policy and the Mughal empire began to crack. He dismissed many Hindu officials who had been employed by former kings. He pulled down many Hindu temples and brought all the idols of Hindu gods and goddesses to his palace and put them underground in the main gateway, so that no one could come to see him without treading them under the feet. Aurangzeb levied a tax known as *Jizia* which was to be paid by Hindus only. This discriminatory and oppressive policies against the Hindu subjects made the Rajputs angry and they gradually alienated from him. Jawaharlal Nehru rightly said, "A civilization decays much more from inner failure than from external attack".[6]

The above facts show that human prosperity flows with the rivers. But the rivers also bring downfall to mankind too. They often become the cause of great human sorrows and miseries caused by devastating floods and erosions. This phenomenon is attributable, in most cases, to rivers that take their rise in the glaciers and snow covered watersheds which are normally charged with large volume of waters by melting of snow and glacier during warmer seasons. These rivers while rushing down the plains cause devastative floods being unable to discharge the heavy volume of water carried by them. The floods and erosions are often extensive and destructive. The Koshi is one such river which is often called as the 'Sorrow of Bihar' for its habitual flood and fury caused to the people of Bihar. The Narayani and Ghogra rivers of Bihar which are the branches of rivers from Nepal are also equally destructive. They are fed by numerous rivers emerging from the large mountain ridges covered with snow in the Himalayas of Nepal and during summer days they carry heavy volumes of water beyond their capacity to release. This results in extensive inundation and submersion of human habitation in the plains of Bihar through which they flow. The occurrence of floods during recent times has become almost regular feature. The devastative flood of the year 2007 is one of the biggest natural calamities in the recent memory of the people. The flood condition continued for more than a month between early August and mid-September, 2007. It washed away thousands of hearths and homes rendering lakhs of people homeless. It also destroyed extensive cropped areas in the districts of Gorakhpur, Champaran, Darbhanga etc. and took a toll of 626 human lives. It is estimated by experts that about nine million cusecs of water was discharged by the rivers in spate during the period of flood.

The Yellow river of China is another classic example of extreme human woes caused by flood and erosion for which the river Yellow is known as the "Sorrow of China". This river is recorded to have changed its course for 26 times of which nine were major and widely destructive. During the 12th century its course changed from the south towards Huai river basin causing extensive topographic change. These are only a few examples out of innumerable natural calamities caused due to inundation by rivers in the history of human civilization.

Notes

1. Jawaharlal Nehru (1946), *Discovery of India*, Calcutta: Nehru Memorial Fund.
2. *Ibid., op. cit.*
3. B.N. Luniya (1998), *Evolution of Indian Culture*, Agra: Lakshminarayan Agarwal, p. 221.
4. Jawaharlal Nehru, *op. cit.,* p. 136.
5. *Ibid.*, p. 146.
6. *Ibid.*

3
Socio-Cultural Affinities

The socio-cultural system of India is, by and large, based on the Vedic traditions in varied forms and degrees among majority of Indian societies barring a few non-Hindu communities. Similarly, the culture and tradition in Nepal are also based largely on Hindu Vedic system. The majority of population of Nepal being Hindus and Nepal being recognized as a Hindu kingdom, the socio-cultural system of Nepal as a whole is established on the Hindu Brahminic base. According to Nepal Census 2001, 80.6 per cent of the population belong to Hindu religion, 11 per cent Buddhist, 4.2 per cent belong to Muslim religion and the rest 3.6 per cent are indigenous population.

One of the most despicable features of Vedic system is the caste system which divides Indian Hindu society into various high and low castes. Herbert Risley, eminent British Anthropologist, has defined caste as "a collection of families or groups of families, bearing a common name, claiming a common descent from a mythological ancestor, human or divine, professing to follow the same hereditary calling and is regarded by those who are competent to give an opinion, as forming a single homogeneous community".[1] Thus, it is a corporate group, exclusive and rigorously hereditary. It is a group of people who are socially exclusive to other groups and the membership to it is strictly hereditary with rigid rules governing the choice of occupation and of life partner. The term 'caste', although a household word in India, has been derived from the Portuguese word 'Casta' meaning breed or race. The caste system of India has its origin in "*Varna*" and "*Jaati*". The former refers to racial difference and the later means birth or descent. The term *Varna* is used to differentiate between races, such as *Arya varna* and *Dasa varna* etc. while the word *Jati* implies the hierarchical orders in the society. The *Rig Veda* explains how the four orders of the Hindu society originated. It is said that the *Brahmana* came from the mouth of the Cosmic Man, the *Kshatriya* was created from the arms, and the *Vaishya* from the thighs and lastly the *Shudras* come from the feet. This division of society into four hierarchical orders was fitted to the occupational roles to be adopted by the people. The *Brahmanas* became the priests, the *Kshatriyas* the fighters, the *Vaishyas* became the traders and the *Shudras* were ordained to serve their masters. In course of time, out of the four castes sprang up many other sub-castes because of the intermarriage between the higher castes and the lower ones, the progenies of whom were placed in a middle order. For instance, if a *Vaishya* woman married a *Shudra* man, their children belonged to *Ayogava* caste and were placed at a middle order in society.

Like India, the Nepalese population consists of multiple races and ethnic groups. She has more or less sixty different ethnic groups with their distinct dialects. According to Nepal Census 2001, the caste distribution and percentage of Nepal's population is shown in Table 3.1.

Table 3.1: Caste Distribution and Percentage of Nepal's Population in Census 2001

Caste	*Percentage*	*Caste*	*Percentage*
1. Bahun	12.74	2. Thakuri	1.47
3. Chhetri	15.80	4. Damai	1.72
5. Sonar	0.64	6. Sarki	1.40
7. Kami	3.94	8. Newar	5.48
9. Rai	2.79	10. Limbu	1.98
11. Magar	7.40	12. Gurung	2.39
13. Tamang	5.64	14. Thakali	0.06
15. Sunuwar	0.42	16. Sherpa	0.68
17. Bhotia	0.08	18. Tharu	6.75
19. Teli	1.34	20. Yadav	3.94

Source : Nepal Census 2001.

Racially, they can be divided into two broad groups, *viz.*, Caucasoids and Mongoloids.[2] Linguistically, the Caucasoids speak

Indo-Aryan or Nepali language while the Mongoloids are the speakers of Tibeto-Burman languages of great many dialects not intelligible to each other. The percentage of Nepal's population on linguistic basis are: Nepali 49 per cent, Maithili 12 per cent, Bhojpuri 8 per cent, Tharu 6 per cent, Tamang 5 per cent, Newari 4 per cent, Magar 3 per cent, Awadhi 2 per cent, Bantawa 2 per cent, Limbu 1 per cent, and Bajjika 1 per cent. The Caucasoid group belongs to Hinduism and are governed by Vedic system of social order with elaborate caste system. The Mongoloid group profess Buddhism and partly Animism or indigenous faith and are free from the rigour of caste system. Table 3.2 presents the overall picture of social stratification of Nepal at a glance.[3]

Table 3.2: Social Stratification of Nepal

Race	*Caste*	*Rank*	*Language*	*Religion*
1. Caucasoid	Bahun			
	Jaisi			
	Thakuri	High	Indo-Aryan	Hinduism
	Chhetri			
	Kami			
	Damai	Low	Indo-Aryan	Hinduism
	Sarki			
2. Mongoloid	Newar	Middle	Tibeto-Burman	Hindu/Buddhist
	Tamang			
	Sherpa	Middle	Tibeto-Burman	Buddhist
	Yolmo			
	Limbu			
	Rai	Middle	Tibeto-Burman	Animist
	Yakha			
	Magar	Middle	Tibeto-Burman	Hindu/Buddhist
	Gurung			
3. Madhesis or Mixed Caucasoid	Tharu, Bhojpuri Maithili	High/Low	Indo-Aryan	Hinduism

Source : Census of Nepal, 2001.

Table 3.2 shows that in the overall caste composition of the Nepalese population there are three caste groups *viz.*, the high caste, the middle caste and the low caste. Among the Caucasoid Hindu societies there are further inter-caste differences. But the

Mongoloid group maintains one rank and there is no high or low caste people among them except among the Newars as they are partly Hindus and partly Buddhists. The Mongoloids occupy a middle place between the high and low ranks of overall class stratification of Nepalese population. Table 3.2 also shows that the major portion of the population belong to Hindu religion. "There are over ninety-two local languages and dialects in Nepal, and over a hundred different social groups based on caste, ethnicity, religion and language".[4]

Another popular way of looking at caste stratification of Nepal is to divide the whole Nepalese population into two halves *viz.*, the Tagadhari and the Matawali. The former group includes the Bahun, Thakuri and the Chhetri who traditionally wear Brahmanical sacred thread across the shoulder and occupy higher rank in the hierarchical order. The latter group comprises the rest of the vast population who are composed of all the three religions *viz.*, Hinduism, Buddhism and Animism. Among the Tagadharis there exists further differences in rank and file. For example, the Bahun rank at the top followed by Jaisi, and Thakuris and then comes the Chhetris. Again, within the Bahun category there are Upadhyayas and Jaisis of which the former rank above the latter. In this way, very elaborate class stratification is strictly followed among the Hindu societies of Nepal even to this day. If a low caste person pretends to belong to higher caste and induces a high caste person to partake food, or even water at his house he becomes liable to a heavy punishment of fine or imprisonment or confiscation of his property.

The caste system of Nepal was re-established and revamped on a strong footing and made rigid social system by Jung Bahadur Rana, the Prime Minister of Nepal. He promulgated in 1854 *Muluki Ain*—a Civil Code based on caste and class of people which firmly institutionalized the caste system in Nepal, and recognized over a hundred different social groups based on caste, ethnicity, religion and language.[5] He defined the social ranks and status of every caste and community. The Brahmnins were assigned an exalted position in the society and they were exempted from capital punishment. The Gorkha soldiers on returning to their country from military service in India had to pay fee of Rupees three to obtain back all rights and privileges of their caste the rules of which they had inadvertently broken. This tax was called *Pani patia*. There was a system called '*Banda*' under which a man could agree to become a bonded servant in some body's house for a term of two or three years, as the case may be, in lieu of an advance money of rupees five or six hundred taken by him. The slavery system (*Kamara*) used to be rampant in Nepal which has now been abolished. The cow is a sacred animal in Nepal esteemed as the mother-cow, and called by Nepalese *Gau mata*. Killing a cow is considered an offence equally heinous as killing a human being for which the prescribed punishment was death.

Of late the caste system in India has undergone some change and the feeling of caste differences in the society has reduced because of modern education, western way of life and diversified occupational pattern. Some sociologists of India, like Prof. M.N. Srinivas have expressed the view that "the caste system is on its last legs and that educated, urbanized and westernized members of the upper classes have already escaped its bond".[6]

In Nepal the caste system is based on Vedic *varna* principle and it is practised more rigorously than in India. It is said to have been introduced by one Hindu king named Dharmadatta. In contemporary Nepal, the caste system has maintained its stronghold almost as before, marginalising at least eighty per cent of its low class population by a small group of high caste.

In Nepal, caste system rigidly divides orthodox Hindus into four major classes. The highest place in the caste hierarchy is occupied by Upadhyayas. But if an Upadhyaya Brahmin enters into marital union with a lower caste Jaisi, Thakur or Chhetri woman then the children of such union are never given the status of their father. The children of a Brahmin father and Jaisi mother will be classed as Jaisi, and from a Thakuri mother will be classified as Hamal and enjoy the status of Thakuri and not of their father. It is interesting to note that the father will never lose his social status by marrying a low caste woman and that such marriage is socially permissible which can be performed with full Vedic rites, and also that the Upadhyaya father and the lower class mother and their children can stay in the same house, but the father cannot eat the boiled rice cooked by the low caste mother.[7]

As in India, Nepal as a whole follows the patriarchal form of society. The father is the head of the family who exercises authority over the family affairs as a whole. The mother occupies next subordinate position after the father. She looks after domestic works and takes care of the young and the old. Marriage is mostly fixed by negotiation and the parents of the boy give a gold ring to the girl as a sign of betrothal. No marriage can be settled without the astrologer's nod, who after thoroughly casting the horoscopes of the boy and the girl gives his green signal. The betrothal is done in the presence of a few members of the families of both the boy and the girl and their close relatives. The ceremony is called Shahi Mundri conducted by the priest in case of Hindus and by Lama in the case of Buddhists. The marriage ceremony is held at night in the bride's house. Child marriage is prevalent among the Brahmins residing in the villages. It is considered good to get a girl married before she reaches the age of thirteen. Marriage is traditionally banned within the circle of agnates and cognates. Polygamy is permissible in Nepal which is practiced by comparatively rich people. Divorce is rare in Nepal which is permissible only when both husband and wife agree to it. Adultery and elopement are quite high and the punishment prescribed for it is rigorous. "The erring wife is imprisoned for life and the dishonoured husband is expected to cut down the seducer with his Khukri, the first time he encountered him".[8]

The property of the family belongs to the head of the family, usually the father. The sons, when grown-up, might claim the property or induce the father to divide it among them. The daughters are excluded from the inheritance of father's property. The old and the infirm are respected and taken care of, and their opinions are obeyed. The women are, by and large, respected in the society. They occupy equal status and participate with other male members of the family in all types of activities and do not use *purdah*. The Nepalese women are free to do any type of work the male members do, they work in the field, in the market, in office and anywhere according to their capability. They are physically strong and capable of carrying heavy loads along hilly paths and even courageous enough to take part in wars as soldiers. It is said that during Anglo-Nepal war, the wives of Nepali soldiers helped their husbands in hurling down stones and boulders from the top of the hills killing and stalling British troops from advancing further. Lt. Colonel Eden Vansittart speaking about the Nepalese women said—"During the assaults on the fort, women were seen hurling stones and undauntedly exposing themselves; and several of their dead bodies and one wounded were subsequently found amidst the ruins of the fort".[9]

Traditionally, the status of women is largely determined by that of their husbands in both Nepal and India. For example, if the husband is holding a title or a job of socially higher status, the wife is also given that status. The normative principle of the society is based on the notion that—"in childhood a woman must live under the care of her parents; in youth under the protection of her husband and in old age under the guardianship of her son". But having said that, it does not mean that Nepalese women are subservient to the male population like that in Muslim community. They respect their husbands and co-operate with them and also take part in decision-making on the affairs of the household. The gender discrimination in Nepalese community is the minimum and the women are given equal status with men. In India the Muslim clerics introduced *Purdah* system for their Muslim women which was partially imitated by Hindu women by wearing veils around their heads with the end of *Sari* or a scarf. This is a social etiquette among the elderly Hindu women of many societies. Gradually, this practice became a part of social nobility and a woman without veil were considered to be devoid of social decency and decorum. In Nepal women never use *Purdah* or even veil which may be due to absence of Muslim culture. However, they often cover their heads with a thin cloth, a kind of scarf called *Muyetra*, keeping their faces open. While appearing before elderly people or in the social gatherings married women cover their heads with scarf.

The cow is considered like a human being and as a mother in Nepal. The killing of a cow is an offence equal to murder of man and the punishment is death. Maiming, or injuring a cow in any manner is punishable with imprisonment for life.

Historically speaking, the caste system in India became extremely rigid during Gupta period (300-500 A.D.). The Brahmin community were considered as belonging to the highest caste whose duty was to do priesthood or become teachers or temple worshippers. The Kshatriyas were to do soldiery, the Vaishyas to do trade and commerce and the Shudras were to cultivate and serve the people of higher castes. Ever since that time ascendancy of the Brahmin class over the other castes became rigidly institutionalised in India. In Nepal although the caste system appears to have been there since the second century A.D. (Raja Dharma Dutta who constructed the Pashupatinath temple is attributed to have introduced *Varna* system) the real casteism is said to have entered Nepal during the time of Rudradeva, the Thakuri king who being influenced by the Hindu evangelist, Shankaracharya, persecuted Buddhist population. Thousands of Buddhist temples were destroyed, libraries were burnt down and Buddhist monks and nuns were brutally killed. In India during *Bhakti* movement, the caste system came under severe attack although it remained rigid. The advent of British rule and spread of modern education, and social enlightenment gradually had its impact upon many kinds of social evils. The movement of social reforms launched by Raja Ram Mohun Ray, Ramkrishna Paramahansa, Vivekananda, Mahatma Gandhi, B.R. Ambedkar etc. had some positive impacts on Indian caste system. Moreover, the Government of India has promulgated law banning untouchability under which a person is liable to be punished with imprisonment or fine or both. Today, the abominable caste system has lost much of its rigour in the Indian society although it has not yet disappeared entirely. Sex discrimination is still there in the rural areas of Maharashtra and Telengana States where women are not allowed to enter into certain temples for prayer and worship. In the north Indian states like Bihar, Uttar Pradesh, Himachal Pradesh, Haryana etc. class system is very intense and the lower caste or *Dalits* are treated very badly.

To sum up, despite advancement in science and education in Nepal, the social discrimination on account of caste or religion has not disappeared from Nepalese society. The stigma of untouchability remains like a perpetual blotch on the forehead despite the overthrow of the dark age of Rana rule. The evils of illiteracy, ignorance and superstition rule the roost over a vast majority of Nepalese population as ever before. More than half a century of the advent of people's democratic rule in Nepal has not succeeded in bringing reforms among people against these disgraceful social evil. Early marriage, child labour, witchcraft and shamanism are deeply rooted in rural Nepal.

Bigamy and polygamy are not restricted in Nepal although they are not much prevalent in the society. These practices are normally adopted by the husbands in case of the first wife fail to bear children or in case of rich and financially sound families only. The blame of being infertile to bear child is squarely put on the women although men also suffer from infertility. Slavery or bonded labour as a social institution was deeply rooted in Nepal in the past. This has been abolished during Rana rule. But in a non-egalitarian society like Nepal, the scourge of caste, class and status differences cannot be ruled out. Social inequalities in the form of informal slavery like domestic helpers, '*Dole*' (palanquine carrier, '*Dhakare*' (load carrier), etc. in the households of high caste nobility and landed gentry of Nepal continue to exist in full force. In Nepal, the long standing impacts of orthodox rule of the Hindu dynasties are writ large even on the Buddhist societies who seem to have gradually departed from their egalitarian spirit. For example, the Newar community in spite of being Buddhist have adopted some sort of caste divisions among them. The Tamangs have no caste system among themselves, but outside their society they consider the Hindu menial class people as untouchables.

The Nepalese mourn for thirteen days on the death of near relatives. Men shave their heads, eye-brows and beards on the death of their parents, sons and brothers. If unmarried daughter dies the father mourns for thirteen days but in case the daughter happens to be married, the father mourns for one day only. The father-in-law, on the other hand, take the place of her father and mourn for full thirteen days. The disposal of dead body is, normally done by burning. The Gurung and Magar either bury or burn their deads. The Limbus also follow both the systems.

Nepal's economy is primarily based on agriculture. Most of the land is owned by rich landlords who never cultivate land by themselves and rent out their lands to landless peasants. There is a rich tradition in Nepal which encourages the aristocracy and rich landowners to do nothing but tend to the renting out of their land.[10] Economically, there are two classes of society—the rich and the poor, the high and the low classes or the landlords and the landless farmers. The land tenure system of Nepal was primarily responsible for this divide in Nepalese society. Ever since the time of Prithvi Narayan Shah, the first Gorkha king, there were four types of land settlement system, *Birta, Jagir, Guthi* and *Raikor*. The *Birta* lands were chiefly allotted to the Rana's kinsmen of ruling family who enjoyed rent free lands. This was abolished in 1950, immediately after the fall of Rana Government. The *Jagir* system was short term land grants given for military services in lieu of cash salaries. This system was devised by Prithvi Narayan Shah in order to reduce the burden of paying cash. *Guthi* system was land grants given to religious institutions. *Guthi* lands were directly administered by Temples or Monasteries. The land revenue realized by Temples or Monasteries was shared between the state and the religious institutions concerned. The *Raikar* land was allotted to certain classes of Government employees as part of their emoluments. This system has also been abolished in 1951. Because of the above systems of land settlement to certain classes of people, the bulk of the land were accumulated in the hands of a few people, who became the landlords. Immediately after the popular Government came into power in 1950, the Government of Nepal took-up drastic measures of land reformation in the country. Some of the salient steps are listed below in brief:

1. Abolition of *Zamindari* system.
2. Imposition of ceiling on land ownership of more than 1.7 hectare of land in Terai, 1.02 hectare in Kathmandu areas and 1.5 hectare in the hill areas.
3. Security of tenancy right so that landowner cannot withdraw land from the tenant at his will.
4 Fixation of land rent at the rate of 50 per cent of produce.
5. Abolition of sub-tenancy.

The above provisions were implemented in every district with effect from 1964.

Nepal is free from the scourge of dowry system that exists in India. The relationship between the bride and the bridegroom and their families remain cordial and stable and there is no divorce, separation or torturing the bride on that ground. The practice of

Sati is unknown in Nepal. Restriction on widow marriage is prevalent among the Brahmins and the Kshatriya of orthodox families. The Brahmin widows have to pass their life under rigidly imposed social code of conduct like, wearing white *saris*, shaving their heads, shunning ornaments and eating restricted foods, etc. The maidens in the Newar community are traditionally married to God Siva before they get married to men and therefore, they never become widow on the death of their husbands and as such no social restrictions are imposed on them. They can either remarry or remain single with all the liberties as enjoyed by a maiden. The rest of the population of Nepal forming the larger group of 'Matawalis' observe no social restriction whatsoever on widows or on their remarriage.

Most of the festivals in Nepal have their roots in religions like Hinduism and Buddhism. The Hinduism comprises 82 per cent of Nepal's population while Buddhism is the second religion with 9 per cent of population. The Hinduism being the largest religion, it has definitely influenced majority of the festivals. The chief Hindu festivals are—*Dasain*, *Tehar*, *Shivaratri*, *Janmashtami*, *Teej*, *Gai-Jatra*, *Indra-Jatra*, *Ganesh Chaturthi*, *Mohani*, *Maghe Sankranti*, *Holi* etc. *Dasain* is the biggest and longest festival in Nepalese calendar celebrated during September/October which continues for fifteen days starting from *Shukla Paksha* of the month of *Ashvin* and ending on *Purnima*. *Vijaya-Dashami* which symbolizes the 'Victory of good over evil' is the major part of this festival and is celebrated as a national festival by both Hindu and Buddhist people of Nepal. *Tehar*, the second largest festival of Nepal which signifies the festival of lights is also celebrated by both Hindus and Buddhists as a national festival. It occurs on the *Trayodashi* of *Kartik*, *Krishna* to *Shukla Dwitiya* every year. This five day festival assumes great importance not only for the welfare of human being but also for birds and animals like crow, dog, cow etc. signifying they are all the part and parcel of human being. *Bhai-Tika* is another important part of *Tehar* festival when the sisters of each family put Tika on the forehead of their brothers, garland them and serve with delicious eateries (*Selroti*, sweet meats etc.) prepared by their own hand. In return the brothers give gifts, money, and ornaments to their sisters. The Buddhist communities celebrate *Buddha Purnima* (*Buddha*

Jayanti), and *Losar* (New year). The festival of Losar falls on the 25th day of the 10th month of the Tibetan calendar, corresponding to the month of December. This festival is celebrated for seven days as a thanks giving to Lord Buddha for good harvest and pay homage to their ancestors. The *Buddha Purnima* is celebrated to commemorate the birth, enlightenment and passing away of the Lord Buddha. Besides Nepal this festival is observed in various parts of the world like—Bodh Gaya, Sarnath, Sikkim, Bhutan, China, Japan, Sri Lanka, Delhi, Sanchi and all other places wherever there is concentration of Buddhists. The Newar community of Nepal celebrate the festival of *Mohani*, *Gai-Jatra*, *Kumari Puja* etc.

Notes

1. Herbert, Risley (1999), *People of India*, (Reprint), New Delhi: Asian Educational Service.
2. T.B. Subba, "Nepalis in the North-east, Political Aspirations and Ethnicity", in *The Nepalis in North-East India*, Ed. A.C. Sinha and T.B. Subba, p. 58.
3. *Ibid.*
4. Sujeev, Shakya (2009), *Unleashing Nepal*, Penguin Books, p. 124.
5. *Ibid.*
6. M.N. Shrinivas (1960), "The Indian Road to Equality", in *Economic and Political Weekly*, Mumbai, Vol. XII, June, pp. 867-72.
7. Christoph, V.F. Haimenndorf (1947), "Status of Interaction among the Hindu Caste of Nepal" in Tribe Caste and Peasantry, " ed. K.S. Mathur and B.C. Agarwal, Lacknow, p. 154.
8. Eden, Vansittart, *The Gurkhas*, p. 49.
9. Eden, Vansittart (1915), *The Gorkhas*, Calcutta: Government Press, p. 33.
10. Sujeev, Shakya *op. cit.*, p. 16.

4
Ethno-Cultural Overview

In the beginning of the first millennium B.C. when human culture and civilization in the Far East countries were still in incipient stage, India played a 'civilizing and humanizing' role in the South-Asiatic countries like Indo-China, Malaya, Indonesia, Sri Lanka Burma, etc.[1] "The torch of Indian civilization travelled beyond Pamirs into Turkistan and Mongolian regions of the nomadic peoples that settled in the vast territories extending between the shores of Caspian Sea and the Great Wall of China".[2]

As the Indian culture reached all-over the north and the south Asia, Nepal a tiny Himalayan country perched on the border of India could hardly remain without being swept away by the wind of enlightenment. For Nepal, a country of Buddha's birth, it came as a new spiritual awakening among the non-Aryan tribes who migrated and lived there in obscurity. Like ancient Greece which acted as a torch of new civilization in Europe, India became the fountain-head of new and vibrant civilization for the Asian countries. Speaking about the early spread of Indian culture and religion throughout the neighbouring countries B.N. Luniya writes, "Indian philosophy and culture went abroad not to destroy or ruin but to awaken and fulfil".[3] Jawaharlal Nehru writes, "One has not only to go back in time but to travel in mind if not in body, to various countries of Asia, where India spread out in many ways, leaving immortal testimony of her spirit, her power and her love of beauty".[4] Echoing a similar note Rabindranath Tagore wrote, "To know my country, one has to travel to that age, when she realized her soul and thus transcended her physical boundaries, when she revealed her being in a radiant magnanimity which illumined the eastern horizon, making her recognized as their own by those in alien shores who were awakened into a surprise of life; and not now when she has withdrawn herself into a narrow barrier of obscurity, into a miserly pride of exclusiveness, into a poverty of mind that dumbly revolves around itself in an unmeaning repetition of a past that has lost its light and has no message for the pilgrims of the future".

The geographical proximity helped Indian missionaries to reach out to Nepal with their art, culture and religion. In later years many Buddhist missionaries and Hindu propagators visited Nepal and stayed there establishing centers for cultural promotion. In olden days there used to be little political interference and the movement of culture and religion knew no physical or political boundary. As the saints and seers from India were maintaining a continuous and close intercourse with Nepal down the centuries, culture and religion flowed like river and watered the fertile soil of Nepal. The geo-political boundary between the two countries never existed. No historical records ever indicated any line of demarcation between the territories of India and Nepal. Some sources say that, the Gupta empire spread as far as Terai areas of Nepal in the north and that emperor Samudragupta exercised his sway over Nepal which paid regular tribute to him. Lumbini, the birthplace of Lord Buddha which is presently in Nepal, was within the territory of the king Suddhodhana, father of Prince Siddhartha whose kingdom was supposed to be within India. This being the situation in the past, Nepal came under immediate and direct influence of Indian culture and religion.

Ashoka, the Emperor of Mauryan dynasty abdicated his royal throne for a Buddhist monk as early as third century B.C. and went to Nepal with his daughter Charumati to spread the teachings of the Tathagata. He built several *Stupas* at places like Pattan, Kirtipur, Lumbini etc. to commemorate and glorify the name of Lord Buddha, some of which can still be seen in Nepal. Ashoka reigned in India about two thousand and three hundred years ago, but the *Dharma-Chakra* (Wheel of virtue) of Ashoka Pillar which is inscribed in the Indian National flag keeps his memory still afresh in our minds. The same feeling is echoed in Nepal by the beautiful *stupas* built by him which still exist. Charumati, daughter of

Ashoka, married Nepal prince and settled down in Nepal to perpetuate the memory of Lord Buddha. The inscriptions written on the pillars declared Ashoka as the *Devanampriya Priyadarshin* meaning the "Beloved of God, of gracious Mien". He was the epitome of love and non-violence. Never before, nor ever afterwards in the history, has a king proclaimed his sorrow for the dead in the war and abdicated his throne to become a mendicant, as was done by Ashoka, the great.

According to Nepalese history, Lord Buddha was born at Lumbini in Nepal during the rule of Kiratas. After attainment of spiritual knowledge in India Lord Buddha and his disciple Ananda visited Kathmandu valley and stayed for some time at Patan. During this time he preached his new found faith among the Kiratas and the Murmis (Tamangs) who were living in their principalities known as *Kipatas* or *Dhyang*. It is said that the work of art is the handmaid of religion. Buddhism had its own form of art and architecture which are prominently seen till today in Kathmandu and Patan embodied in the buildings, temples, *stupas* and *chaityas*. Simultaneously, Buddhism spread Buddhist art throughout north and south India, the evidences of which can be seen in the caves of Ajanta and Elora. Numerous beautiful Buddhist *stupas* were erected all-over the Deccan during the times of Andhras. The great *stupa* at Amravati at the mouth of Krishna river is yet another specimen of Buddhist architecture. The fertile valley of the Krishna river was the cradle of civilization in the eastern Deccan and this area became one of the greatest centres of Buddhism. Today, the entire *stupa* of Amravati has fallen in ruins. Some parts of the ruins made of marble stone including the dome of the *stupa* decorated with intricate carvings depicting scenes from the life of Lord Buddha, have been shifted to the museum of Madras and also to the British Museum in London. An eminent authority remarked, "This is the most voluptuous and the most delicate flower of India's sculpture". At Nagarjunikonda another relic of Buddha has been discovered which include a *stupa*, two *chaityas* and a *vihara*. Kanishka, the Kushana king is reputed to have been a great builder and patron of Buddhist art. It is believed that the art of Gandhara which makes free use of Buddha image flourished during his reign. The Buddhist tradition attribute Kanishka to be a great patron of Buddhism and adorn him with the title of 'Second Ashoka'. The Buddhist art and architecture was brought to Nepal by Emperor Ashoka in the form of *stupas* which are still extant in Kathmandu and Patan.

Thus, India has ever been the primary source of ideas and inspirations to Nepal. We find that every new development whether political, social or religious that took place in India, reached Nepal within no time and this was mainly due to close proximity and long border with India. The two epics of India *viz.*, *Ramayana* and *Mahabharata* have greatly influenced the people of Nepal throughout the centuries. Nepal was so closely associated with the temporal and spiritual ethos of Indian life that she found frequent mentions in India's great epics like the *Ramayana* and *Mahabharata* and *Puranas* etc. In the epic of *Mahabharata*, there is a mention of a place named Viratnagar where the Pandavas performed the penance of *Agyatavasa* which means exile in disguise. Viratnagar was the kingdom of King Virat, as the name suggests, and today this place is an industrial town in Nepal. So, also the place called Janakpur where Sita was born (according to *Ramayana*), is an important town in the Terai of Nepal.

History tells us that the Kiratas, the first ever known tribe of Nepal, migrated to Nepal in seventh century B.C. from the north-east region of India. The Kiratas were the people of the north-east India around Pragjyotishpura who were pushed into the mountainous regions of Nepal by the Aryans as they advanced from the Gangetic plains like the Celts, the oldest tribe of the British Isles who were driven by the mighty Romans and Germans towards European fringes during 50 B.C. K.L. Baruah identifies the Kiratas with the country inhabited by the tribes from the foot of the Garo Hills and Khasi Hills to hill tracts of Tipperah along the eastern coast of Brahmaputra.[5] The landmass stretching from Sun-Kosi river in the west to the Arun river in the east of Nepal was known as Kiratadesha or the country of the Kiratas, which constitutes the eastern Nepal today. This territory is also called Limbuana by the Nepalese and the aboriginal people who reside there from time immemorial are known by the name of Limbu or Subba. The term Subba is not the real name of a tribe, but is a title conferred on the head of the tribe by the Gorkha king with the permission to rule a certain part of the newly acquired territory. In Nepal, the term

Subba is an official designation of a civil authority equivalent to Deputy Commissioner in India.

Dr. S.K. Chatterjee observed that the Sino-Tibetans known as Kiratas originally belonged to the Brahmaputra valley of Assam.[6] According to E.A. Gait, Ghataka, one of the Kirata kings ruled in Kamrup, the ancient Assam who was defeated and slain by Naraka Asura.[7] King Ghataka, the ruler of Pragjyotisha was famous for his glory and splendor. After having firmly convinced that Naraka's purpose was to usurp his throne King, Ghataka marched with his army and started showering arrows on his political adversary. Naraka being a redoubtable warrior fought gallantly with bows and arrows and swords. Finally, Naraka defeated and killed all the soldiers and Commander-in-Chief of Ghataka and captured twenty-five thousand elephants, cavalry horses and jewels, golds and ornaments. The Kirata king Ghataka was beheaded. After the death of Ghataka many of his Kirata subjects deserted the country and fled away eastwards to the sea-shore.[8]

After the Aryans took over the Gangetic valley they pushed away the Kiratas towards further-east. The Aryans and the Indo-Mongoloid settlements extended to the valleys of Brahmaputra and Borak rivers through North-Bengal in their eastward march where the two races lived side by side for thousands of years. This whole area of the north-east India including Nepal, Bhutan and Sikkim may be termed as a 'Culture Zone' where the two primeval racial groups, the Indo-Mongoloid and the Indo-Aryans lived together. They lived side by side mixing each other culture and languages, at times fighting each other and at others, living peacefully and ever meeting and mixing their blood in legitimate marriages or otherwise, and paved their way to the inevitable process of moulding-up new cultures of their own, most of the Indo-Mongoloid cultures having been influenced by Indo-Aryan faith and culture.

The vast concourse of humanity historically known as the Mongoloid or the Indo-Mongoloid, as Dr. Suniti Kumar Chatterjee prefers to call them, constituted the aboriginal population of the whole eastern Himalaya including Tibet, and the Sub-Himalayan region of North Bihar, Sikkim, Bhutan, Nepal, North Bengal and the whole of the North-East region. The settlement pattern of this

'Culture Zone' is characterized by purely Indo-Mongoloid in the hill regions of the north, which gradually changes into a mixture of Indo-Aryans as one proceeds towards the southern belts of Brahmaputra valley, Bihar and Bengal. Thus, the geography too has played its role in ethnic distribution of population as can be distinctly seen from their customs, religions and their physical appearances marked by stronger Mongolian strain in the north while Aryan features predominating in the south. The Indo-Mongoloids are believed to have occupied as far as the Bay of Bengal in the pre-historic times as evidenced from the accounts of two Arab travellers viz., Ibn Houkal and Istakhri who referred Bay of Bengal as the Tibetan Sea in the 10th century AD.[9]

From the above historical analysis it becomes amply clear that the Kiratas who are variously called as Paleo-Mongoloid, Proto-Mongoloid or Indo-Mongoloid etc. were the people of the North-East India from where they migrated into Nepal. Dr. Regmi also stated that the Kiratas came to Nepal from north-east India. They gradually migrated to the hills of Sub-Himalayan countries like Nepal, Sikkim, and Bhutan etc. as the comparatively more powerful Aryans gradually dispossessed their habitats. According to an account, however, the Kiratas came to Nepal in the 7th century B.C. from the south-east which indicates Mongolia or some Chinese territory. Dr. S.K. Chatterjee obviously used the cultural term Indo-Mongoloid to mean that the Kiratas were the aborigines of India who were frequently mentioned in the *Vedas*, *Puranas*, the Epics and *Tantra* literatures of ancient India. Prof. J.N. Choudhury opines—"Dr. Chatterjee possibly implied no more than the fact that these tribes lived within the confines and greater orbit of the Indian culture since time immemorial, as is evident from distinct reference to them in ancient Indian literature".[10] Significantly, this provides us with the clue that the earliest human population and their culture moved from the south to the north, i.e. from India to Nepal ever since pre-historic times.

The most ancient records would seem to indicate that long before the Kiratas[11] came to settle in Nepal some unknown tribe must have been inhabiting that land. Perhaps, they were one of the many branches of the great waves of Mongolian conquest, which spread through the length and breadth of Asia. They might have broken-up from the mainstream, crossed over the bleak snows of the mighty Himalaya into the fertile valleys of Nepal and settled down there adopting the country as their own. Dr. Regmi, eminent historian of Nepal, echoes the same view and states that this tribe had a close affinity with the Mundas, Kol, Bhil tribes of Chhotanagpur. To quote him—"Undoubtedly, the earliest settlers in Nepal valley were of the same stock as the Mundas, Kols and Bhils of Chhotanagpur region in today's south Bihar. It seems also certain that the Dravidians comprised the second wave emigrants and they might have penetrated into the valley in their northward expansion from the Gangetic plains. But these were literally swamped by the Kiratas at the later stage who came from north-east India and spoke a language of Indo-Tibetan origin. They were mixed race and probably the same as the Mons and Khmers of the Indo-Chinese origin".[12]

In respect of social institutions we find that the Nepalese social system, like India, is predominantly based on the Vedic traditions, except for a section of non-Hindu population. The Nepalese population is composed of multiple races, and ethnic groups, each having distinct dialects not understandable to each other and separate social customs of their own. The caste distinction is the benchmark of Hinduism and the same came in its entirety when Hinduism entered into Nepal. Socio-culturally, the Nepalese population can be divided into two broad divisions, *viz.*, Tagadharis and the Matawalis. The former group include the Brahmins, Thakuris and the Kshatriyas who ritually wear sacred thread around the shoulder and occupy the highest place in the social order. The latter group comprises the rest of the larger half of the population who belong to the middle and the lowest ranks of social hierarchy. The group falling in the middle rank of social hierarchy include, by and large, the indigenous communities like the Newars, Magars, Gurungs, Rais, Limbus, Tamangs, Thakalis, Sunuwars, Lepchas etc. who profess Buddhism, and those in the lowest rank group fall communities like Kami, Damai, Sarki etc. and they belong to Hinduism. The Tagadharis are chest Hindus and are strictly governed by Vedic system of social order while the Matawalis are ritually liberal in their religious pursuits.

As in India, Nepal also has the patriarchal form of society. The father is the head of the family who exercises authority over the family affairs while mother occupies the next subordinate position. Marriage is fixed by negotiation and polygamy is permissible in society, though not in much practice. Women are, by and large, respected in society and are free to move about without veil or *purdah*. They can also take-up any profession or do any work the male member does without social bar. Nepal is free from the scourge of dowry system (tradition of giving valuable gifts to bridegroom by the parents of the bride), but there are other social evils which still plague the Nepalese society like child marriage, forced labour, illiteracy, superstition, practice of shamanism etc.

One of the earliest confederations of Nepal was that of Shakya clan whose capital was Kapilavastu in the Nepal-India border. Today Kapilavastu is a small town within the territory of Nepal. Prince Siddhartha belonged to this Shakya clan who was born at Lumbini in present Nepal and became Gautama Buddha in his later life. Gautama Buddha, after attainment of divine enlightenment at Sarnath visited Nepal during the reign of the seventh Kirati king, by name Jitedasti. The Kiratis and other aborigines of Nepal welcomed Lord Buddha and accepted Buddhism as their religion and since that time Indo-Nepalese cultural fusion started in Nepal.

According to Hindu and Buddhist traditions, the valley of Nepal, in the early days, was a lake called the Nag Hrad brimmed with water. Manjushri, a Buddhist saint, converted the lake into a fertile habitat by cutting a canal to flow out the water to the river Bagmati. Manjushri himself being a Buddhist Bhikshu, installed Dharmakar as the king of Nepal who having no issue appointed one Dharampal as his successor. Dharampal is said to have come to Nepal with a Hindu saint of India called Krakuchand who had with him 700 disciples of the Brahman and Chattri castes.[13] They settled down in Nepal and professed Hindu religion and culture. This may be called the genesis of Hindu culture in Nepal valley. Another Indian king named Raja Dharmadutta from south India is said to have built the temple of Pashupati and brought Brahmin priests from India to worship Pashupatinath.[14] Even to this day the priests who worship in the Pasupatinath temple are the Hindus from south India. Dharmadutta is also credited to have introduced the four caste or *varna* system in Nepal which is based on Indian Vedic social code. According to this system, the Hindu society is rigidly divided into four different social hereditary classes or castes. The highest class in social order is the Brahmin who functions as priest (need not necessarily be priest); closely followed by the Kshatriyas whose profession is to be soldiers and protect the country. These two classes are called as Tagadharis in Nepal as they are exclusively permitted to wear the sacred Brahmanical thread. Then comes the traders and merchants and the last of all are the lowly farmers and untouchables.

Jayadeva, the Lichchavi prince, fled to Nepal after the fall of his kingdom at Vaishali[15], present Bihar. He defeated the Kirati king of Nepal and ruled over the country for a considerably long period of time. *Jataka* stories tell us that Vaishali, the original capital of Lichchvis in Bihar, was a beautiful city surrounded by three walls, several gates and watch towers. Although, it is controversial matter as to when the Lichchavis kingdom began in Nepal, from the findings at the ancient capital at Handigoan it has been conjectured that the Lichchavis ruled in Nepal on two occasions, the first time from 200 C.E. to 500 C.E. and the second, from about 750 to 1200 C.E.

The Lichchavis were Kshatriyas and had a close relationship with the Shakya clan of Kapilavastu. The wife of Suddhodhana was a Lichchavi princess. Prabhakar Vardhan a Lichchavi king of Nepal is credited to have extended his kingdom up to the basin of the Ganges. This fact may be true as the edicts of Emperor Samudragupta written on the pillar at Allahabad reveals that Nepal was an independent country on the northern frontier of his kingdom. Although most of the Lichchavi kings were devout Hindus, they did not impose Brahmanic social codes or values on their non-Hindu subjects. Manadeva, like other Lichchavi kings, had a liberal view about religion. Although, he himself believed in the worship of Vishnu, his wife set-up *Siva Lingas*, the pillars representing the phallus near Vishnumati river in 474.[16] Buddhism existed side-by-side with Vaishnavism, Shaivism and the Shakta cult. Sivadeva II another Lichchavi king was a devout Hindu king and he saw to it that the duties of Mahayana Buddhism were not neglected and that Buddhists were properly looked after.[17]

But the Thakuri kings who replaced the Lichchavis were not liberal in matters of religion like the Lichchavis. They were conservative Hindus and did not like other religion to exist in Nepal. The Thakuri dynasty was started by Amsuvarman and this dynasty had eighteen kings. Viswadevavarman, the thirty-first and the last of the Lichchavi dynasty had no male child, so he gave his kingdom to his son-in-law named Amsuvarman. As soon as Amsuman Varman, the Thakuri king ascended the throne of Nepal in 634 A.D. the politico-religious scenario of Nepal began to show changes. The Thakuris were staunch followers of Hindu culture and religion and they adopted a state policy that patronized Hindu religion against all other faiths professed in Nepal. During the reign of Rudradeva (635 to 656 A.D.) one Shankaracharya, a bigoted Hindu from India visited Nepal who incited the king to persecute against all people, who professed the religion of Buddha irrespective of age and sex. The Thakuris destroyed Buddhist literatures, burned Buddhist temples and images and butchered the priests and monks.[18] This was one of the most significant events in the history of Nepal so far as religious persecution is concerned. Towards the year 750 A.D. the political scenario of Nepal took a sharp turn as the Lichchavis took over the power for the second time. With the coming into power of the Lichchavis, the religious persecution of Buddhists perpetrated by the Thakuris came to an end and both religions, Hinduism and the Buddhism flourished side by side for another spell of about one hundred years.

The Malla dynasty of Nepal (1200-1769) witnessed for the first time the rise of Hinduism in Nepalese soil under the patronage of the Malla kings. The kings followed a policy of not only encouraging and developing Hindu religion, but also persecuting and discouraging the growth of Buddhism. King Jayasthiti Malla was a hard core bigot and followed the policy of persecuting followers of Buddhism and Buddhist Monks. He ordered banishment of all celibate monks from Nepal and burning down of monasteries. It is said that a great many of Buddhist scriptures were destroyed by Shankaracharya in the 8th or 9th centuries. Shankaracharya was a famous Brahmanical bigot who waged incessant attacks against Buddhism in India and Nepal and succeeded in converting the Newari king into Hinduism through whom he carried out his mission of Buddhist persecution systematically. After a few years he went to Tibet with the same mission when he had a controversy with the grand Lama there who transfixed Shankaracharya's shadow on the ground with a knife. Shankaracharya's throat was pierced by knife to which he succumbed.[19] After Jayasthiti Malla, his son Jyoti Malla became the king who was very tolerant to Buddhism despite being a Hindu. During his reign two Buddhist Bhikshus, *viz.* Kyanchen Lama and Chhiring Lama came to Nepal from Gyarong province of Tibet and re-established Buddhism in Nepal.

The Shah dynasty (1769-1846) saw further decline of Buddhism and simultaneous growth of Hinduism in Nepal. Buddhism was considered as a part of Hinduism and there was an attempt to merge Buddhism within the religious pantheon of Hinduism. Hindu deities like Bhairava and Mahakala, Siva and Mahadeva, Ganesha, Indra, Garuda etc. found the place in Buddhist temples where their idols were worshipped together with Buddha. A sterling example of unification of Hinduism and Buddhism is found in a temple called Mahakala dedicated to Mahadeva and situated on high road close to Tundikhel. The idol inside the temple is that of Siva, but on his head is a small figure of Buddha Akshobhya.

In 1848 A.D. the Shah dynasty was replaced by Rana dynasty and together with this Hindu religion was raised to status of state religion of Nepal by the Rana rulers. Nepal was declared as the Hindu kingdom in the world. Buddhism suffered further setback, many of the indigenous tribes of Nepal such as the Magar, Gurung, Newar etc. changed their religion from Buddhism to Hinduism. This resulted in further dwindling down of the Buddhist population and increase in Hindu population of Nepal. The process of increase in Hindu population continued ever since than till recent times. According to the census 2001, the ethnic populations and their percentages to total Buddhist population in Nepal, is shown in Table 4.1.

The Nepalese, as a nation will for ever remain grateful to one tribe called the Khas who gave them the language they speak today in Nepal. The present day Nepali language which is the *lingua-franca* of the country of Nepal was originally the speech of the

Table 4.1: Buddhist Population of Nepal in Census 2001

Ethnic Group	*Total Buddhist*	*Percentage*
Tamang	1,257,461	98.06
Magar	1,268,000	60
Gurung	3,000,000	95.9
Newar	190,629	15.3
Sherpa	130, 000	92.8
Bhote	98,000	98
Thakali	35,000	65
Chhant	18,000	64.2
Jirel	19,600	87
Lepcha	50,800	88.8
Hyolmo	195,4009	8.4

Source : Census of Nepal, 2001.

Khas people who migrated to Nepal in the early twelfth century A.D. from the north-west frontiers of India *via* Tibet and established a kingdom for themselves at a place called Sijā in the province of Jumla. The Khas is an ancient race which finds mention in *Mahabharata*, *Purana* and also in the famous *Rajatarangini* of Kalhana. In course of time their dialect, known in Nepal as Khas Kura being a branch of Indo-Aryan language became popular and acceptable to all, even before the advent of the Gorkhas. After the conquest and unification of Nepal by the Gorkhas, the Khas Kura that was spoken by majority of the people was widely accepted all over the country and came to be known as the Gorkhali language. The Gorkha king, Prithvinarayan Shah gave this language the status of official language in the kingdom of Nepal. The present form of Nepali language has been called by Dr. Suniti Kumar Chatterjee and also by the eminent Nepali historians as *Khas Apabhramsha* because of its close affinity with Kumaoni, Garhwali and some other western hill dialects. The Khas people are found in Garhwal and Kumaon districts in India whose dialect is akin to Nepali language.

Thus, Nepal is a country that was originally inhabited and ruled by peoples coming from two different places and directions—one from the north, being the Mongolians of the Tibeto-Burman race and the other from the south as the Kiratas, Aryans and Dravidians. For centuries continuous batches of peoples from the north and the south were finding their ways into Nepal settling down side by side meeting and mixing together for generations, at times fighting each other, at another living peacefully and mixing their cultures and languages, which paved the way to the inevitable historical process of building a new nation, that is the Nepalese as they are known today.

After the Thakuris reigned for 225 years Harisingh Deva, king of Simraun (India) conquered Nepal in 1324 A.D. and founded Ayodhya dynasty. Simraun was an ancient capital of a powerful Hindu kingdom of Mithila (modern Tirhut) which Harisingh Deva lost to Mohammedan Emperor of Delhi, Gheyasu-din-Tughlaq. On being defeated in the war he withdrew to the northern mountains and displaced the Thakuri kings of Bhatgoan, Patan and Kathmandu one after another. After the death of Shyamasingh Deva, the 4th and the last king of Ayodhya dynasty, the throne passed on to Malla dynasty by matrimonial relations. Joyasthiti Malla, the famous king of this lineage is credited to have introduced a true and precise Hinduism in Nepal and laid the foundations of a Brahminical order of society. With the establishment of numerous Hindu shrines and temples across the country there came hoards of Brahmin priests and pilgrims from India and settled in Nepal. As a result, the casteless and colourless (*jaati/varnahin*) Buddhist and indigenous tribes of Nepal gradually came under the influence of Brahmanical system. Many non-Hindu indigenous tribes like the Newars, Magars, Gurungs, Thapas etc. accepted Hinduism as their religion and started practicing Hindu rites and rituals. The rest of the communities who continued to hold on to Buddhism like the Tamangs, Gurungs, Newars, Sherpas, Bhutias, Lepchas etc. and also those who followed their indigenous faith like the Rai, Limbu, Khambu etc. also gave way to liberal view and began to observe Hindu festivals such as *Dasain*, *Tehar* etc. like national festivals of Nepal. The Buddhism of Nepal, itself became adulterated with the induction and worship of Hindu Gods and Goddesses.

When we analyse the history and make a comparative reading of the chronological developments of events that took place in India and Nepal, we find a very close resemblance between the two. In Nepal, Buddhism was already in the wane ever since the Lichchavis' entry into Nepal, after which she received further setback, as more and more Hindu followers began to arrive in the wake of the Brahminical ascendancy. The contemporary India experienced the same situation like Nepal characterized by gradual decline of Buddhism and revival of Hinduism. The advent of imperial Gupta rule during and after 5th century A.D. may be considered as the watershed for the revival of Brahmanism and the beginning of Hindu cultural renaissance in India. During fifth century A.D. when Fa-Hien came to India he found Buddhism flourishing and after two hundred years when Chinese pilgrim Huen- Tsang visited India and the North-eastern region he saw a gradual decline of Buddhism. The Buddhist centre of learning, Takshashila, Pataliputra were in ruins and the Hindu temples surpassed the Buddhist structures in their grandeur and dignity. During post Harsha period Buddhism deflected its course from Mahayana towards Tantrika Buddhism. The high ideals of Mahayana Buddhism which aimed at salvation of all, soon yielded to gross superstition and immoral practices of Tantrism. From the trend of events that happened in India one can see clearly that the culture and religion of Nepal had systematically and continually been influenced by the changes that prevailed in India ever since millenniums past. Simultaneously with Indian trend the Buddhism in Nepal became adulterated by Tantrism involving the practice of magic rites, appeasement of various gods and goddesses, ghosts and demons etc. which degenerated the Nepalese Buddhism in the 11th and 12th centuries A.D. Even today, a section of the Newar community follow the Vajrayana Buddhism while the Tamang, Gurungs and other Buddhists practice Shamanic Tantrism. In India, the corrupted Buddhism could not last long; and after the termination of Pala dynasty in north India Buddhism became literally weakened due to lack of royal patronage and ascendancy of Hinduism. The invasion of the Muslims in India during the beginning of the 13th century and their policy of religious intolerance leading to destruction of monasteries by Muslim rulers put a severe jolt to Buddhism in India.

The Malla kings ruled over Nepal valley—Kirtipur, Lalitpur and Bhaktapur for more than four hundred years until they were vanquished by the Gorkha king Prithvinarayan Shah, the scion of Rajput race of India. The advent of Shah dynasty in Nepal and the rise in power of the Gorkhas for two and a half centuries after unification of Nepal by Prithvinarayan Shah heralded the era of final consolidation and perpetuation of Brahminism in Nepal. Under the royal patronage of the Rajput kings Hinduism rose to a new height and heralded a new spiritual life among the people of Nepal. The Rajputs were not only ruthless in their policies and administration, but also zealous defenders of religion and staunch protagonists of Hindu culture and religion. It was the Rajput Gorkhas who proclaimed Nepal as the only Hindu kingdom in the world and its subjects the staunch worshippers of Lord Pashupatinath, the guardian deity of Nepal. Through, the promulgation of '*Mulki Ain*' the Brahmins were accorded highest rank in society and the law was made stringent and discriminatory against those in the lower ranks in society. Religious intolerance had a profound impact on the relationship between the people professing Hinduism and other religions. The Rana rulers looked at the movements of Europeans with suspicion and distrust and believed that they would bring Christianity into Nepal. It was their popular saying that the *Firingis* (Foreigners) come to Nepal with bayonet in one hand and Bible in the other. With thc usurpation of powers of the king by the Rana Lords, religion in Nepal became so practical and ritualistic that it not only confined to religious and cultural activities, but also permeated every sphere of life of the people including political and administrative affairs of the Government of Nepal.

The agrarian economy of Nepal was most neglected. The farmers were exploited by landlords taking advantage of the defective land tenure system which was practiced ever since the reign of king Prithvinarayan Shah. He made land central to the feudal and economic structure of Nepal and controlled access to it through the *pijani* system. He introduced the system of *Jagir, Birta, Guthi* and *Rakam* in the land tenure settlement which were directly responsible to herald feudalism in Nepalese agrarian economy. The *Jagir* system was short term land grant which were mostly given for military services in lieu of cash salaries. This was an ingenious way devised by Prithvinarayan Shah to reduce the cash burden on his kingdom that lacked strong cash economy. The *Birta* system was land grants given out by the state to individuals for their services to the state with the right to rent out to farmers for production of crops. The *Guthi* land grants were given to temples and monasteries for the benefit of the local community. The *Rakam* land grants were given to craftsmen and skilled workers as payment for their labour. These systems of land settlement to private individuals created a class of feudal landlords in Nepalese society who never cultivate the lands by themselves, but rent out to landless farmers at exorbitant rates and exploit them in various ways. This system also did away with direct relationship between the state and the peasantry and adversely affected the traditional system of *Kipot* under which certain communities like the Rai, Limbu and Tamang used to hold community lands for their livelihood. Large tracts of *Kipot* land were converted into *Birta*, *Jagir* and *Guthi* and the indigenous natives of the soil were dispossessed of their source of livelihood. The *Jagir*, *Birta*, *Guthi* land settlement were given tax free and so the state could not levy taxes on the *Jagirdars*, *Birtadars* and *Guthidars*, instead the tax were collected from the poor peasants who cultivated the land as tenants.

The name Pashupatinath literally means the Lord of beasts and is just another appellation of Lord Siva. He can be considered as the hallmark of Nepalese cultural and spiritual synthesis who commands profound faith and reverence from every citizen of the country irrespective of caste, creed and religion. He is a symbol of solidarity between the Hindus, Buddhists and the animists. He imbues a psyche that everyone who is in the precinct of his temple or the place of worship is under the banner of a Nepali Hindu. All official documents, notifications and proclamations were made in the revered name Lord Pashupatinath. The sacrificial worship to Lord Pasupatinath, the guardian deity of Nepal, invariably preceded all important tasks scheduled to be done by the royal family; for they believed that the blessings of Lord Pashupatinath would help successful completion of the project. The temple of Pashupatinath is constructed at a place which, according to Hindu scripture, Lord Siva had visited in the guise of a deer and it overlooks the bank of river Bagmati below, where dead bodies of Hindus are cremated day in and day out. Old and ailing Hindus come to this place in order to die with their feet dipped under the water of Bagmati as they breath their last, which they consider is the best way to reach heaven after death. Nepalese tradition has it that Jaiprakash Malla, the last king of Malla dynasty after being vanquished by

Prithvinarayan Shah breathed his last with his feet immersed in the holy water of Bagmati. The environment around the temple is no different from that of Viswanath temple of Benaras, with the outskirts of the temple dotted with numerous small temples of Hindu gods and goddesses and the *sadhus* and pilgrims hanging around, while inside the temples are a band of south Indian Brahmin priests engaged in worship. This practice of engaging Indian priests for worshiping the Pashupatinath temple had been there for the past three hundred years which still continues. Recently in January, 2009, the newly formed Maoist Government led by Puspa Kamal Dahal (Prachanda) made an abortive attempt to replace the Indian priests by a set of local Nepalese Priests which evoked a great commotion between the supporters of the two sides. The dispute went up to the Supreme Court of Nepal which issued an interim order asking the Government to allow the south Indian priests to continue the worship. In the long run, the matter was decided in favour of the south Indian priest and accordingly Pandit Mahabaleswar Bhatta and two others—Ganesh Bhatta and Ramkrishna Bhatta were reinstated in their positions in presence of a number of Hindu leaders including Indian film star and Member of Parliament Shri Govinda.

Hinduism and Buddhism have co-existed side-by-side in India and Nepal since time immemorial and at no point of time the one has replaced the other wholly. Hinduism entered Nepal together with its elaborate caste system and spread throughout the length and breath of the country under the royal patronage of different Hindu dynasties. But in spite of the supremacy, it enjoyed throughout the centuries Hinduism could not supplant Buddhism from the soil of Nepal. Buddhism continued to hold its own against all adversaries and existed like a smouldering fire on the altar of Lumbini, the birth place of Buddha. In a country where Hinduism had always been the religion of the Crown and the high class people while Buddhism had ever been the faith of the humble and down-trodden, nevertheless, the former group has had, never attempted to trample over the latter group in any way. It was mainly due to the reason that Buddhism in Nepal was at no point of time wholly displaced by Hinduism, not even during the reign of Rudradeva, known for Hindu bigotry. He was a Thakuri king, who persecuted the Buddhist monks and ruthlessly destroyed monasteries and Buddhist literatures. Except this lone event of religious persecution, there has been no blood-shed or war in Nepal in the name of religion. This is one of the unique features of Nepalese cultural history. The two major religions—Buddhism and Hinduism have continued to enjoy the deepest faith and reverence of the Nepalese people ever since the inception. For the Nepalese people believed that Buddhism is not an anti-Hindu faith but is an adjunct to Hinduism with different ethical tenets. Buddha is considered as one of the ten Incarnations (*Avatars*) of Hindu pantheon and the Buddhist ideology as a branch of Hindu philosophy. This may be the secret of the long and peaceful co-existence of the two faiths side by side flourishing and enriching respective doctrinal ethos. This is the beauty of the cultural synthesis of society which has no parallel in any part of the world except India and Nepal. The nitty-gritty of Nepalese culture and religion can better be comprehended from the following passage taken from Henry Ballantine's *Nepal: The Gurkhas Mysterious Land*—"....for here at last, was a spot where there was neither Jew nor Gentile, where beneath the shadow of the 'Abodes of Gods' the world's two great sects, forgetting their differences, had clasped hands; where Hinduism and Buddhism had bound together in one volume their Sanskrit *shastras* and the sayings of Shakya Muni, and where the Mongolian from Peking with the Malabaris from Rameswar bent their knees side by side in the same sacred precincts (of Swayambhunath temple) consecrated alike to Buddha and Siva".[19] The temple of Swayambhunath, referred to above, is an ancient temple of Buddhist origin. Its genesis can be traced back to the legend of Manjushri who converted the lake of Kathmandu valley into a habitable place by cutting a canal to flow out its water down to the river Bagmati. It is believed that there was a lone lotus flower floating on the surface of the lake and when the water was drained out the lotus sank down and rested at an elevated place. The present Swayambhunath temple is said to be located at the spot where the lotus had rested. It is a green hill top, about two kilometres west of Kathmandu that this spectacular dome like structure of Swayambhunath is situated with its two big eyes constantly staring down the valley of Kathmandu over the centuries past, as a silent witness to the rise and fall, growth and decay of the numerous kingdoms and the tribes that lived in this small Himalayan country. Swayambhunath, meaning self-existent, is a famous pilgrimage for both the Buddhists as well as the Hindus although originally being a Buddhist temple. On the top of the holy shrine there are five images of Lord Buddha in five different postures while at the entrance there stands a big prayer wheel about which, it is believed that one turn of the wheel equals to two and a half lakh prayers. The devotees visiting the temple turn the prayer wheel to get blessings of Lord Buddha.There are many images of Hindu gods and goddesses around the shrine which seem to be later additions by some Hindu kings, ostensibly with an objective of instilling a sense of religious solidarity among the people. The festival of *Buddha Jayanti*, (birthday of Lord Buddha) is celebrated at Swayambhunath by both Hindus and Buddhists with sanctity and fervor. In the same way, *Siva-ratri*, the festival of the Hindus, is celebrated by both communities with equal pomp and gaiety. *Indrajatra* which is celebrated in order to propitiate Indra, the Hindu god of rain is joined by Hindus, Buddhists and the animists. The celebration continues for eight days and is attended by the king of Nepal. It is believed that on this day the Gorkha king, Prithvinarayan Shah conquered Kathmandu and unified Nepal. *Dasain* and *Tehar* are the two national festivals of Nepal which are observed by every citizen with equal fervor irrespective of caste, creed and religion. This indicates the spirit of national integration and solidarity of the Nepalese people. The traditional rituals of *Vijaya-dasami* and *Bhratri-dwitia* are Nepal's most auspicious festivals when the family members and close relatives meet each other and reciprocate their love and blessing through the rituals of offering *Tikas* (sticking grains of rice mixed milk cream on the forehead). Although the two festivals have their roots in the Hindu mythology, over the centuries, they have assumed universal ethos among all citizens and have become a national festival of the Nepalese community as a whole.

Thus, the Nepalese are a conglomeration of many communities, cultures and religions with as many dialects of their own and yet they speak one Nepali language and feel themselves as one people and one nation. This is what may be called, in the true sense of the term, the unity in diversity of Nepal, and this particular feature makes Nepal verily akin to India. The history of Nepal is an account of inter-mixture of multiple races, religions and languages that has galvanized into one nation and one State. In this respect, Nepal may be called a miniature India with similar Vedic socio-religious base and identical art, culture, customs and language. Both the countries have passed through a similar geo-political process, of having received waves of invaders from the outside world in the past who settled down in their new found lands, mixed-up their bloods, cultures and faith and became merged with the local dwellers. The bracing climate and somewhat flat topographic condition of the place gradually attracted other settlers from the north and the south ever since and before the Christian era. From the north came the people of Tibeto-Burman linguistic group while from the south migrated more dominant and culturally advanced Aryans, Dravidians and Indo-Mongoloid races. For centuries continuous batches of people from the north and the south were finding their ways into Nepal settling down side by side meeting and mixing together for generations, at times fighting each other, at another living peacefully and mixing their cultures and languages that paved the way for building up of a new Nepali nation. The Kiratas who are variously called by historians as Indo-Mongoloids, Palaeo-Mongoloids or Proto-Mongoloids were the first historically known people to enter Nepal from the north-eastern frontiers of India. A few centuries thereafter, the Kiratas were followed by other more advanced Hinduised people from India called the Lichchavis, Thakuris, Mallas and Shahs one after another they vanquished or subdued the ruling chieftains, established and extended their own dominions over various parts of Nepal and ruled there. They also brought with them Hindu religion and initiated the people into their religion and culture and developed the Brahminical social system in Nepal. The geographical proximity too helped Indian missionaries to reach out to Nepal with their culture and religion. The advent of Hindu Rajputs in Nepal during 14th century A.D. and the rise in power of the Gorkha dynasty finally heralded an era of consolidation and perpetuation of Brahminism in Nepal. The unification of greater Nepal by the Gorkha king Prithvinarayan Shah in 1769 A.D. and thereafter, the continuous regime of the Shah dynasty for the next 240 years put

Nepal on the solid foundation to be known as the only Hindu kingdom in the world. With the assimilation of the indigenous Nepalese people with Indian rulers and immigrants, Nepal came to be like a miniature India with common history, culture, religion, language and even ethnic composition.

While that was the real history commonly shared by India and Nepal in the past, unfortunately today, the people of the two countries are, blissfully unaware of the historical fact that they were the descendants of the same ancestors. More than ninety per cent of the present population of Nepal, barring those of Tibetan origin, are the progenies of Kiratas, Lichchavis,Thakuris, Shahs, and the Ranas of India who migrated to Nepal during the last couple of millenniums. There are more than ninety-two local languages and dialects in Nepal and over one hundred social groups based on caste, ethnicity, religion and language who bear distinct imprints of their counterparts living in India. They seem to have totally forgotten about the grand ethnic and cultural assimilation of the past, nor they seem to make any effort to impart this historical knowledge to their school children. The Indian students read the history of world in their schools, but never the history of Nepal. The map of Nepal is invariably superimposed on the top of India's map as though it is a part of India, but the Indian geography does not speak a word about Nepal. A host of Nepal's rivers like the Kosi, Gandaki, Kali and Bagmati are the lifelines of the people of Uttar Pradesh and Bihar, but Indian geography does not speak a word about these rivers. The history of India and Nepal are so closely interlinked with each other, but our Indian history does not make even a fleeting reference to Nepalese history and its people who are from common ancestors. It is high time that the educationists from India and Nepal put their heads together and devise a suitable syllabus for the students of both the countries to study the ethno-cultural relations between India and Nepal.

Notes

1. B.N. Luniya, *Life and Culture in Ancient India*, p. 460.
2. B.N. Luniya (1998), *Evolution of Indian Culture*, Agra: Lakshminarayan Agarwal, p. 235.

3. *Ibid.*, p. 231.
4. Jawaharlal Nehru, *op. cit.*, p. 200.
5. K.L. Baruah, *Early History of Kamrupa*, p. 8.
6. S.K. Chatterjee, *Kirata-Jana-Kriti,* 194, Calcutta: Asiatic Society.
7. E.A. Gait (1926), *History of Assam,*Calcutta.
8. G.P. Singh (1990), *The Kiratas in Ancient India*, New Delhi: Gyan Books, pp. 355-56.
9. J.N. Choudhury (1988), "Prehistoric and Early Tribal migrations in North-east India", in *The Archaeology of North-East India,* Ed. Jai Prakash Singh, NEHU, Shillong.
10. *Ibid.*
11. Since, the Kiratas appear in Nepal from the dawn of Nepal's history it deserves deeper study. Who were the Kiratas ? Where they came from? To get the answer to the questions we have to take a look into the ancient Vedic history. In *Rig Veda* there is a reference to a battle between Aryans and Kirata which was fought around Prayaga where the Kiratas were finally vanquished. The Kiratas are said to have withdrawn towards the eastern Himalayas. Arjuna was stopped and defied by Kiratas in the disguise of Siva as he was ascending the Himalaya towards the north. In *Ramayana,* Bhima subjugates the seven kings of the seven Gandakis and seven Kosis in Nepals Himalaya. D.R. Regmi Says: "It appears that before the Kirata invaders landed in Nepal there were already peoples of Indo-Aryan origin settled there". B.H. Hodgson observed that the Kiratas are Mongolian people because they are of Tibetan, Chinese and Mongoloid origin. J.W. McGrindle identified Kiratas as Mongoloid race and Sylvan Levy also referred to racial connection with the Mongoloisd people. G.P. Singh, however, asserts that the Kiratas are neither Mongolians nor did they come from China or Tibet.
12. D.R. Regmi, (1969), *Ancient Nepal,* Calcutta: Rupbani Press.
13. Eden Vansittart (1915), *Gurkhas*, Calcutta: Government Press.
14. Lt. Colonel Eden Vansittart, *Gurkhas,* p. 12.
15. Some historians including K.P. Jayaswal maintain that towards the 200 A.D. Nepal was under the suzerainty of the Lichchavis who had their capital at Vaishali. D.R. Regmi thinks that there is ample ground to believe that a major part of the north Bihar which passes through obscurity all these centuries might have been a part of Nepal.
16. Rishikesh Shaha, *Ancient and Medieval Nepal*, p. 156.
17. *Ibid.*, p. 164.
18. Eden Vansittart, *op. cit.*, p. 13.
19. Henry Ballantine, *Nepal : The Gurkhas Mysterious Land.*
20. H. Ambrose Oldfield (1880), *Sketches from Nepal,* Vol. II, Reprint 1974, p. 129, Delhi: Cosmo Publication.

5

Uniformity of Faith and Religion

India and Nepal are both deeply religious countries. Hinduism is their main religion while Buddhism is also widely professed in Nepal and in lesser degree in India. The existence of numerous Hindu and Buddhist temples and shrines in the valley of Kathmandu and its surroundings, and the fluttering of thousands of Buddhist prayer-flags all-over the hills and valleys of Nepal are the indicators of how extensively has the religion influenced the lives of the people of this country. Similarly, in India, the plethora of places of worship and pilgrimages and the mushroom of ancient Hindu temples scattered all-over the north and the south India speak loud and clear of the profound religious and spiritual fervor ever hunting the sentiments of Indian people. "Religion has been and continues to be the life-blood of societies all-over the world", says the book, *The World's Religions: Understanding the Living Faiths*. John Bowker, in his book, *God: A Brief History*, observes—"There has never been any human society in which God has not been a part, usually a controlling and creative part". Thus, religion has been a golden mean that has brought India and Nepal so close to each other in the past and the present.

Kapilavastu, the capital of King Suddhodhana, father of Gautama Buddha is situated in the Terai of Nepal, a few miles away from Lumbini, the famous birthplace of Lord Buddha which is also in Nepal. It is a sacred place of pilgrimage for the people of India as well as Nepal. Historians say that Lord Buddha visited Nepal during the rule of Kiratas. After Buddha, a Jain saint named Bhadrabahu is said to have come to Nepal about 2307 years ago in order to spread the message of Lord Mahavira. In *Mahabharata* there is a mention of a place named Viratnagar where the Pandavas performed the penance of "*Agyatavasa*" which means exile in disguise. Viratnagar was the kingdom of the king Virata and today Viratnagar is an industrial town in Nepal. So also, Janakpur where Sita was born is a growing town in the Tarai of Nepal and is an important place of pilgrimage for the Hindus. A magnificent Janaki temple was constructed by some Indian prince at a cost of Rs. nine lakh. Because of this reason this temple is called Naulakha temple by the Nepalese people.[1]

History tells us that Ashoka the great, visited Nepal more than 2200 years ago in order to worship at the birthplace of Lord Buddha at Lumbini and to preach the teachings of the Tathagata. According to legend Ashoka (273-32 B.C.) of Maurya dynasty visited it around 250 B.C.[2] At Lumbini he erected a pillar with an inscription which can be read even to this day. In the inscription the Emperor Ashoka is called as the—*Devanampriyena priyadarshin.*[3] The two *stupas* or monuments constructed by him at Pattan and at Kirtipur are still there to be seen. Charumati, the daughter of Ashoka married a Nepal prince and settled down in Nepal to propagate Buddhism. Her name has been perpetuated by a place called '*Charuhil*' or *Chabhil*, (named after Charumati) located not very far from Kathmandu where she is believed to have stayed. A *Stupa*, in the shape of a large inverted bowl, constructed by her at this place, still exists.[4] Today Nepal is another country in the world where Hinduism is major religion. From this point of view also Nepal has a very close religious affinity with India. The phrase "Hindu and monarchical kingdom" of the definition is, however, going to change drastically under the new Constitution of Nepal which is being redrafted after the political changes have taken place in 2008.

Buddhism is still a major religion in Nepal followed by a fairly large section of the population. There are ten different types of religions and faiths presently found in Nepal. The percentage and number of people who follow various religions, according to census 2011, are shown in Table 5.1.

The Nepali capital Kathmandu and its surroundings have a large number of Hindu and Buddhist temples and *pagodas*. The Bodhnath Stupa, situated a few km away from Kathmandu on way to Charuhil is bigger in size and shape than the Stupas of Gaya

Table 5.1: Religions of Nepal, Number of Follower and Percentage

Religion	*Number of Followers*	*Percentage of Followers*
Hinduism	2,15,51,492	81.3
Buddhism	23,96,099	9.00
Islam	11,62,370	4.4
Kirat	8,07,169	3.1
Christianity	3,75,699	1.4
Prakriti	—	0.5
Bon	13,006	—
Bahal	1,283	—
Sikhism	609	—

Source : Census of 2011, Government of Nepal.

and Sarnath and has a large compound enclosed by stone walls with four gates at four corners.[5] The temple of Pashupatinath in Kathmandu occupies an exceptional place in the cultural history of Indo-Nepal unity. It is believed that the temple of Pashupatinath was built by king Dharma Dutta who came from South India in 4th century A.D. It was renovated by Adi Shankaracharya towards the eighth century. Every year on *Sivaratri* day it draws large number of pilgrims from different parts of India. Interestingly, all the priests who perform religious rites in the temple are from south India especially from Mysore and Maharashtra.[6] It goes without saying that this temple of Pashupatinath is a glorious symbol of ancient cultural and religious unity between India and Napal. The famous Buddhist temple of Swayambhunath on the top of the hillock near Kathmandu, the Gujweshwari and the Lumbini temples are of special attraction for the pilgrims from India. Similarly, the ancient pilgrimages of India like Kasi, Gaya, Haridwar, Kedarnath, Setubandha, Rameshwaram etc. draw numerous Nepalese pilgrims round the year. The Kamakhya temple of Guwahati, Assam, assumes a special religious importance for the people of Nepal, it being one of the *Pithas* where the pelvic part of Parvati's body had fallen. The king of Nepal and his high officials traditionally come to worship Kamakhya Devi of Assam (India), since long ago where Lalmohoria Panda, special priest appointed by the King of Nepal performs *Puja* for them. Interestingly, the title of Lalmohoria priesthood is held by inheritance from father to the son as an established institution at Kamakhya temple even to this day. At present, one Ram Chandra Dev Sarma holds with pride the Lalmohor, the order of priesthood, which he inherited from his father late Loknath Panda, the son of the original Lalmoharia, late Suklal Panda.[7] The king of Nepal is a life Patron of a number of Indian temples such as Jagannath temple of Puri and Rameswaram temple and he enjoys special privilege of worship in those temples at any time of the year. There is, thus a mutual understanding and a sense of co-sharing between India and Nepal in respect of construction, development and preservation of a number of Hindu temples and shrines of India.

The temple of Samrajeshwara Pashupateshwara Mahadeva which was constructed by Nepal king is reminiscent of the glorious royal history of Nepal. The temple stands, till today, at Lalita Ghat along the river Ganga at Benaras, India. It is one of the outstanding temples of India and even known as the temple city of India. Its *pagoda*-style of architecture distinguishes it from other Indian temples with its exquisite wood carvings, and elaborate erotica, are definitely the work of master craftsmen brought from Nepal. This temple is a replica of Pashupatinath temple of Kathmandu which is a world heritage site and visited by thousands of tourists and devotees every year. This temple was built in 1841 by Ran Bahadur Shah, the third king of Nepal's longest ruling Shah dynasty. Towards the end of his reign Ran Bahadur Shah was banished to Benaras for four years with his queen Lalita and during this period he built this temple in his queen's name together with a resting place for pilgrims and old-age home for widows and abandoned women. The temple and its adjuncts are presently in a dilapidated condition due to long neglect and lack of maintenance. Recently this, 167 year old historic temple, has received the attention of the Nepalese Government which has decided to restore and renovate this temple complex.

During the reign of Rudra Deva, the 7th King of Suryavamshi dynasty (653-656 A.D.) Adi Shankaracharya, saint of India visited Nepal who under the patronage of the king, started the movement for revival of Hindu religion in Nepal. He set-up a *matha* and made regular arrangements for worship in the temple of Pashupatinath in the Bagmati valley and since that time the tradition of appointing priest from the south India is continuing till today.[8] He was a diehard

Hindu bigot and strongly opposed to any faith other than Hinduism. He instigated against the Buddhist religion and advised the king to persecute against the Buddhist followers. Accordingly, the king destroyed Buddhist literatures, burnt down Buddhist temples and butchered many Buddhist monks. But the persecution of king Rudra Deva could not succeed in overthrowing Buddhism from Nepal.

When we analyze the history and make a comparative reading of the chronological developments of events that took place in India and Nepal we find a very close resemblance between the two. In Nepal, Buddhism was already in the wane ever since the Thakuri's entry into Nepal, after which she received further setbacks, as more and more Hindu followers began to arrive Nepal in the wake of the Brahminical ascendancy, while the contemporary India experienced the same situation like Nepal characterized by gradual decline of Buddhism and revival of Hinduism. The advent of imperial Gupta rule during and after 5th century A.D. may be considered as the watershed for the revival of Brahminism and the beginning of Hindu cultural renaissance in India. During the fifth century A.D. when Fa-Hien visited to India, he found Buddhism flourishing and after two hundred years when Chinese pilgrim Huen- Tsang came to India and to the north-eastern region he saw a gradual decline of Buddhism. The Buddhist centres of learning, Takshashila, Pataliputra were in ruins and the Hindu temples surpassed the Buddhist structures in their grandeur and dignity. During post- Harsha period Buddhism deflected its course from Mahayana towards Tantrika Buddhism. The high ideals of Mahayana Buddhism which aimed at salvation of all, soon yielded to gross superstition and immoral practices of Tantrism. From the trend of events that happened in India one can see clearly that the culture and religion of Nepal had systematically and continually been influenced by the changes that prevailed in India ever since millenniums past. Simultaneously with what happened in India, the Buddhism in Nepal too became adulterated by Tantrism involving the practice of magic rites, appeasement of numerous Gods and Goddesses, ghosts and demons which degenerated the Nepalese Buddhism by the 11th and 12th centuries A.D. Even today a section of the Newar community follow the Vajrayana Buddhism while the Tamang, Gurungs and other Buddhists practice Shamanic

Tantrism. In India the corrupted, Buddhism could not last long; and after the termination of Pala dynasty in north India Buddhism became literally weakened due to lack of royal patronage and ascendancy of Hinduism.

Saint Gorakhnath was a Hindu seer from India who lived in a small shrine located in the cave of a hillock in western Nepal. He was a god-like sage and after his death the shrine where he worshipped came to be known as Gorakhnath temple. The village was also called Gorkha and subsequently the whole principality under the Shah dynasty came to be known as Gorkha principality.[9] Perhaps, it was owing to the blessings of the Lord Gorakhnath that the political history of Nepal took a sharp turn culminating into the consolidation of a greater Nepal during the mid-seventeenth century. The Gorkha principality under the Shah dynasty rose in power in quick succession and within a short period the Gorkha king Prithvinarayan Shah succeeded in carving out a composite Sub-Himalayan kingdom called Nepal which included all the territories and chieftainships conquered by him. That was, more or less, of what the country of Nepal is constituted today. The name Gorkha by which the Nepalese are alternatively known was derived from the principality of Gorkha, the origin of Shah dynasty. The term 'Gorkha,' as a race, connotes the idea of valour because the brave king Prithvinarayan Shah who conquered and consolidated Nepal into a single country belonged to the Gorkha race. The Nepalese people feel proud to be called as Gorkhas which name became renowned in the world for bravery and elan while fighting as part of British Indian Army during the First and Second World War.

The world history offers us harrowing tales of wars, deaths and destructions in the name of religion like those of the massacre of Jerusalem by the king of Babylon, the Thirty-years war of Europe and the loot and destruction of Hindu temples by the Muslim invaders. The invasion of the Muslims in India during the beginning of the 13th century and their policy of religious intolerance leading to destruction of monasteries and temples had a severe impact on both Hinduism and Buddhism in India. In comparison to these tumultuous religious rivalries of medieval India, religion had never been a matter of conflict in Nepal except the one instance that occurred during the reign of Thakuri King Rudradeva in mid-seventh century A.D. as mentioned in the preceding paragraph. The Indian history tells us that from the eleventh century onward the Muslim invaders demolished and mutilated a great many Hindu temples and shrines causing irreparable loss of life and property. For example, during the eleventh century A.D., Sultan Mahmud of Ghazni massacred cities and shrines of the north and south India as many as seventeen times and carried away gold and silver idols on horse backs. The destruction of the temples of Mathura, Kannauj and Kathiawar where the temple of Somnath was renowned for fabulous wealth were among the most haunted by the Muhammadan invaders. However, the motive force behind the incursion of Sultan Mahmud was not against Hindu religion, but for his selfish greed for wealth like that of Nebuchadnezzar, the king of Babylon who destroyed Jerusalem and took away the golden vessels, "bowls, dishes, lamp stands" all that were made of gold and silver including "bronze pillars, shovels, sprinkling bowls and wick trimmers" from the temple. The Muslim atrocities were, no doubt, barbaric but they were basically of tolerant attitude in so far as Hindu religion is concerned. The following words of Amartya Sen, the Nobel Laureate of India, are worth quoting here—"It would be as silly to deny the barbarities of the invasive history, as it would be to see this savagery as the main historical feature of the Muslim presence in India".[10] The Muslim rulers of India, such as the Mughals could hardly be characterised as destroyers rather than builders despite many Hindu shrines and temples in India were demolished or partially demolished and remodeled to use them as mosques. The Mughals were undoubtedly great builders. Works of exquisite Muslim architectural design introduced by the Mughals can still be seen in buildings, monuments and mosques constructed by them in India. Mughal Emperor Shah Jahan's construction of the Taj Mahal at Agra and the Jama Masjid of Delhi are the master pieces of Mughal architectural engineering. It was an amalgam of Islamic, Persian and Indian architecture. Emperor Akbar built many buildings and monuments of which Humayun's Tomb (for his father's memory), Agra Fort, the Fort of Fatehpur Sikri and Buland Darwaja are famous.

In respect of Nepal, there was little or no impact whatsoever of the Muslim religion on any faith or religion of Nepal although attempts to invade the country were made by some Muslim kings during their rule in India. But they failed to establish their sway over any part of Nepal because of military prowess of the Gorkhas and their mountain fastness.

If we take a glimpse into the history we find that Buddhism flourished in Nepal during the rule of Lichchavi kings (400-750 A.D.). People of different ethnic groups living in central Nepal such as Tamangs, Gurungs, Magars, Lepchas, Newars, Thamis etc. came under the religion of Buddhism. Kirati people like Limbu, Rai, Yakhkhas also adopted Buddhism. Lichchavi king Manadeva had a liberal view of religion and visited both Hindu and Buddhist temples. Religious tolerance was the rule in Nepal and all people freely adopted and worshipped the religions of their own choice without fear and hindrance from anybody. The two faiths—Buddhism and Shaivism—flourished side by side in Nepal. It is stated that Brahma, Vishnu and Siva had taken their abodes in the green hills above the river Bagmati near Manjupatnam. Lichchavi king Amsuvarman gave his daughter Vrikuti in marriage to the Tibetan king Tsrong Tchong Gampo.

The Malla dynasty of Nepal (1200-1769) witnessed for the first time the rise of Hinduism in Nepalese soil under the patronage of the Malla kings. The kings followed a policy of not only encouraging and developing Hindu religion but, also persecuting and discouraging the growth of Buddhism. King Jayasthiti Malla was a hard core bigot and followed the policy of persecuting followers of Buddhism and Buddhist Monks. He ordered banishment of all celibate monks from Nepal and burning down of monasteries. It is said that a great many of Buddhist scriptures were destroyed by Shankaracharya in the 8th or 9th centuries. Shankaracharya was a famous Brahminical bigot who waged incessant war against Buddhism in India and Nepal and succeeded in converting the Newari king into Hinduism through whom he carried out his mission of Buddhist persecution systematically. After a few years, he went to Tibet with the same mission when he had a controversy with the grand Lama there who transfixed Shankaracharya's shadow on the ground with a knife.

Shankaracharya's throat was pierced by knife to which he succumbed.[11] After Jayasthiti Malla his son Jyoti Malla became the king who was very tolerant to Buddhism despite being a Hindu. During his reign two Buddhist Bhikshus, *viz.* Kyanchen Lama and Chhiring Lama came to Nepal from Gyarong province of Tibet and re-established Buddhism in Nepal.

The Shah dynasty (1769-1846) saw the further decline of Buddhism and simultaneous growth of Hinduism in Nepal. The Malla kings ruled over Nepal valley—Kirtipur, Lalitpur and Bhaktapur for more than four hundred years until they were vanquished by the Gorkha king Prithvinarayan Shah, the scion of Rajput race of India. The advent of Shah dynasty in Nepal and the rise in power of the Gorkhas for two and a half centuries after unification of Nepal by Prithvinarayan Shah heralded the era of final consolidation and perpetuation of Brahminism in Nepal. Under the royal patronage of the Rajput kings Hinduism rose to a new height and heralded a new spiritual life among the people of Nepal. The Rajputs were not only ruthless in their policies and administration, but also zealous defenders of religion and staunch protagonists of Hindu culture and religion. Buddhism was considered as a part of Hinduism and there was an attempt to merge Buddhism within the religious pantheon of Hinduism. Hindu deities like Bhairava and Mahakala, Siva and Mahadeva, Ganesha, Indra, Garuda etc. found the place in Buddhist temples where their idols were worshipped together with Buddha. A sterling example of unification of Hinduism and Buddhism is found in a temple called Mahakala dedicated to Mahadeva and situated on high road close to Tundikhel. The idol inside the temple is that of Siva but on his head is a small figure of Buddha Akshobhya.

In 1848 A.D. the Shah dynasty was replaced by Rana dynasty and together with this the status of Hindu religion was raised to state religion of Nepal by the Rana rulers. Nepal was declared as the only Hindu kingdom in the world. Buddhism suffered further setback, many of the indigenous tribes of Nepal such as the Magar, Gurung, Newar etc. changing their religion from Buddhism to Hinduism. Amongst those Tibeto-Burman linguistic groups who were most influenced by Hinduism were as follows:

Community	*Total Population*	*Hindus*	*Percentage*
1. Magar	16,22,421	12,10,276	74.60
2. Newar	12,45,232	10,47,561	84.13
3. Rai	6,35,151	1,58,803	25.00
4. Gurung	5,43,571	1,56,263	28.75

This conversion into Hinduism resulted in further dwindling down of the Buddhist population and subsequent increase in Hindu population of Nepal. The process of increase in Hindu population continued ever since then till recent times.

Synthesis of Two Religions

The two principal religions, Buddhism and Hinduism co-existed in Nepal throughout the past centuries and in fact, they merged into one another as stated above, This happened mainly because of the innate spirit of tolerance of one another's point of view that permeates the life of the Nepalese people. This spirit of respecting other's faith and religion is strongly reflected in their practice of animal sacrifice and the ceremony of *shraddha* performed by the Buddhists living side by side with the Hindus. The infusion of Tantricism brought in the practice of animal sacrifice in the Buddhist fold which helped them coming closer to Hinduism. On the part of Hindu king Narendra Malla, he struck his coins bearing the images of both Buddhist and Hindu deities. Again the name of 'Lokanatha', a Buddhist deity occurs on the coins of King Yogendra Malla of Lalitpur who is a Hindu king. In this context, it may be pointed out that the Lokanatha and Vajrayogini though belong primarily to the Buddhist pantheon are worshipped by the Shaivites as well.[12] Though *Stupas* and *Chaityas* are primarily worshipped by the Buddhists, they receive the equal trust and respect from the Hindus also. The classic example of religious synthesis in Nepal are—the half sunken Buddha in Pashupatinath Temple, the sleeping Vishnu in Buddhanilakantha and the statue of Buddha and numerous representation of Vishnu in Changunarayan.

Thus, over the centuries there has been a lot of assimilation of Buddhist culture and religion with those of the Hindus who ruled the country. The Hindu and Buddhist religions have influenced each other and the people worship, on many occasions, the deities of each other religion without discrimination. For example, the idols of the following Hindu deities are found installed inside many Buddhist temples and worshipped by both Hindus and Buddhists:

1. Bhairava and Mahakala two forms of Siva and Mahadeva.
2. Devi Bhairavi or Kali, consort of Bhairava.
3. Ganesha, the son of Bhairava and Bhairavi.
4. Indra, a form of Vishnu.
5. Garuda, the vehicle of Vishnu.

Another unique symbol of unification of religion in Nepal is found in a Hindu temple called Mahakala dedicated to Mahadeva or Siva and situated on the high road close to Tundikhel. The main idol inside this temple is that of Siva, but on his head there is a small figure of Buddha Akshobhya. The Hindus look on Mahakala as a form of Vishnu while the Buddhists regard him as Vajrapani. Thus, the people of two religions worship together the same deity under the same name within the same temple, but each assign to that deity characteristics that belong to his own creed.

The Buddhists regard the weapon *Vajra* (*Dorje*) as a symbol of power and their Lamas use it during the performance of every religious rites. There is a story about how this *Vajra* which is the weapon of Hindu deity, Indra came to be used by Buddhists. It is said in the scriptures that a contest took place between Buddha and Indra in which Indra was defeated and Buddha wrested from him the *Vajra* and since then it came to the possession of Buddha.

The festival of *Kumari puja* is celebrated in Nepal every year. The *Kumari puja* although is a Hindu cult it has merged within the Buddhists pantheon who worship with equal fervour.

Notes

1. Raghunath Singh (1950) *Jagrat Nepal* (Hindi), Benaras.
2. Ram Rahul (1978), *The Himalaya as a Frontier*, New Delhi, p. 58.
3. Raghunath Singh, *op. cit.*, Benaras, p. 158.
4. *Ibid.*
5. *Ibid.*, p. 264.
6. Sriman Narayan (1971), *India and Nepal*, p. 46, Delhi: Hind Pocket Book.

7. B.L. Upadhyaya (2004), *Khan Mihali*, Chandmari, Tezpur: Sonitpur Comprint.
8. Ram, Rahul (1978), *The Himalaya as a Frontier*, New Delhi: Vikas Publishing House, p. 57.
9. K.K. Muktan (2002), *The Legendary Gorkhas*, Guwahati: Spectrum.
10. Amartya Sen (2005), *The Argumentative Indian*, p. 58.
11. H. Ambrose Oldfield (1880), *Sketches from Nepal,* Vol. II, Delhi: Cosmo Publication, Reprint 1974, p. 129.
12. Prof. G.C. Shastri, *Hinduism and Buddhism in Nepal.*

6
Uniformity of Language and Literature

The Nepali language is the *de-facto lingua-franca* of Nepal and the official language of the country, as Hindi is in India. According to some chronicles Nepali or Khas Kura was introduced as official language of Nepal by Gorkha king Prithvinarayan Shah since 1768. Nepali is spoken throughout the length and breadth of Nepal by all sections of communities although a large number of her tribes have their own separate dialects. There are 123 languages in Nepal spoken as mother tongue as per Nepal census 2011 of which Nepali is spoken as mother tongue by 44.6 per cent of the total population followed by Maithili 11.7 per cent, Bhojpuri 5.98 per cent, Tharu 5.77 per cent, Tamang 5.11 per cent, Newar 3.2 per cent, Bajjika 2.99 per cent, Magar 2.98 per cent, Doteli 2.97 per cent and Urdu 2.61 per cent. Nepali is also spoken by over five million Indian nationals allover India besides it being the State language of Sikkim, a State within India where two-thirds of its population speak Nepali as their mother tongue. Nepali is also one of the two recognized official languages of West Bengal, the other being Bengali. In Bhutan, the neighbouring country of India, a large chunk of its population are speakers of Nepali language. In short, Nepali is the dominant language of the lower Himalayan and sub-Himalayan regions of India. It is recognized as one of the major literary languages of India and is included in the Eighth Schedule of the Constitution of India. Like India, the Nepalese population consists of multiple races and ethnic groups. She has more or less sixty different ethnic groups with their distinct dialects. According to Nepal Census 2011, the percentage of the speakers of major languages in Nepal is shown in Table 6.1.

Table 6.1 : Major Languages in Nepal in Speaking Per cent

Language	*Speakers*	*Language*	*Speakers*
Nepali	44.6%	Maithili	11.7%
Bhojpuri	5.98%	Tharu	5.77%
Tamang	5.11%	Newari	3.2%
Bajjika	2.99%	Magar	2.98%
Doteli	2.97%	Urdu	2.61%

Source : Nepal Census, 2011.

The present-day Nepali language which is the *lingua franca* of the country of Nepal was originally the speech of the Khas people who migrated to Nepal in the early twelfth century A.D. from the north-west frontiers of India *via* Tibet and established a kingdom for themselves at a place called Sija in the province of Jumla. The Khas is an ancient race which finds mention in *Mahabharata*, *Purana* and also in the famous *Rajatarangini* of Kalhana. In course of time their dialect, known in Nepal as Khas Kura being a branch of Indo-Aryan language became popular and acceptable to all, even before the advent of the Gorkhas. After the conquest and unification of Nepal by the Gorkhas the Khas Kura that was spoken by majority of the people was widely accepted all-over the country and came to be known as the Gorkhali language. The Gorkha king, Prithvinarayan Shah gave this language the status of official language in the kingdom of Nepal. The present form of Nepali language has been called by Dr. Suniti Kumar Chatterjee and also by the eminent Nepali historians as *Khas Apabhramsha* because of its close affinity with Kumaoni, Garhwali and some other western hill dialects. The Khas people are found in Garhwal and Kumaon districts in India whose dialect is akin to Nepali language.

Nepali and Hindi are both Indo-Aryan languages and they are written in Devanagri script which is derived from the root Brahmi character. The word Brahmi, as the name suggests, implies to a popular belief that the word owed its origin to God Brahma who is often represented as holding a palm-leaf in his hand indicating his knowledge of writing. The art of writing in India goes back to the most ancient times. Old potteries discovered in India belonging to the Neolithic age are inscribed with Brahmi script. Many inscriptions found in Mahenjo-Daro have not so far been deciphered. The Ashokan inscriptions are found written in two scripts, Kharosthi and Brahmi. The term Kharosthi means "as lipped" or spoken and it is originated from the Aramaic script in the 5th century B.C. Kharosthi was introduced in India by the Persians who came to rule over north-western India under the leadership of Cyrus and Darius.

Like most of the languages of the northern India, Nepali has its origin in Sanskrit language. The word Sanskrit is derived from *sanskara* which means refined or perfected. Sanskrit is a rich, efflorescent and highly advanced language with rigid grammatical rules which Panini laid down more than 2700 years ago. It is a language of languages, or the mother language of almost all Indian languages. Dr. Prodosh Aich, an eminent historian remarked, "The Sanskrit language is of wonderful structure, more perfect than the Greek, more copious than the Latin and more exquisitely refined than either, yet bearing to both of them a strong affinity, both in the roots of verbs and in the forms of grammar, than could possibly have been produced by ancient; so strong indeed that no philologer could examine them all three without believing them to have sprung from common source".[1] This fact of Sanskrit having common origin with Gothic and Celtic group of languages was first discovered by William Jones, President of the Asiatic Society in 1786, who worked as British Judge in Calcutta High Court, and thereafter no one has ever questioned this discovery. R.L. Turner, Professor of Sanskrit of the University of London stated that Sanskrit is the root of Nepali language and about 5000 out of 26000 words that he collected are derived from Sanskrit language. Sanskrit is also the mother language of many other foreign languages such as the Poshto language of Afghanistan, Urdu of Pakistan, the Singhalese of Sri Lanka, Bengali language of Bangladesh. Sanskrit as a language of religion, occupied an important place in the history of Nepal.

The ancestry of Sanskrit goes back to the Indo-European language which was spoken by a group of people called Caucasoid that lived in the territory lying between present Turkey, Iran and Russia known as Central Asia. During second millennium B.C., a branch of these people came towards the east *via* Persia, Iran and

Afghanistan and entered into India who were known as Indo-Aryan and their language was Sanskrit. Another branch went towards the west and entered Europe and spoke Greek, Latin and Aramaic languages which, later on, broke-up into many languages like, Germany, French, Spanish, English, Italian etc. The Indo-Aryans wrote *Veda*, *Upanishad* and other scriptures in Sanskrit and spoke Prakrit, natural or simple form of Sanskrit. In course of time as they spread out to different regions and settled down for long time so that their original language Sanskrit was broken-up into many branches like Hindi, Panjabi, Gujarati, Marathi, Bengali, Nepali etc.

This being the origin of most of the present Indian and European languages it will be pertinent here to discuss, in brief, about the growth of Hindi and Nepali literatures. Tracing out the chronological development of Hindi literature the scholars have broadly divided the trajectory of Hindi literature into four periods—viz., *Adi Kala* (Early Period), *Bhakti Kala* (Devotional Period), *Riti Kala* (Scholastic Period) and *Adhunik Kala* (Modern Period).

The *Adi Kala* begins from tenth century A.D. and continues till about seventeenth century A.D. and represents the beginning of Hindi poems which highlighted on the religious ideologies and the heroic deeds of Rajput rulers and warriors in the form of narrative verses. Poets like Swayambhu, Somdutta Suri, Sharangadhara etc. figure prominently during this period who composed poems propagating moral tenets of Hindu religion.

Bhakti Kala starts from fourteenth century A.D. and represents the period of devotional movement in the country with composition of *Bhakti Kavya* or devotional poems. Religious missionaries like Guru Nanak, Kabir, Dharamdas, Sundardas etc. were the poets who inspired the spiritual feelings of the people in this period.

The *Riti Kala* represents the period of classical rhetoric tradition in Hindi literature with various styles, diction and rhetoric like *rasa, alankara, nayikabheda* etc. In respect of traditional styles two groups of poets prominently figured out, *viz.*, those who followed the *Ritibandhaka* (conservative) style and those who preferred *Ritimukta* (non-conservative) style in writing poems.

The *Adhunik Kala* is further divided into four phases—*Bharatendu Yuga* (1868-1893), *Dwivedi Yuga* (1893-1918), *Chhayavada Yuga* (1918-1937) and the *Vartaman Yuga* (1937 onward). Bharatendu Harishchandra (1868-1893) who brought in a modern outlook in Hindi literature is known as the "Father of modern Hindi literature". Mahavir Prasad Dwivedi (1893-1918) who is responsible for introducing refined style of writing Hindi prose is regarded as the architect of modern Hindi prose. Another poet Maithili Sharan Gupt revived the ancient epic tradition with long narrative poems like his *Panchavati*, *Jayadrathbadh* etc. Harivansh Rai Bachchan (b. 1907) enriched the world of Hindi poetry with his three monumental collections—*Madhushala*, *Madhubala* and *Madhukalas*.

In the similar way, Nepali literature has been divided into four different periods by Dilliram Timsina and Madhav Bhandari,[2] and other Nepali scholars. The periods are—*Prarambhika Kala* (Initial Period), *Utthana Kala* (Renaissance Period), *Vikasa Kala* (Development Period) and *Adhunika Kala* (Modern Period).

1. *Prarambhika Kala*—This period is taken from the year 1312 on the basis of evidence of the earliest Nepali written record that was found in the copper inscription of 1312. Before this period there were oral folk literature which were mostly anonymous and verbal. Nepali folk tales and songs like Jhyaure geet, Balon, Sangini, Deuda etc. came down the generations by mere words of mouth. Hence, the beginning of the written Nepali literature is taken from this period. This was a period of military prowess and victory of Gorkha king Prithvinarayan Shah who conquered small pieces of principalities scattered from east to west and unified them into a greater Nepal. It is said that this was a period when brave Gorkhas ran over from the river Tista in the east and to the Sutlej in the west to clean their blood stained *khukuris*. So far as literature is concerned, some scholars ascribe this period to be of *Beer Rasa* (chivalrous theme). Poets like Subananda Das and Saktiballav Arjyal wrote poems about the valour and victory of the brave Gorkha warriors. They were appointed panegyrists in the court of the King Prithvinarayan Shah and composed poems and songs in praise of the king. The other poets and prose writers of this period were Premnidhi Pant, Radhaballav Arjyal, Udayananda Arjyal etc. The

outstanding works among the prose literatures were Premnidhi Pant's translation *Prayaschitta* and Prithvinarayan Shah's *Divyopadesha*.

2. *Utthana Kala*—This was a period of great political intrigue and blood-shed in the history of Nepal. The political turmoil that was created by 'Kot massacre' in 1846 by Jang Bahadur Rana leading to the advent of Rana rule in Nepal, cast a pale of deep fear and insecurity in the minds of the intellectual section of the Nepalese society. The writers and poets naturally turned towards Gods providence which induced them to write devotional poems for moral and spiritual awakening of people. Poet Bhanubhakta Acharya (1814-1868) composed *Ramayana*, *Ramgeeta*, *Bhaktamala*, *Badhushiksha*, and *Prashnottari;* which exhorted the common men towards devotion to God. For this reason, scholars like to call the literature of this period as of *Bhakti Rasa* (devotional theme). Besides Bhanubhakta, other eminent poets of this period were Raghunath Pokhreal (1811-1861), Patanjali Gajuryal (1822-1887), Jadunath Pohkreal, Basanta Padhya (1803-1986) and Motiram Bhatt (1866-1896) etc.
3. *Vikash Kala*—This may be called the golden period of Nepali literature. For, during this period there was a great development and unfolding of Nepali literature into various forms like prose, poetry, novel, drama, short story, journals and news-papers etc. The first Nepali grammar was published from Darjeeling by Rev. A.Turnbull in 1887, which was followed by other grammar books by Jaiprithvi Bahadur Singh in 1911, by Viswamani Dixit in 1912 and by Hemraj Sharma in the same year. Journals and News-papers were published from various places of Nepal and India—*Gorkha Patra* in 1901 from Kathmandu, *Gorkha Khabar Kagat* from Darjeeling in 1901, *Sundari* and *Madhavi* from Benaras in 1906 and 1908 respectively. Trichanda College, the first college in Nepal was established in 1915 which brought western ideas into Nepal. In 1913, Gorkha Bhasha Prakashini Samiti was formed for publication of Nepali books. Many writers of Nepali literature were born of whom the prominent prose

writers were—Rajlochan Josi (1848-1929), Homenath Khatiwada (1854-1927), Lakshmi Datta Pant (1865-1905), Tirtha Pande (1879-1922), Gopinath Lohani (1873-1917), Krishna Prasad Regmi (1883-1928) etc. and among the poetry writers—Chiranjivi Sharma (1867-1940), Somenath Sikdel (1884-1969) etc. This period ends up with the eminent poet Lekhnath Paudyeal (1884-1965) who was awarded the title of '*Kavi-Siromani*' by the Government of Nepal in 1951 and also 'Tribhuvan Puraskar' posthumously in 1969.

4. *Adhunika Kala*—This period represents the rise of nationalism in Nepal and also allround growth and enrichment of Nepali literature in India and other places. Balkrishna Sam (1902-1981), the pioneer nationalist of Nepal, who was born in Rana family renounced his high ranking Rana title of 'Shamsher' and adopted only the short form'Sam' and suffered imprisonment for joining anti-Rana movement. He edited Nepali news-paper '*Gorkha Patra*' and wrote books, such as Ago ra Pani, *Chiso-Chulho* etc. Lakshmi Prasad Devkota (1909-1959) wrote *Muna-Madan*, *Kunjini*, *Sakuntala Bankusum* which are monumental work of literature. Among other prominent litterateurs of this period are Mahananda Sapkota (1899-1978), Rupnarayan Singh of Darjeeling (1904-1954), Sivkumar Rai of Darjeeling (1916), Madhav Prasad Ghimire (1919), Bhimnidhi Tiwari (1911-1973), Hari Prasad Gorkha Rai of Kohima (1910), Guru Prasad Mainali (1900-1971), Lainsingh Bangdel of Darjeeling (1933), Lil Bahadur Chetri of Assam and many others.

From the above periodical divisions of Hindi and Nepali literatures we can see that there is a close similarity between the growth and development of the two languages although the beginning of the written literature was preceded by Hindi literature by about three hundred years. If proper research in Nepali written literature is carried out, it may lead to discovery of still older records. According to one source, the earliest inscription in Nepali language written in *Devanagari* script was recorded by Lichchavi kings around 733 A.D. which, however, has not yet been accepted by Nepali scholars. Both the literatures begin with the preponderance of *Beer Rasa* (Chivalrous themes) that were found during the periods of Rajput kings in India and the Gorkha king in Nepal. The second period of both Hindi and Nepali literatures are again characterised by the same *Bhakti Rasa* (Devotional theme). The third period of Hindi literature represents growth in the style of writing poems, such as *alangkara*, *nayikabheda*, *riti-bandha* and *riti-mukta* etc. while the Nepali literature is characterised by the growth of various forms or branches of literature, such as prose, drama, novel, short story, journals etc. The fourth or the last periods of both Hindi and Nepali literatures are same as development and expansion of literatures. At this juncture, it must be mentioned that the development of Nepali literature was greatly restrained and stagnated by the Rana rulers who, for fear of anti-Rana campaign, literally gagged the press and the right to expression of the people.

Nepali language has a very close affinity with Kumaoni, Garhwali and some other western hill dialects of India bordering Nepal. This fact led Dr. Suniti Kumar Chatterjee and a number of eminent historians to believe that Nepali is derived from the Middle Indo-Aryan language known as *Khasa Apabhramsha*. The *Khasa Apabhramsha* has its link with Nepali language ever since the 12th century A.D when a hill tribe known as the *Khasa* migrated eastward along the Himalayas, entered south-west Tibet and north-west Nepal and established a kingdom there.[3] Sir G.A. Grierson, in his celebrated work, 'Linguistic Survey of India', held the similar view.[4] It may be mentioned that Nepali language is also known in Nepal as *Khas Kura* (i.e., speech of the Khas) and a great number of people living in Kumaon and Grahwal even today call themselves Khasas and speak a language akin to Nepali. The earliest known document in Nepali language is a royal deed of gift dated 1356 A.D. From the records available, it is believed that like many other Indo-Aryan languages including western Hindi dialects, Nepali took its definite shape by the 11th century A.D. and that by the time the Gorkha king Prithvinarayan Shah had brought political unification of greater Nepal, Nepali language had spread throughout the country of Nepal. Apart from Nepali, there are numerous other languages spoken in Nepal. Like in India, Nepalese population consists of multiple races and ethnic groups, each group speaking its own dialects. She has more or less sixty different ethnic groups with their distinct dialects. According to Nepal Census Report, 2001, there are ninety-two different dialects spoken in Nepal. The percentage of population on linguistic basis are : Nepali 49 per cent, Maithili 12 per cent, Tharu 6 per cent, Bhojpuri 8 per cent, Tamang 5 per cent, Newari 4 per cent, Magar 3 per cent, Awadhi 2 per cent, Bantawa 2 per cent, Limbu 1 per cent, and Bhajjika 1 per cent. Most of these dialects have no script of themselves and some of them have adopted Devnagari script.

Today, Nepali is one of the richest literary languages of not only Nepal, but also of India. After Nepali language has been recognized as one of the State Languages of India, the Indian Sahitya Academy is giving away Sahitya Academy award in Nepali literature every year. The similarity of Nepali language with Hindi is so much that Brian Hodgson, the British Resident at Kathmandu said—"The eight-tenths of its vocabularies are substantially Hindi". The Nepali language, by virtue of its close affinity with Hindi language and Devanagari being the script of both the languages, Hindi and Napali are read and understood in both India and Nepal. Hindi films are as popular in Nepal as in India. The Hindi Daily newspapers of India are widely read and well circulated all-over the towns and cities of Nepal. It is a tradition that whenever Indian political leaders visit Nepal they deliver speeches in Hindi and never in English, for example, Lal Bahadur Shastri in 1965. Shri Atal Bihari Bajpei, Former Prime Minister of India, once speaking before a delegation of the Assam Gorkha Sammelon, in New Delhi said—"Some days ago I visited Kathmandu, when I felt as if I were in my own country."[5] Indira Gandhi in 1966 visited Nepal and addressed public meetings in Hindi. In India itself, at least thirty per cent of its population do not understand Hindi which is its own National Language. Shri H.D. Deve Gowda, the Prime Minister of India himself does not know Hindi. He stood at the ramparts of New Delhi's Red Fort and read out his Independence Day address to the nation in Hindi of which he scarcely understood a word. The speech written for him in Hindi with his native Kannada script, was pronounced in such accents that it was understandable neither to the North nor to the South Indians. Such situations have been repeated by many other high dignitaries of India which is well nigh conceivable anywhere in the world.

In Nepal besides Hindi, three other Indian languages *viz.*, Bhojpuri and Maithili and Tharu are also spoken in the Terai areas. According to Nepalese census record there are thirty different languages spoken in Nepal of which 14 are Indo-Aryan, 14 Tibeto-Burman and one each of Munda and Dravidian origin. In terms of linguistic distribution of population, 80.30 per cent Nepalese speak Indo-Aryan language, 17 per cent speak Tibeto-Burman and a very negligible number of people speak Munda and Dravidian languages. (Harka Gurung,[6] "Nepali Nationalism: A matter of Consolidation, in Himal, March, 2001).

In respect of language both India and Nepal occupy unique positions—such as, it is only in Nepal that the Vice-President of the country took the Oath of Office and Secrecy in a language other than its national language. Shri Paramananda Jha, the first Vice-President of Nepal took oath of office in Hindi, in July, 2008. It is also only in India that the President of the country, the Head of the State, did not know the language of the State. Dr. A.P.J. Abdul Kalam, the Nuclear Scientist and President of India could not speak Hindi. The Constitution of India recognizes as many as twenty-three languages as Indian languages. India's currency notes bear eighteen languages in their own scripts to mark out its denomination. India with its vastness of size, extreme diversity of physical features, endless variety of races, and the great magnitude of its population with different languages and dialects, is a unique nation and a greatest democracy in the world.

Notes

1. Dr. Prodosh Aich, *That Language named Sanskrit in Aseemaa, Journal*, Vol. 6, p. 6.
2. Dilliram Timsina, and Madhav Bhandari, *Hamro Sahitya Ra Sahityakar.*
3. Dr. G. Tucci (1956), *Preliminary Report on Scientific Expedition to Nepal*, (Reprint), Rome.
4. G.A. Grierson (1916), *Linguistic Survey of India*, Vol. IX, Part IX.
5. Assam Gorkha Sammelon (1969-1981), *Bulletin*, p. 212.
6. Harka Gurung (2001), "Nepali Nationalism, A Matter of Consolidation", in Magazine, *Himal*, March.

7
Uniformity of Art and Architecture

The art and the religion always go hand in hand like the soul and the body. The Nepalese art, architecture and sculpture betray a deep influence of Indian art and architecture which are but the hand maids of religion. As Buddhism and Hinduism came to Nepal at different periods of time they also brought art and culture from India, the land of their origin. In addition to that, Nepal also had her own distinct form of architecture. In this chapter, an attempt has been made to portrait the rich heritage of India and Nepal and to analyse the history of development and assimilation of art and architecture of the two countries at different ages.

The history of Indian art and architecture goes back to the Indus Valley Civilization. Any history of Indian architecture must inevitably begin from the time when the earliest known wave of immigrants settled in modern Sind and Punjab.[1] About five thousand years ago an itinerant herd of people, probably a branch from Sumerian origin entered into India and settled down in the fertile valley of the river Sindhu. They planned and built cities which were historically famous and now known as Mahenjodaro and Harappa between 3000 and 2000 B.C. The discovery of the ruins of ancient city under the barren land in Sind, around Dorki and Larkana in 1923, unveiled the past record of the ebb and flow of Indian civilization. The momentous discovery of the ruins of potteries, seals, building bricks, decorative pieces etc. opened up the store-house of knowledge and stunned the historians with the fact that some 3000 years ago there was a civilization in India which was far more advanced and of higher standard of art and craftsmanship than the people of 1000 years later had known. They lived in planned and well-built cities and used advanced articles. Each of the two cities of Mahenjodaro and Harappa was nearly a square mile in size, set within crenellated defensive walls all around. The cities were divided into twelve blocks by 30 feet wide streets cutting criss-cross and running in the north-south and east-west directions. They had developed a system of pictographic writing and the script used by them consisted of about 270 symbols which remain undeciphered till today. The Indus valley people were also artistically advanced. They used beautifully painted potteries, jewelleries, necklaces, armlets, bangles, pendants made of gold, silver and jade. Large number of seals, amulets have also been discovered out of the ruins with beautiful designs depicted in them which give an idea of their high artistic inclination. The seals were used for security and for identification of ownership of property and they were cast in steatite. The cities they lived were fairly big in size and were well planned with buildings and garden lay outs, water tanks and footpaths. The city was served with extensive system of drainage; the bathrooms being connected to drains under the walkways and manholes being provided at places for cleaning of drains. The 'Great bath' was an imposing structure consisting of a large quadrangle in the centre with galleries and rooms on all sides. In the centre of the quadrangle was a large swimming pool, 11.7 meters long, 7 metres wide and about 2.4 metres deep. From this fact one can well understand the standard of architectural knowledge that the Indian people had some three millenniums before.

The next stage of Indian art and architecture can be traced in the Mauryan period of Indian history, particularly during the reign of Ashoka. It is, in fact, from the period of Ashoka that we can properly begin the history of Indian art, architecture and sculpture. Historian B.G. Gokhale, said—"The Maurya art burst, as it were, on the scene with a tremendous force shown through both its technique and material used".[2] Ashoka was a great builder and his monuments can be grouped under three heads, *viz*. (a) the *stupas* or domical mounds of masonry; (b) monolithic sandstone pillars; and (c) caves with highly polished walls cut out on hard rocks.[3] The Ashokan *stupas*, caves and pillars constructed by Ashoka at various places of India and Nepal which can be seen even today are the glaring examples of high engineering and artistic skill of those days. Ashoka erected four *stupas* in Patan and Lumbini, the birth place of Buddha which can be seen till today. The imposing stone pillar of Sarnath with majestic figures of lions, horses and deers and the wheel of *Dhammachakra* (adopted as the State Insignia by the Government of India) forcefully announce the grandeur and beauty of Mauryan art and sculpture. The capital of Ashokan pillar showing the figures of four lions standing back to back and the smaller figures of animals on the abacus represent a high class of Indian art. V.A. Smith praised the art in the following words—

> "It would be difficult to find in any country an example of ancient animal sculpture superior or even equal to this beautiful work of art which successfully combines realistic modelling with ideal dignity and is finished in every detail with perfect accuracy".[4]

The transportation and erection of a long and huge pillar are the proofs that the engineers and stone cutters of Ashokan age were not inferior in skill and resources to those of any country of that time. The caves of Barabar in Gaya district diligently cut into the monoliths of hard granite rocks, to the extent of 30 to 40 feet depth not only inspire awe and admiration of the visitors, but also represent the ancient cave-architecture of India. The *stupas* were constructed to commemorate the events of great religious significance or as memorial monuments enshrining the post-cremation relics of saints. Erecting of *stupas*, large or small, was a common practice during Ashokan time. There are great many numbers of *stupas* constructed by Ashoka in India, Nepal and Afghanaistan. The two famous *stupas* of Sanchi and Bharhut in Madhya Pradesh are consisted of two hemispherical domes of brick with a shaft and an umbrella each on the top. They are surrounded by railings running all around and opening into four gate-ways for the devotees to burn candles on holy occasions. Along the railings are displayed stately and graceful works of sculpture depicting scenes from the life of Buddha and important events of his life.

Thus, the Mauryan period can be rightly called a landmark in the history of ancient Indian architecture. It is from the period of

Ashoka that started the era of building monuments, palaces, *stupas* and pillars with the medium of stones and rocks. The pillars were cut out of huge sandstones dexterously chiselled and polished into elegant designs and erected at various places associated with Buddhism. The column of the pillars used to be not less than fifteen metres in length with a crown at the top artistically carved out depicting some animals like lion or elephant or a lotus as symbols of love and peace. As to the aesthetic quality of the Ashokan sculpture, V.A. Smith spontaneously uttered the following words of praise—"It would be difficult to find in any country an example of ancient sculpture better than or even equal to this beautiful work of art, which successfully combines realistic modelling with ideal dignity and is finished in every detail with perfect accuracy".[5] The palaces and buildings constructed by Ashoka in Pataliputra were exquisite samples of Mauryan architecture. Fa-Hien visited Ashoka's palace and was struck by the beauty and grandeur of the buildings.

The Mauryan period is also remarkable from the point of view of cave-architecture. Large caves were excavated from hard and refractory rocks for the purpose of cave temples, monasteries and dwellings for the Buddhist monks. Dwelling in the caves provided them with much needed seclusion from the bustling world and strengthened the sense of sacrifice and devotion to god. These man-made caves are not only the reminders of hard labour and toil, but also the living monuments of wonderful work of architecture. The remains of these ancient caves are still found in Nagarjuna Hills and Barabar Hills around Gaya. The Barabar caves are seven in number and are situated on the hills on the bank of river Phalgu.

The advent of Greeks into India heralded a new epoch in the sphere of Indian art and sculpture. The Greek form of art added a new depth and liveliness in the Buddhist sculpture and made a remarkable impact in the field of Indian art. The images of Buddha with prominent fold-lines on his draperies looked lively and real that resembled the images of Apollo, Jesus and Mary. In course of time, the use of Hellenistic form of art in India resulted in the establishment of a new school known as Gandharba school of art and sculpture which remained quite for some time in this country.

This Gandharva form of art, however, failed to receive wide acceptance in India and hence it did not influence Indian sculpture so much. Practically, it disappeared by 400 A.D.

During Gupta period a new and distinctive form of art came to be used in India. The Gupta age (320 to 550 A.D.) has been characterized as an age of renaissance of creative arts, painting, sculpture and architecture. A new form of art was developed which soon attained its maturity, balance and perfection of expression. This form of art is traditionally referred as the Gupta Art. It brought about a marked difference from the Gandharva style in the idol of Buddha with curly bunch of hair in sharp contrast to his earlier shaven head. This new form went a long way to add maturity, beauty and grace to Indian art. It also effected a change in the drapery of Buddha with transparent and plain stripes in place of Hellenic deep folds which gave a distinct and independent look to Buddha idol. The frescoes of Ajanta and Elora are some of the classic examples of the noble and cultural heritage of the Gupta age. The frescoes beautifully depict scenes from the life of Buddha which reveal the entire range of expression from exalted joy to profound sorrow. These eternal picture galleries represent, in the true sense of the term, beauty and elegance, simplicity of expression and keen aesthetic imaginations of the artists as the basic characteristic of the Gupta art.

The Mughal period occupies a special place in Indian history in the domain of art and architecture. It adds a new dimension to the Indian architecture and brings about a harmonious blending of the form and style of all structural works. The Islamic religion has had a deep bearing on the Mughal architecture of all times which is basically characterized by distinctive domes and minars on top of all religious buildings. Thus, we can see the tombs, mosques and mausoleum built by the Mughals bear impressive and beautiful domes and *minarats* on the top. On many occasions, the Muslim rulers converted Hindu temples into mosques by dismantling a part of the structure and adding-up some Islamic designs on them. Some times, the Hindu temples having splendid *Sikhar*, strident (*Trisul*), lotus or *Kalash* on the top were replaced by bulbous domes and *minarats*, and at others, dark, gloomy and cave-like Hindu temples were converted into wide, open and airy prayer halls with many doors and windows. This is how a new architectural form was born in India to be known as Indo-Islamic architecture. This was basically an architecture of aesthetic blending of two religious forms and motives into one. While it is not possible to say how much the new Indo-Islamic architecture owed to Hindu style and how much to Muslim style, but it is a fact that the Muslims had wonderful capacity to absorb Hindu art in their own, without which there would not have been a happy synthesis of the Mughal and Indian art. The Indo-Islamic architecture encompasses a wide range of styles from various backgrounds that helped shape the architecture of the Indian sub-continent. The Indo-Islamic style of construction has had a far reaching influence of the Indian architecture.

The advent of British rule in India ushered in yet another feature in the domain of Indian art and architecture. Under the patronage of the British rulers and the technical skill of European engineers who served under the Britishraj, the Indo-Islamic architecture took a new turn towards modernization. It heralded a renaissance in Indian architecture that aroused the national spirit to explore a new creative impulse of self-expression that would produce a magnificent work of engineering. In the beginning, the English, French and Portuguese constructed Churches, bungalows and official buildings in European architectural forms. High rise Gothic designed churches with many colored window panes and multi-storied Government buildings became a new attraction to Indian architects. Eminent British architects like Edwin Lutyens, Edward Baker and Charles Wyatt etc. who were equally inspired by the grandeur and elegance of Mughal architecture, wisely brought about a happy blending of Eastern and Western styles. This resulted in the adoption of new models of the British India architecture, the examples of which are found in the Victoria Memorial, Parliament House, Rashtrapati Bhawan and many other buildings in India.

The Nepalese art and architecture can be broadly classified into three structural designs—the *pagoda* design, the *stupa* design and the *shikhara* design. The *pagoda* style consists in multi-roofed structure with wide eaves supported by carved wooden struts. The number of roofs can go up to five and they are pyramidal in shape while the windows are either latticed or grilled. The classic specimen of this design can be seen in the 'Kasthamandapa', a house of wood in pagoda style built by Malla king. The city of Kathmandu, the present capital of Nepal was named after Kasthamandapa. Another specimen of *pagoda* style is the nine-storey Basantapur palace built by Prithvinarayan Shah. It is believed that the architect who originally designed the *pagoda* style was one Balbahu. The *pagoda* design is indigenous to Nepal which was adopted by China and some other Asian countries later on. According to historical records, a team of Nepalese architects led by Arnico (*Balbahu*) went to China on the invitation of Chinese Government in 1271-1368 for construction of *pagoda* designed buildings. To commemorate this, the Chinese Government unveiled a statue of Arnico at Baita (White Tower) temple in Beijing on 17th May, 2005.

The *stupa* design consists of hemispherical mound of brick with a shaft and umbrella on the top. It has a round passage with railings running allround and opening into gateways at places. The Swayambhu and Bodhnath Shrines of Nepal are the fine examples of *stupa* style. We have already seen that the art and architecture go hand in hand with the religion of the country. The *stupas* that are found in Nepal are identical in their design with those of India as they are basically of Buddhist concept. The Sanchi *stupa* of India and the Bodhnath *stupa* of Nepal are similar in their fundamental shapes and designs as both of them are Buddhist shrines. This is how the culture and religion of India have impacted upon the art and architecture of Nepal throughout the ages.

The *shikhara* design of temples show a marked influence of Hindu architecture from India with lotus, *kolas* or *trisuls* on the top of the domes. This kind of temples are found everywhere in India and Nepal. The Krishna temple of Patan constructed by Malla king is a typical example of this design.

The history of Nepalese art and architecture begins as early as the period of Mauryan empire. The existence of pillars and *stupas* constructed by the Mauryan emperor, Ashoka at various places in Nepal are the historical evidences of Indian architecture in Nepal. Ashoka visited Lumbini, the birthplace of Lord Buddha and constructed a *stupa* there. His daughter Charumati stayed in Nepal for propagation of Buddhism and established many *stupas* and *Viharas* around the city of Lalitpura. On the outskirt of Kathmandu there is a place called '*Charuhil*' which is named after Charumati who used to stay there. She has constructed a *stupa* made of stone in the traditional shape of Ashokan *stupas*, (in the shape of an inverted bowl), which is one of the oldest *stupas* of Nepal. Many of these *stupas* and pillars are still in existence, which speak themselves of the travel of Indian art and architecture into Nepal in early third century B.C. These monumental works of Ashoka that are extant today in Nepal bear a close resemblance to those of Indian pillars of Sarnath, Gaya and other places in India. They are most remarkable for their skilful stone works and artistic excellence and show overwhelming influence of Indian art. Sir John Marshall said—

> "To know Indian art in India alone, is to know but half of its story. To apprehend it to the full we must go back to the period of Buddhism that flourished in other countries like Nepal, China, Japan, Kambodia, Java etc".[6]

The Bodhnath *stupa* of Nepal is one of the oldest and biggest *stupas* which is believed to have been built during Mauryan period. It is not known as to how many ancient *stupas* like this might have been ruined and disappeared in India during the foreign yoke for want of proper care and neglect, but the contemporary *stupas* of Nepal like the Bodhnath *stupa*, still remain in tact. The Bodhnath *stupa* is traditionally looked after and maintained by the Tibetan authority. It is constructed in the same shape and design with the Sanchi *stupa* of India which represent Buddhist architecture, but it is much wider in dimension and stature than the Sanchi *stupa*. Unlike the Sanchi *stupa* it has a staircase that leads to the top of the dome where a circular platform with a circular canopy stands wherefrom one can take a panoramic view of the city of Kathmandu. At the base a ten feet wide raised verandah runs around the *stupa* facilitating the devotees to walk and around.

The three ancient cities of Nepal *viz.*, Bhaktapur, Lalitpur and Kathmandu are the veritable galleries of ancient art and architecture in their own rights. The old architecturally designed buildings, the tall and dark edifices and the stone paved footpaths running in between the buildings give an impression of some medieval cities, if not ancient ones. The rows of *pagoda* styled temples standing along the street in Lalitpatan exude an atmosphere of distinctiveness reminiscent of some Japanese city. The city of Bhaktapur is especially important for its temples and display of unique art in wood carving which catches the eyes of every visitor. The huge gate-way with a pair of lions skillfully cut out of stone at the entrance of Bhaktapur greets the visitors to fore-tell of the treasure trove of art and sculpture that is in store for them inside the city. The city of Bhaktapur abounds in elaborate and intricate works of brass and wood carving all over the doors, windows and door-seal and window-seals which have no parallel anywhere. The designs are distinctive and typical to Nepal being the products of local Newari artisans. It is however a matter of concern that these heritage works of art of Nepal are undergoing disrepair and decay. It is heartening to note that the *Durbar* squares of Kathmandu, Patan and Bhaktapur, the three hubs of Nepalese ancient art and architecture have been declared as the World Heritage Sites by UNESCO and will be preserved, protected and maintained by the same.

The tradition of painting frescoes is another area of art in Nepal which has come down since ancient times. This work is carried out by the Buddhist monks with professional skill and expertise and has a close similarity with the works of Ajanta and Ellora caves painted during the Gupta rule between 4th and 6th century A.D. It is most probable that present work of Buddhist style of painting in Nepal has its root in the ancient fresco painting of Gupta rule. This tradition of Buddhist art and painting has been kept alive in present days by Buddhist Lamas who are imparted training in this art in the monasteries. These Lamas are awarded the title of 'Khaiba Lama' after the successful completion of training. Their function is to paint frescoes, thankas, prayer flags etc. and to install and decorate Buddhist altars for performance of special rituals. *Thangka* painting is an unique art exclusively painted by the Buddhist painters of Nepal that reflects Buddhist theology, culture and belief. There are varieties of *Thangka* painted with bright colours mixed with gold, silver and various hues displayed in shops in Kathmandu, Pokhara and other business centres for sale. The Newar artists paint exquisite *thangkas* and put on sale in Kathmandu and Pokhara markets.

Wood carving is another exquisite art of Nepal. The perfection of this art reached its nadir during the late Malla dynasty. Intricately carved doors and windows of temples, palaces and private houses can still be seen in Kathmandu which represent the high standard of wood craft that Nepal had achieved. Examples of excellent wood workmanship are also preserved in the museums of Kathmandu, Patan and Bhaktapur.

Notes

1. Satish Grover (1980), *Buddhist and Hindu Architecture of India*, New Delhi, p. XI.
2. B.G. Gokhale (1952), *Ancient India,* Calcutta: Asia Publishing House.
3. K.L. Mukherjee, *History of India*, Calcutta, p. 110.
4. B.N. Luniya (1998), *Evolution of Indian Culture*, Agra: Lakshminarayan Agarwal.
5. B.G. Gokhale, *op. cit.*
6. Jawaharlal Nehru (1946), *Discovery of India*, Calcutta: Nehru Memorial Fund.

8
Political Relations

The political relations between India and Nepal dates back to the pre-historic times. Mention of military alliance between the two countries can be found in the epic of *Mahabharata* where Bhagadatta, king of Kamrupa and an ally of Kauravas, is said to have participated in the battle of Kurukshetra with one *Akshauhini* of soldiers consisting of the Kiratas and Cinas from Nepal. The *Mudrarakshasa*, another ancient Sanskrit literature recounts that during the reign of Chandragupta Maurya (322-298 B.C.), a brigade of Kirata army was raised from Nepal through the diplomacy of Chanakya which helped Chandragupta to capture Pataliputra and to establish Mauryan empire.[1] In the Indian history we have evidences of the diplomatic ties with India as far back as 7th century A.D. According to Chinese tradition, the king Harshavardhana of India died in 647 A.D. without an heir. Arunashva, one of his Ministers usurped his throne and also robbed a Chinese Mission led by one Wang Hieun-tse who came to India shortly after Harsha's death. In order to take revenge of this ill treatment meted out to him, the Chinese Ambassador rushed to Nepal, raised a strong force of seven hundred Nepalese soldiers (Kiratas) and one thousand Tibetan soldiers and marched to Magadha against Arunashva. In the battle they defeated Arunashva and took him prisoner to China.[2] During Gupta, period, Nepal was a vassal country to the Indian emperor Samudragupta who was said to have exercised his sway over Nepal. It is said that Nepal, as a vassal to Gupta emperor, used to pay regular tributes to Samudragupta. According to K.P. Jaiswal, about 200 A.D. Nepal was annexed to Vaishali (part of present Bihar in India) a kingdom of Lichchhavi and it remained within India for seven generations until Vaishali was amalgamated with Gupta empire and Jayadeva, the Lichchavi king shifted to Nepal. The political relations between India and Nepal became increasingly closer and wider as different royal dynasties from India began to come to Nepal and establish their kingdoms in Nepal. After the Lichchavis ruled over Nepal for about three hundred years, the Thakuri dynasty came to Nepal in 634 A.D. and since that time the politico-social scenario of Nepal witnessed a gradual change leading to closer social contact and influence of Brahminical system which continued more vigorously ever since the advent of the Shah dynasty in 17th century A.D.

The Indo-Nepal war, 1814-16 brought Nepal to direct confrontation with the East India Company which culminated into a close military relationship with India. The treaty of Sigauli dated 2nd December, 1815 as ratified by the king of Nepal on the 4th March, 1816 which stated—"There shall be perpetual peace and friendship between the Honorable East India Company and the Raja of Nepal"[3] marked the beginning of Indo-Nepal relationship that was to endure for nearly two centuries to come. Article 8 of the Treaty mentioned, "In order to secure and improve the relations of amity and peace hereby established between the two States, it is agreed that accredited Ministers from each shall reside at the court of the other". Thus, for the first time the door to the Himalayan kingdom which was hitherto closed to an European, was opened. The Nepalese believed that "the Europeans often come with bayonet in one hand and a Bible in another, both are to be distanced from". The *Durbar* of Nepal also allowed Gorkha young men to be recruited in the Indian Army after the conclusion of the treaty of Mutual Concession, 1884. According to this treaty, the East India company agreed to supply arms and ammunitions to Nepal in exchange of the Gorkha recruits.The East India Company was so impressed by the fighting skill and bravery of Gorkhas that it went headlong with the work of recruiting them even before the conclusion of war. They raised the first Gorkha Battalion in 1815 which was named Nasiri Battalion and this was quickly followed by two other battalions called Malaun and Kumoun battalions. Out of this nucleus Gorkha battalions, the British gradually built up a super-power Gorkha Brigade comprising as many as ten

Gorkha Regiments which served the British well throughout their rule in India and built-up a reputation of high tradition of gallantry, loyalty and fidelity. During the First World War they left their dead in France, Gallipoli, the Suez and Mesopotamia, and in the Second World War, they distinguished themselves in Burma, Kohima, Italy and North Africa for their legendary bravery, tenacity and elan. After India's Independence, the Gorkha Brigade was broken-up into two halves, one half consisting of four Regiments were taken by the British and the other half comprising six Regiments continued to serve with India as an integral part of Indian Army.[4] They figured conspicuously during Pakistani invasion of Kashmir in 1948, Chinese aggression in 1962, Indo-Pak War in 1965, in the Bangldesh War, 1971 and in Kargil War of 1999. They made supreme sacrifices with their lives and blood and earned awards and medals by their extreme valour, fighting skill and dedication. Today the Gorkhas are indefatigably guarding the borders of India in the glaciers of Siachen, in the borders of Kashmir, and along the McMahon line in Arunachal Pradesh. Indian borders are safe in the hands of the redoubtable Gorkhas. This is one of the classic examples of Indo-Nepal co-operation that had begun centuries ago and sustains till today. We shall deal with this topic in more details in the following chapters.

Politically, both India and Nepal suffered prolonged subjugation under foreign and autocratic rulers. India came under British rule since 1857 while Nepal was ruled by the Rana family under the titular king of Shah dynasty both being of Indian origin. India and Nepal both had to struggle hard for their political emancipation and make supreme sacrifices of life and property for over a century. India became Independent in 1947 and this was closely followed by an overthrow of the autocratic Rana rule by the civic revolt in Nepal in 1950. India played a significant role in the struggle of the Nepalese insurgents in bringing down the 104 years old Rana rule. The history of freedom struggle of India and Nepal is essentially a story of long and sustained goodwill and co-operation between the peoples of both the countries.

It was the Indian political leaders who first ignited the fire of nationalism in the hearts of Nepalese young men who came in close contact with them in early 20th century. Ever since the close of the nineteenth century some educated and politically conscious Nepalese young men were attracted by the ideals of Arya Samaj movement in India, under the leadership of Swami Dayananda Saraswati. One Madan Singh Gorkha was the first young man to spearhead the cause of Arya Samaj movement whose doctrine was *Swaraja, Swabhasa* and *Swadharma*. This doctrine of trinity instilled a strong national feeling among the youths from Nepal who came under the personal influence of Indian national leaders like Lala Lajpat Rai, Bal Gangadhar Tilak, Jawaharlal Nehru etc. The elite section of Nepalese people were averse to the Rana autocratic rule and desperately wanted to launch similar kind of political movement in Nepal in order to overthrow the Rana rulers. They wanted to rouse political consciousness among the people of Nepal and launch freedom movement like that in India. But they could not do this because the Rana rulers were ruthless in suppressing all kinds of political movements. They never allow any activity that might lead to the growth of nationalistic ideas among the people. In order to check the infiltration of democracy and progressive ideas into Nepal from outside, the Ranas kept the country strictly isolated from outside contacts. So initially, the political activists had to base their political platforms in Indian cities like Benaras, Dehradun, Calcutta and Darjeeling from where they could infiltrate national consciousness into Nepal. They, in collaboration with the Indian Nepalese of these places, formed political and cultural organizations and through these platforms they carried out their political activities. The pioneer organizations were—the Hillmen Association of Darjeeling, formed in 1921, the Gorkha Association of Calcutta formed in 1926 and the All India Gorkha League started in 1921 at Dehradun. These Associations were shown as having social and literary objectives and were joined by both Indian Gorkhas and the Nepalese youths who came to India for study. Through these organizations the Nepalese youths and Indian Gorkhas joined their hands in the mission of arousing national and political awareness among the people of Nepal as well as the Indian Nepalese. Side by side with these organizations, the press played a significant role by publishing news-magazines and periodicals in Nepali language. The pioneers among them were the Gorkha Saathi from Calcutta, 1911, the

Gorkhali and the *Janmabhumi* from Benaras, 1914 and 1921, the *Tarun Gorkha* from Dehradun, 1927. These periodicals, besides other topics, published articles on Mahatma Gandhi's doctrine of non-violence and non-co-operation, *swadeshi* movement and through them instilled national feelings among the Gorkhas. These magazines and pamphlets were clandestinely sneaked into Nepal which helped in the preparation of groundwork for the future anti-Rana movement in Nepal.

As early as 1920s when Mahatma Gandhi launched the Civil Disobedience Movement in India, a group of Nepalese young men including B.P. Koirala, Matrika Prasad Koirala, D.R. Regmi, S.P. Upadhyay and Krishna Prasad Bhatarai joined the movement from their base at Patna. Another enlightened Nepali gentleman, Tulsi Mehr, being greatly inspired by Mahatma Gandhi's philosophy of life started Khadi and Village industry movement in Nepal. He established "*Charkha-Guthi*", an institution for imparting training to the womenfolk of Nepal in spinning and weaving khadi clothes. This was viewed by the Rana rulers as an attempt in spreading *swadeshi* movement in Nepal. It was considered as a serious offence in Nepal for which Tulshi Mehr, a staunch follower of Mahatma Gandhi in Nepal, was awarded life imprisonment. Inspired by Mahatma Gandhi's 'use *swadeshi* garment' movement Tulshi Mehr founded Charakha Guthi, an institution for the propagation of *khadi* and village industries in Nepal.[5]

In those days-Matrika Prasad Koirala was an active member of the Indian National Congress and occupied an important place in the Bihar Congress Party. He participated in the general conference of the Indian National Congress held at Pandu, Assam in 1926. He was actively involved in the freedom struggle of India and suffered imprisonment in Patna jail. Krishna Prasad Bhatarai, who later on became the Prime Minister of Nepal, also suffered imprisonment for his involvement in freedom struggle of India. His brother Biseswar Prasad Koirala was an active member of the Indian National Congress and suffered imprisonment for four years at different places of India. In 1930, the British came to know of his involvement in Indian politics and arrested and jailed him at Bankipore jail where he spent with Dr. Rajendra Prasad. Afterwards, he was shifted to Hazaribag jail where he met Jagjivan

Ram who later became Defence Minister and Deputy Prime Minister of India. During his stay in Hazaribag jail he received the sad news of his father's (Krishna Prasad Koirala's) death but he was not allowed to visit his home. The political leaders from Nepal established a very intimate relationship with the top socialist leaders of India, like Jaiprakash Narayan, Dr. Ram Manohar Lohia, Acharya Kripalani, Achyut Patvardhan, Ashoke Mehta, Principal Hem Baruah, Dr. Hareswar Goswami and Bipinpal Das of Assam.[6]

In the wake of Gandhiji's campaign for breaking the salt law in 1930, Khadag Bahadur Bist, a Nepali firebrand leader, was arrested in May, for attempting to loot the Government salt depot at Dharsana,150 miles from Bombay and was imprisoned at Sabarmati jail together with his thirteen Gorkha associates. After his release from jail, he was again found involved in some insurgency activities for which police rounded him up and recovered from his possession many secret documents. Khadag Bahadur Bist was a close associate of revolutionary leader Sachindra Sanyal of Calcutta. Another group of young Nepalese from Benaras including Manmohan Adhikari, Puspalal Shrestha etc. actively participated in freedom movement of India from Benaras platform and suffered imprisonment. It must be considered as a rare event in the history of political movement when the citizens of one country get involved in the political movement of another country and suffered imprisonment.

Similarly, we have instances galore of political leaders of India supporting the cause of Nepal's political emancipation from the tyrannical rule of the Ranas of Nepal. The Indian freedom movement in which the Nepalese young leaders actively participated, proved to be an opportunity for them to learn how to launch similar movements against the autocratic rule in Nepal. They not only learnt the art of political movement from the veteran leaders of India like Mahatma Gandhi, Govind Vallabh Pant, Sardar Vallabhbhai Patel, Jaiprakash Narayan, Dr. Ram Manohar Lohia etc., but also continued to receive constant inspirations and valuable guidance from them during the civil movement in Nepal. To cite an instance, some Nepalese young men under the leadership of Pandit Sukraraj Shastri formed an association named Nepali Praja Parishad in 1935. A delegation of this organization consisting of

Sukraraj Shastri, Gangalal and Dharma Bhakta met Mahatma Gandhi and Dr. Ram Manohar Lohia in India and after receiving necessary guidance and blessings from Mahatma Gandhi they returned back to Nepal. But no sooner had they set their feet on the soil of Nepal than they were arrested and put in jail by the Nepalese Government. The intelligence network of the Nepalese Government was in close link with that of the Government of British India from where the Police collected information regarding the whereabouts of these Nepalese leaders. By the 1st October, 1940, Narashamsher Rana, the Director General of Police arrested nearly 500 Nepalese insurgents under the charges of conspiracy for waging war against the Rana Government and put them into the prison cell. After a brief trial Yudh Shamsher Rana, the Prime Minister of Nepal pronounced the final judgement of the case in the *Singha Darbar* before a jam-packed audience which included top Civil and Military officials. According to the judgement order: Sukraraj Shastri, Dasarath Chand, Dharma Bhakta, Gangalal and Subba Puran Chandra were found guilty of treason and conspiracy against the Government and awarded death sentences with appropriation of their properties; Tek Prasad Upadhyaya, Ram Hari and Sankar Prasad Sarma were awarded life imprisonment, appropriation of properties and ex-communication. The other twenty-six accused persons were awarded imprisonment of various lengths and severities while the rest of the arrested persons were acquitted. The historic judgement sent out a message of shock and terror down the hills and valleys of Nepal. After a period of two months, the fateful day came on the 30th January, 1941—early in the morning, the above named five gallant patriots of Nepal were executed in public view and with this ended the anti-Rana movement of Nepal not to resurrect again in the soil of the Himalayan kingdom for a considerable time. This day of 30th January, 1941 will remain forever as a *Black Day* in the history of democratic movement in Nepal.

The seed of nationalism that was sown by the Indian leaders, however, did not remain dormant for long in the politically fertile soil of Nepal. The advent of Quit India Movement of 1942 in India provided a new impetus to the Nepalese leaders who had by that time acquired sufficient knowledge and experience about organizing and launching political movements. The Nepali leaders did not lose time and opportunity. A fresh wave of political movement swept across the important towns of Nepal in 1942. In the wake of internment, by the Nepalese Government, of the Indian political leaders like Jaiprakash Narayan, Dr. Ram Manohar Lohia and their companions who had fled into Nepal during Quit India Movement, the Nepalese openly took to the streets in support of the Indian leaders. The people of Saptari, the Head-quarters of Eastern Tarai, demonstrated in front of Hanuman Nagar jail demanding immediate release of the Indian leaders who were interned by the Government of Nepal. Soon, in the month of January, 1947 a political organization by the name of Nepali Rashtriya Congress came to be formed at Calcutta which launched Civil Disobedience movement in Nepal starting first from Viratnagar, the bordering district of Nepal and then gradually spreading into other districts. Sensing that the mighty British Raj is pulling out its legs from India, the Ranas soon realised their shaky position *vis-à-vis* the people's solidarity against the Rana rule in Nepal. As a sequel to this, in May, 1947, the Prime Minister of Nepal, Padma Shamsher announced the formation of a Political Reforms Committee with a view to framing a new Constitution for Nepal on the basis of elected Panchayats. A panel of Indian legal experts including Sri Prakash and Dr. Ram Ugraha Singh was invited to Nepal to assist the Reforms Committee.[7] On the 26th January, 1948, the Prime Minister of Nepal, Padma Shamsher Rana, for the first time in Nepal's history, promulgated a written Constitution for Nepal. According to this constitution there would be established a Council of Ministers, a Bicameral Legislature and a High Court in Nepal. The constitution also envisaged the establishment of a comprehensive Legislative Structure beginning from the Gram Panchayat as the lowest unit of Central Legislature consisting of two Houses. This must be called a big step forward for paving the way for a democratic Government in Nepal which provided a positive booster to the political workers who contributed to it. The promulgation of the Constitution, however, was not without strong opposition from a section of the Rana rulers due to which Padma Shamsher had to quit from the Government by handing over charges of Prime Ministership to Mohan Shamsher, the leader of the opposition group. Immediately on assumption of the office the Prime Minister, Mohan Shamsher announced the banning of the Nepali Rashtriya Congress, withdrawal of the autonomy given to the Kathmandu Municipality by Padma Shamsher and the arrest of all the prominent leaders of the Nepali Rashtriya Congress including B.P. Koirala.

Thereafter, in April 1950, a new political Party, "Nepali Congress" was formed out of the erstwhile Nepali Rashtriya Congress and the Nepal Prajatantrika Congress and thus a new combined force stoodup again much to the consternation of the Rana Government. The anti-Rana movement in Nepal got a new momentum for a final thrust that came in 1950 when the Nepali Congress launched an open liberation movement with the secret connivance of the King Tribhuvan Vir Vikram Shah. On 6th November, 1950, the king exiled himself with his family members and took refuge in the Indian Embassy at Kathmandu who were later on brought to Delhi by special plane. This followed an armed confrontation between the Rana Government and the insurgents of the liberation force called "Mukti Sena" which captured the Governor and other officials of Birganj. They also seized the Nepal Radio Station and announced the establishment of a parallel Government. The people's war ultimately culminated into an agreement with Rana rulers according to which the Government of Nepal agreed to recognize King Tribhuvana as the king of Nepal and to form an interim Cabinet, half of whom would be the popular representatives, and to hold election to the Constituent Assembly by 1952.

The King Tribhuvan was welcomed back to Kathmandu on the 18th February, 1951 with great pomp and jubilation for the peoples' victory which marked the end of Rana rule in Nepal and heralded a new era of Monarchical Democracy in Nepal. Once again India played a sterling role in the task of pulling down the impregnable edifice of the one-family Rana regime and the establishment of a popular democratic Government in Nepal. On the other hand, the contributions made by the Nepalese leaders in India's struggle for freedom from the colonial rule cannot be underestimated. This fact will go down in the history of India and

Nepal as an example of unique partnership, goodwill and sacrifice between the peoples of the two countries.

Following the end of the Rana regime, Nepal embarked on the highway of popular democratic system of Government. The king promulgated a new constitution of Nepal according to which the first democratic election to Nepalese National Assembly was held in early 1959. In the election, the Nepali Congress emerged as the biggest party which received people's mandate to form the Government. Accordingly, Biseswar Prasad Koirala, its President, took over as the first Prime Minister of democratic Nepal. But Nepalese Government was destined to suffer yet another jolt of political hiccups. In the wake of the departure of Rana rule from Nepal, the king found himself as, "the monarch of all I survey", and a selfish desire for an absolute monarchy sprouted up in his heart. Hardly a couple of years had passed when King Mahendra Vir Vikram Shah promulgated, in December, 1960, a new constitution that envisaged a party-less Panchayati system of Government. This system gave absolute power to the king as the Head of the State with sole authority over all Government institutions including the Cabinet (Council of Ministers) and the Parliament. The system of Governance went against all norms and principles of democracy which the people could hardly accommodate.

Wranglings for Democracy

The party-less Panchayati system of Government as promulgated by the King became a singular bone of contention among the people of Nepal. The system of Government empowering the Monarch with absolute authority over the democratically elected Parliament was not acceptable to the people at large as it ran counter to all principles of democracy. For this reason, there was large-scale protests and anti-monarchical demonstrations launched by different political parties demanding multi-party system of democracy. The political forces which gave rise to the demand for multi-party democracy in Nepal were generated partly from within the political parties of Nepal and partly were indirectly inspired by India as she wanted that Nepal should be a full-fledged democratic country under the monarch. The constitution for Panchayati system promulgated by the King envisaged a non-party government which explicitly implied a blanket ban on all political parties. Therefore, the people's movement was mainly directed towards the lifting the ban on parties and not against the King. The movement for democracy picked-up its momentum in 1979 with wider support from the students community, the elite and the middle class people. Taking out procession, students strike and demonstrations became a daily feature which exude an atmosphere of political unrest and breach of public tranquility. Under this situation in May, 1979, the King announced the decision of holding referendum to choose between party-less Panchayati system and the multi-party government. Accordingly, the referendum was held in May, 1980 in which over 67 per cent voters participated and the result was in favour of retention of the existing system of Party-less Panchayati system of Government. This was sharply reacted by all the political parties led by Nepali Congress Party which launched Civil Disobedience Campaign in May, 1985. There was large scale arrest of political leaders which led to calling off of the campaign. In June 1985 the agitation picked-up once again in a virulent form with explosion of bombs and killing of people in front of the palace by Janavadi Morcha, a political party of Nepali progressive leaders based in India. The election held by the Government to elect members of the Panchayat in 1986 was boycotted by the Nepali Congress and the Marxist-Leninist Party. On 6th April 1990, a massive demonstration launched by students and political parties in Kathmandu clashed with security forces which killed as many as fifty persons.

Eventually, the king was forced to accept multi-party system of Government in 1991 and Nepal went for another general election in which the Nepali Congress Party emerged once again victorious with 110 out of 205 seats in the House. During all these years of political imbroglios, the Government of India worked for a political consensus in Nepal and stood behind the people of Nepal in their effort to establish a stable democratic government.

The Civil War

In 1996, Nepal's political movement assumed a new dimension with the launching of insurgency activities by an extremist group called the Maoist. This was an armed rebellion with an objective to abolish the monarchy and replace the existing Parliamentary Monarchy with a new Democratic Republican Government through mass revolution called 'People's War'. This led to a major Civil War in Nepal under the leadership of Baburam Bhatarai and Puspa Kamal Dahal (Prachanda) causing a state of complete anarchy and chaos in the administration. The Maoist succeeded in bringing under control as many as five districts in the Western Nepal and established a Provisional Government there. In August 2004, the insurgents laid seize on Kathmandu and almost paralysed the Government administration. The Government of Girija Prasad Koirala failed to contain the onslaught and the very foundation of monarchy became shaky. As an extreme measure to protect the monarchy and re-establish himself to power, the King Gyanendra declared a State of National emergency and dismissed the Government by assuming to himself the executive powers of the Government on 2nd January, 2005. Ministers and all politicians were either arrested or put under house arrest, telecommunications were cut-off and the freedom of Press were severely curtailed. King Gyanendra ordered the army to crack down on the Maoist guerillas. The rebels intensified its campaign and the army responded with vigorous action killing hundreds of Maoists, the largest toll ever since insurgency began in 1996. According to an estimate 13,000 people were killed during the Maoist insurgency. The king's anti-insurgency and dictatorial policy measures could not, however, suppress the rebellion, rather it whipped up anti-monarchy sentiment among those who believed in the democratic process of Government. People's uprising, strikes and demonstrations increased all the more and it became difficult for the King to run the affairs of the Government smoothly. India helped Nepal with arms supply during Maoist insurgency but after King Gyanendra dismissed the democratically elected Government and took to himself the executive powers of the parliament, India stopped arms supply in February, 2005 in order to put pressure on the King to restore democracy. Eventually, the king was compelled to withdraw state of emergency and re-instate the Parliament in April 2006 which installed a Seven-Party Coalition Government with Girija Prasad Koirala as the Prime Minister. The Maoist rebels declared unilateral cease-fire and agreed to hold talks with the Government. Immediately thereafter, "peace process to end the decade long standing insurgency of the Maoist were accelerated by holding talks between the Government and the Maoist leaders who were rigid in their stance to abolish monarchy." The Indian Prime Minister's envoy Shri Shyam Saran who visited Nepal on 12th October, 2007 said, "India is committed to help Nepal in her peace process in every possible way and to achieve the goal for a stable, democratic and prosperous Nepal".

After prolonged parleys and political bargaining, on 24th December, 2007, the Seven-Party Alliance Government and the rebel leaders signed a 23 point Agreement and agreed to co-operate in the peace process towards the establishment of a Democratic Republican Government in Nepal. According to the agreement both sides agreed to abolish the institution of Kingship in Nepal and to hold election to form a new Federal Democratic Republic. The Maoists who were running a parallel Government and working from underground also agreed to surrender their arms under the supervision of the United Nations and to take part in the election to form a Constituent Assembly for drafting a new Constitution of Nepal. New Delhi welcomed the peace accord and looked forward for renewed and closer friendship with Nepal. The people of Nepal, for the first time in history, exercised their fundamental right on April 10, 2008 in electing a 601 member Constituent Assembly mandated to write a new Constitution for the country. The voters turned out to cast their franchise in a very large number and the election demonstrated to the rest of the world that an armed conflict can successfully be converted into a peace process with the conscious efforts and determination of political leaders and the whole-hearted support of the people. In the election the Maoist Party came out victorious with simple majority capturing 229 Assembly seats. Table 8.1 shows the number of seats in the Constituent Assembly won by some of the major political parties of Nepal.

On August 15, 2008, the Constituent Assembly elected Maoist Supremo Mr. Puspa Kamal Dahal (Prachanda), as the first Prime Minister of the Republic of Nepal. He was sworn-in on 18th August, 2008 as the Head of the Coalition Government consisted of six

Table 8.1 : Number of Seats Won by Parties

Political Parties	*No. of Seats*	*Percentage*
1. Communist Party (Maoist)	229	38.1
2. Nepali Congress	115	19.1
3. Communist Party (UML)	108	18.1
4. Madhesi People's Rights Forum	54	9.0
5. Tarai Madhes Loktantrik Party	21	3.5
6. Sadbhavana Party (Mahato)	9	1.5
7. Communist Party (ML)	9	1.5
8. Jana Morcha, Nepal	8	1.3
9. Rashtriya Prajatantra Party	8	1.3
10. Communist Party (United)	5	0.8
11. Others	35	8.3
Total	**601**	**100%**

Source : Nepal Election Commission.

political parties, *viz.* CPN (Maoist), CPN (UML), Madhesi People' Rights Forum, National Sadbhavana Party, CPN (United) and Peoples' Front Nepal. On the same day, Shri Manmohan Singh, the Prime Minister of India congratulated Mr. Puspa Kamal Dahal (Prachanda) and expressed his hope for a fruitful and continued relationship with India.

The Maoist Supremo, Prachanda, during his visit to India in April, 2008, gave assurance that he will maintain equal distance from the two giant neighbours India and China. He said, "Nepal has a historical relationship with India and shares open borders. It is very important to have good relations with India". India looked forward for a good relationship.

The first Assembly of the Nepalese Parliament that was held on 28 May, 2008 passed an historic resolution to put an end to the centuries old monarchy and to constitute Nepal into a Federal Democratic Republic. It also decided to convert the Royal Palace of Narayanhiti Darbar into a National Museum. Accordingly on the 11th June, 2008, the deposed king Gyanendra of Nepal handed over the Royal Crown to the Government and vacated the Narayanhiti Darbar to make room for the proposed National Museum. Thus His Majesty, Gyanendra Vir Vikram Shah Dev, the last King of the kingdom of Nepal unceremoniously moved out of his royal palace Narayanhiti Darbar in a black Limousine and made a hurried dash to his private residence in Kathmandu. No farewell given to him, no gun salute boomed for him, nor was there a ceremonial send off. Gyanendra made his exit from Government as a common citizen of Nepal and with this ended the 240 years long, only Hindu kingdom of the world as Nepal became a State.

Democratic process towards the formation of the Republican Government proceeded further with the election of the first President and the first Vice-President of the country. On the 21st July, 2008, the Assembly elected Dr. Ram Baran Yadav, a sixty year old veteran member of the Nepali Congress as the first President of Nepal. Shri Paramananda Jha was also elected on the same day as the first Vice-President of Nepal. Interestingly, the above two leaders who were elected to the highest offices of Nepal came from a community not belonging to Nepalese origin. Both are Madhesis of Indian origin and belong to an ethnic group of India whose population in Nepal constitute hardly 18 per cent of her total population. This must be termed as an epoch making event in the history of Nepal which could not happen even in India, a country accredited as the largest democracy in the world with the high secular and socialistic ideals. Our memory is still fresh when a section of the top leaders of India vehemently opposed Sonia Gandhi, the President of the Indian National Congress from being elected to the post of the Prime Minister of India on the ground of her not being of Indian origin. This issue gripped the sentiment of Indian political leaders so strong that the Bharatiya Janata Party even could not conceive the idea of occupying so high a post of Prime Minister of India by a person of Italian origin. Within the Indian National Congress Party itself emerged a rift leading to vertical split in the party and emerging out a new party called Nationalist Congress Party led by Sarad Pawar. This generous act of Nepalese legislators in electing two leaders of Indian origin to the highest offices of their country, not only shows the magnanimity of heart but also a feeling of trust and close relationship with India. It must, therefore be stated with an amount of certainty that in so far as India is concerned this has added a new dimension to the age old relationship between India and Nepal. We can hope that the bond of friendship and goodwill between the two countries will further be strengthened through the good offices of the President and the Vice-President of Nepal.

The political history of Nepal, however took a 'U' turn as the coalition Government led by Maoist leader Shri Puspa Kamal Dahal did not continue for long. The Government of Nepal came to a dramatic end in May 2009, with the sudden resignation by the Maoist Prime Minister, Puspa Kamal Dahal, pushing Nepal once again into a state of political chaos and uncertainty. The reason for taking this extreme step by Shri Puspa Kamal Dahal may be ascribed due to a hitch between him and the President of Nepal on an issue arising out of the proposal for integration of Maoist rebels (PLA) into Nepal army. The Prime Minister of Nepal, as the executive head of the country, had passed an order sacking Shri Rukmangud Katawal, the Chief of the Army Staff of Nepal from his service on the charge of defying his order to recruit the Maoist rebels in the vacancies of Nepal army while Dr. Ram Baran Yadav, the President of Nepal, as the Supreme Commander of the Nepal Army, abrogated the discharge order of the Prime Minister and re-instated Rukmangud Katawal in his service. The country was aghast at the ding dong battle that took place between the two highest offices wielding their respective powers which no one could say who was right in the absence of the country's constitution that was yet to be written. Nepal plunged into a state of constitutional crisis.

Puspa Kamal Dahal's dramatic resignation from the post of Prime Minister pushed Nepal into another spell of uncertainty and political dead-lock. It also left unresolved one of the important task of constitution making. The differences among various political parties, absence of mutual trust and lack of flexibility of their stances led to the failure of the Constituent Assembly to write the constitution. This resulted in the dissolution of the Constituent Assembly on the ground of expiry of the extended time frame on 27 May, 2012. At this juncture, there remained no other option before the leaders of political parties of Nepal except to go back to the people again to elect a new Constituent Assembly for the completion of drafting the constitution. To this end, the major political parties of Nepal once again engaged in a concerted dialogue to come to a consensus that the only way to end the existing political stalemate was to hold re-election for another Constituent Assembly. Moving towards this direction, the parties agreed to amend the Interim Constitution and to form a non-political Government under the leadership of the Chief Justice of Supreme Court, Shri Khil Nath Regmi. The political parties also reached a consensus that the election would be held on 19 November, 2013 and accordingly the Government appointed Shri Nila Kanta Upreti as the Chief Election Commissioner for smooth conduct of the election.

As per decision taken the election was held on November 19, 2013 to elect the second Constituent Assembly. The election ended successfully with good out-turn of voters. The nationwide average rate of voting was found to be 87.34 per cent which broke the previous record of 68.15 per cent in 1991. The Chief Election Commissioner, Nila Kanta Upreti ascribed the high percentage of turn out of voters to two reasons—one, reform measures in election procedures and better awareness of people created by the election machineries; two, greater urge of the people to form a stable government under the prevailing situation of political uncertainty. The election was conducted, by and large, in a free and peaceful manner except a few minor incidents. Nepali Congress, the oldest party of Nepal, secured the highest number of seats with 105 out of 240 directly elected seats while the Communist Party of Nepal (UML) bagged 91 seats and the United Communist Party of Nepal (Maoist) got only 26 seats. The remaining 18 seats were won by smaller parties and independent candidates. Table 8.2 gives the detailed result of the election.

The United Communist Party of Nepal (Maoist) leader Puspa Kamal Dahal objected against the conduct of election alleging fraud and unfair means and threatened to withdraw from the Constituent Assembly. But the International Observers found the election to be proper and fair. It hailed the election as a "milestone not just for Nepal but for the people around the world". The former President of USA, Jimmy Carter who personally visited the election operation commented as "well conducted election" and congratulated Nepal.

After a few days of political bargaining, the Nepali Congress which had secured simple majority seats in the Assembly elected

Table 8.2: Results of the Constituent Assembly Election held on 19-11-2013

Political Parties		*Number of Seats Won*	*Percentage*
Nepali Congress	—	105	29.30
CPN (UML)	—	91	27.55
UCPN (Maoist)	—	26	17.79
Madhesi Jana Adhikar Forum (Loktantrik)	—	4	3.13
Rashtriya Prajatantrik Party	—	3	2.63
Tarai-Madhesi Loktantrik Party	—	4	2.90
Madhesi Janadhikar Forum (Nepal)	—	2	2.28
Sadbhavana Party	—	1	1.56
Nepal Workers Peasant Party	—	1	1.56
Tarai Madhesi Sadbhavana	—	1	1.56
Independents	—	2	1.19
Total		**240**	

Source : Election Commission of Nepal.

Sushil Koirala as the Prime Minister of Nepal with the support of the CPN (UML). He took over charge on 12 February, 2014 as the fourth member of the Koirala family to become the Prime Minister of Nepal. This reminds us about the great sacrifice and contribution of Koirala family to Nepal. Therefore, it has generated high hope and expectation among the public who have had a dismal experience at the abortive attempts of the last Constituent Assembly.

Undoubtedly, Mr. Koirala, Prime Minister had, before him, a daunting task of giving Nepal a stable government as well as fulfilling the long awaited aspiration of the people of Nepal by promulgating a well-rounded constitution accepted by all. To accomplish this job he had to bring the UCPN (Maoist) and the political parties of hills Janajatis as well as Madhesis into the fold of shared consensus on the contentious issues that would come-up for discussion in the Constituent Assembly. In this connection, Mr. Sushil Koirala together with his ally CPN (UML) promised that the drafting of the constitution would be completed within one year period. Mr. Koirala has another challenging job waiting for him to do. He has to amicably resolve with the leaders of the UCPN (Maoist) the most contentious issue of integrating the Maoist combatant force into national security force which is hanging fire since more than five years. Ever since the civil war ended in 2007 Nepal has witnessed a political whirlpool of frequently toppling of governments involving as many as six Prime Ministers within a period of five years. This time around the present government and the political parties of Nepal have a tremendous responsibility to create conducive atmosphere and strong determination to pull Nepal out of existing political quagmire and resolve all outstanding issues for a durable peace and prosperity in the country. This can, however, be achieved only if the leaders of the UCPN (Maoist) and Madhesi parties, the third front, would show a greater degree of flexibility with a spirit of compromise and sacrifice for national interest. Earlier on 26 July, 2013, as the former Prime Minister of Nepal, Madhav Kumar Nepal, in his address at Indian Council of World Affairs at New Delhi, said—"Therefore, broader understanding on national, political and developmental issues and mutual trust and confidence among the parties and leaders, particularly among the major parties in the country, are the need of the hour. Only through this we can resolve some of the most delicate and contentious issues".

The second Constituent Assembly took charge in November, 2013 under the Chairmanship of Subhas Nembang to complete the half-done constitution. The time-line set for completion of the constitution for the second Constituent Assembly was 22nd January, 2015. The principle of the constitution making procedure as agreed upon by the political leaders was that all decisions should be taken by general consensus among the parties or by vote with the former to take priority over the latter.

Restructuring of State

The most contentious issue in the process of constitution making was regarding the state restructuring, i.e. on the issue of determining as to how many provinces should be there in federal Nepal; how the boundaries of these provinces should be delineated and how they should be named. The Committee on Restructuring of the state proposed for fourteen provinces and twenty-two autonomous regions on which a considerable disagreement cropped-up in the Constituent Assembly. To solve this problem, a High Powered state

Restructuring Commission was formed for reviewing the whole issue and to resubmit a viable proposal. The Commission, however, divided itself into two groups and submitted two different proposals—one group proposed for a 10+1 model, i.e., 10 territorial provinces and one non-territorial province for *Dalit* community. The other group of the Commission proposed for six province model. The UCPN (M) and Madhesi parties supported the former proposal while the Nepali Congress and CPN (UML) stood for the latter. The issue was highly politicized among different political parties which projected various proposals to suit their own interest making it extremely difficult to forge a consensus. The UCPN (M) made an alliance with the small parties of Madhesis and Janajatis in order to strengthen its bargaining power in pushing forward its identity based federalism. Puspa Kamal Dahal (Prachanda) and Baburam Bhattarai played the card of identity for Janajati and Madhesis and pleaded for the eleven province model. Sushil Koirala, Prime Minister and Nepali Congress Party members firmly supported the six province model. Both sides remained rigid on their stances not yielding to other's proposal, at any cost. In between, many small groups and parties belonging to various communities like the *Dalits*, Madhesis, Janajatis, Muslims and the people of backward regions have been fighting for identity, equality and social justice. They made alliance with either of the two groups. One of the political parties named RPP (Nepal) (Rashtriya Prajatantrika Party) is a diehard monarchist advocating restoration monarchy in Nepal and also re-establishment of Hindu state as well as creation of Unitary form of government in Nepal. The Constituent Assembly had to be disolved on several occasions without being able to forge a consensus on the issue of federalism. The proceedings of the Constituent Assembly virtually came to a halt to the utter discomfiture of the Chairman, Mr. Subhas Nembang who tried his best to bring the two groups into a mutual consensus. Puspa Kamal Dahal (Prachanda), leader of the UCPN (M) even threatened to boycott any negotiation that fall short of his demand. There being a complete deadlock of Assembly proceeding Mr. Subhas Nembang found no other way than to take recourse to the second option of deciding the issue by vote. However, Mr. Nembang gave ten days time to Puspa Kamal Dahal

(Prachanda) to come to negotiating table failing which the pending contentious issues would be decided by the process of voting. "It is not the best way out, but I am ready to face any consequence"—said Nembang. After the deadline expired with neither side moving forward for dialogue Nembang took the bold step by tabling the Proposal Draft Committee (PDC). The PDC which will draft a questionnaire on the disputed issue and submit the same to the Constituent Assembly was the first step towards passing the new constitution through vote. While the Nepali Congress and the CPN (UML) with the help of Subhas Nembang were busy in preparing draft questionnaire, the UCPN (Maoist) and the Terai organization, in a joint meeting decided that the two parties will intensify their agitation protesting against the act of adopting the constitution by voting system.

On 30 January, 2015, Ram Baran Yadav, President of Nepal, called upon the conflicting political parties to frame the constitution through consensus and not to recourse to voting procedure. The President stepped-up his role as an intermediary to bring the ruling and the opposition parties together to end the political impasse through dialogue and consensus. The President held talks with UCPN (Maoist) Chairman, Puspa Kamal Dahal and tried to dissuade the opposition leaders from taking any rash step that could derail the constitution drafting process. He reminded Puspa Kamal Dahal that as a signature to the 12 point agreement and comprehensive Peace Accord his party should play a constructive role in the constitution writing process. He said—"The country could plunge into another conflict if either of the parties did not take any step to improve the strained relations". Surya Bahadur Thapa, former Prime Minister of Nepal also called upon the Nepalese Government to settle-up the dispute through mutual discussion which only will bring a durable government. This was a special message to Subhas Nembang, the Chairman of the Constituent Assembly who had decided to proceed according to voting process and formed a Proposal Drafting Committee despite strong protest from the UCPN (Maoist) party.

Prime Minister, Sushil Koirala said that his party is ready to adopt "maximum flexibility" in talks with opposition leaders in order to bring the constitution drafting process into track. He said—

"The biggest challenge of the management of Maoist arms and army has been overcome. So, why are we fighting when we have got to institutionalize democracy and peace in Nepal". In the backdrop of sharp political polarization following the failure to meet the January 22 constitution promulgation deadline, the Prime Minister had been reaching out to the Maoist, Madhesis and the Janajati parties to resume stalled talks. According to Vijai Kumar Gachchedar, Chairman of the Janadhikar Forum, the Prime Minister's 'Flexibility' is not enough, he has to be positive in his approach for dialogue. He said that Prime Minister should commit to move ahead as per the spirit of the 12 point agreement of peace and accord.

The agenda of the Constituent Assembly remained suspended for an indefinite period of time due to the devastating earthquake of 15th April, 2015. On 18th August, 2015, the Constitution Drafting Committee submitted its report to the Chairman of the Constituent Assembly. After threadbare discussion on the report three major political parties of Nepal, *viz.*, Nepali Congress, UCPN (Maoist) and the CPN (UML) came to the agreement that there should be seven provinces in Nepal. This decision was, however, vehemently opposed by the parties of Madhesi, Tharu and Janajati people who decided to go for '*Aam Hartal*' to register their protest. They objected the decision of the Constituent Assembly to create seven federal provinces and demanded that the Terai region should be separated from the hill provinces and be allotted for them two separate provinces; one extending from Jhapa to Parasa to be called Mithila state and the other from Chitawan to Kanchanpur to be called Buddha State. There should be a provision for 83 parliamentary seats for Terai in the new constitution. They were wary that they would be marginalized if clubbed together with hill areas. The Prime Minister, Sushil Koirala, said that this issue could be threshed out later by the Federal Commission proposed in the draft constitution, therefore, it should not hold back the promulgation of constitution since all other issues had been addressed by consensus. The Madhesis and the Tharus showed no sign of compromise and they declared Tarai Bandh, and started demonstrations. They demanded, an immediate halt to the on going constitution drafting process and a commitment from the three major parties to implement the past pacts. The Prime Minister, Sushil Koirala sent formal letters to the disgruntled Madhesi-Tharu parties to come for a formal talk within three days beginning from 27th August, 2015 which was flatly refused by the parties. In reply to this, the Chairman of the Sanghiya Samajavadi Forum, Shri Upendra Yadav said on 30-8-15 that the ongoing Tarai agitation will continue until the rights of the Madhesi, Tharu, *Dalits* and ethnic people are guaranteed. The agitation spread like *wildfire* in the whole Terai areas and demonstrations were held at places like Kailali, Rautahat, Tikapur, Birganj etc. The protesters attacked one Police station with petrol bomb and in retaliation the police opened fire killing one person who was later on identified to be an Indian citizen. This fact gave rise to the suspicion of the involvement of Indians in Madhesi agitation. Curfews were promulgated in many places affecting the normal life of the people. The situation was further confounded by the demonstrations held by the Rashtriya Praja Parishad Party demanding Nepal to be a Hindu state. In the eastern Nepal, again, the Limbus and Rais demanded a separate province of Limbuwan. On 24-8-15 at Tikapur Kailali agitators became violent and clashed with police in which four police personnel were killed including an Assistant Superintendent of Police and several others were injured. The Government called in the Nepal army to quell the agitation. At Parsha large number of protestors shouting slogan and carrying flags and sticks in hand staged demonstration. On 1-9-15, an unruly agitators vandalized Police station, burnt down Government buildings and vehicles at Birganj for which police opened fire killing four persons. The district administration imposed curfew for indefinite period of time. In the agitation at least 40 persons were killed. Shri Tirtha Nath, spokes person of the UCPN (Maoist) criticized the Government action for trying to suppress public opinion with the help of army. Sher Bahadur Deuba, former Prime Minister of Nepal supported the demand of the Tharu community. The former Maoist Prime Minister of Nepal, Baburam Battarai resigned from the UCPN (Maoist) party saying that injustice had been done to the Madhesis by not redressing their legitimate demand.

Thus, in the midst of political wranglings, the Constituent Assembly of Nepal finally adopted the constitution and formally promulgated on the 20th September, 2015 by putting the signature and seal of the President. The people of Nepal, by and large, welcomed the new constitution which they got after a long waiting of seven years. They celebrated the day with bursting fire crackers and illuminating of Government buildings and private houses. USA, China and many other countries congratulated Nepal and expressed their happiness at the adoption of a new constitution. While on the other hand, more than one-third of the citizens of Nepal living in Terai felt disappointed and disgruntled. The Madhesis and Tharus boycotted the day and exhibited their anguish by organizing demonstrations and showing of black flags. At Birganj they clashed with police in which one person was killed.

Undeclared Indian Blockade

The Government of Nepal accused India of imposing an undeclared blockade of essential commodities from entering into Nepal. The daily arrival of at least 300 trucks carrying petroleum products, medicines and food stuff and other essential goods from India to Nepal suddenly stopped. India denied the allegation stating that the trucks were being stopped by the Madhesi agitators from entering Nepal and India has no hand in it. But despite Indian denials, trucks were not entering even from the border entry points where there was no agitation. The Indian Press Media, the *Indian Express* reported that India had demanded specific changes to the Nepalese constitution. In another report, The *Economic Times*, a personnel from Sashastra Sewa Bal (SSB) "confirmed that at least till the third week of September they had orders from above to intercept fuel shipment to Nepal". The blockade severely affected Nepalese daily life for want of petrol, diesel, cooking gas (LPG) kerosene and even food stuff and medicine. In order to meet the situation, the Government of Nepal stopped providing fuel to private automobiles including public transport and taxis for a few days at the beginning so as to distribute fuel to government and prioritized sector. The transport system of Nepal came to halt. Some 2000 factories were shut down for want of fuel. The Nepal

Government accused India of trying to coerce Nepal into accepting unfair demands of the Medhasis and thus, interfering with the internal affairs of Nepal. On 11 November, 2015, UN Secretary General, Ban Ki-moon reiterated his concern over the obstruction of essential supplies on the Nepal-India border. He underlined Nepal's right to free transit, as a land-locked country and for humanitarian reasons. The Government of India denied imposing a blockade stating that the truck drivers coming from India were not entering Nepal for fear of attack and damage of cargo by the protestors from Nepal side. Whatever might be the case—the blockade had a far reaching effect on the daily life of the Nepalese belonging to every walks of life and deeply hurt their sentiment. The Government of Nepal made an arrangement with China for importing petroleum products as an alternative and temporary source which, if actually carried out, would have certainly cast an adverse affect upon the good relationship between India and Nepal.

It is understandable from the above discussion that the political scenario of Nepal is drifting towards a direction not very healthy to the Indo-Nepal relation. The Nepali Congress Party and other democratic parties of Nepal which were hitherto closely allied to India, are now gradually losing their grounds to Communist and leftist parties which have a natural bend towards China, by virtue of common party ideology. The NCP (Marxist) Maoist which had been fighting a civil war in Nepal since 1996 under the leadership of Baburam Bhattarai and Puspa Kamal Dahal (Prachanda) succeeded in capturing the highest number of seats in the Nepalese Constituent Assembly in the general election held on 10th April, 2008. After that, two consecutive Governments were formed both by the Communist parties, once by Shri Puspa Kamal Dahal Maoist supreme on 15th August, 2008 and thereafter by Shri Jhala Nath Khanal CPM (UML) with active support of the Maoist Party on the 6th February, 2011. The Nepali Congress was the only party in the opposition bench of the Nepalese Constituent Assembly together with other minor parties whose political stance, however, fluctuates according to their convenience.

Taking advantage of this political situation, China is increasing her involvement into the affairs of Nepalese Government by extending various grants and soft loans for economic development of Nepal. An agreement has recently been signed between Beijing and Kathmandu according to which China will advance a concessionary loan of 200 million US Dollar to Nepal for construction of Upper Trisuli Hydro-power Project. China has also agreed to extend a grant of Rs. (N) 428 million for implementation of mutually agreed development projects.

In such situation Government of India needs to gear-up its activities to renew the old ties with Nepal by improving economic, political and cultural relations. Nepal has definitely closer and deeper bond with India since time immemorial than she has with China. India's cultural relationship with Nepal is unique which are unparallel and non-existent between any other two countries of the world. The relationship based on solid foundation of historical, cultural and social parameters which the two countries have been sharing with each other. It must, therefore, be noted that our relationship must be based on positive, constructive and people to people basis, and certainly not on an open animosity towards China. Unlike China, Nepal and India have come a long way bypassing many political vicissitudes and fighting for each other's political freedom. History bears witness to the fact that without India's help Nepal alone could not have succeeded in overthrowing the mighty Rana Government so easily. During 1950s, the Government of India played a sterling role in the process of pulling down the impregnable edifice of the Rana rule and thereby, establishing a popular democratic Government in Nepal. Similarly, the Nepalese young leaders made a great sacrifice in the Quit India movement actively participating and courting imprisonment to free India from the colonial yoke. These facts, stand out in glaring letters in the history of India and Nepal which the two countries should never forget.

Criminal cross-border activities is another area that calls for a fresh look from both sides and find a suitable solution to the problem. Because of the existing open border policy between India and Nepal it has become easy for the criminals and smugglers to sneak into the other side to evade arrest or legal action. The existing agreement of extradition was signed during Rana Prime Minister, way back in 1855 in which the offences were ranging from theft and murder to desertion from the Armed forces and accepting bribes by public servants. In October, 1953, the then Indian Ambassador to Nepal, B.K. Gokhale and former Nepalese Prime Minister, Matrika Prasad Koirala had redefined the offences for which the offenders could be extradited from India and *vice versa*. With the changes of time and ramification of the nature of offences that include political offences, economic offences, insurgency, militancy and cyber frauds etc., it was felt by both the countries that there is a need to remodel the whole treaty of extradition. It has assumed greater importance, therefore, that the two Governments sit together and try to iron out the loose ends to put an end to this menace once for all.

Notes

1. P.C. Roy, *Mahabharata,* Translation, Vol. II, Part I, Sec. IV, p. 7.
2. Romila Thapar (1966), *A History of India*, Vol. I, p. 144 .
3. K.K. Muktan (2002), *The Legendary Gorkhas*, p. 1.
4. Out of the ten numbers of Gorha Rifles, the 1st, 3rd, 4th, 5th, 8th and the 9th G.R. were retained in India and the rest 2nd, 6th, 7th and 10th G.R. were taken by Great Britain.
5. Shriman Narayan (1971), *India and Nepal*, Orient Paperbacks, p. 29.
6. B.L. Upadhyaya (2004), *Khanmihali* (Assamese).
7. Shriman Narayan (1971), *India and Nepal,* Orient Paperbacks.

9
Economic Co-Operation

Nepal is an economically backward country. It ranks the 17th poorest country in south-east Asia. Approximately 25 per cent of its population live below poverty line. Its geography, hilly terrain, and extreme cold climate have adversely affected the life and livelihood of its people. Politically, Nepal's economy was severely stagnated for more than a couple of centuries under the autocratic rule of the Shah and Rana dynasties. Dr. Ram Sharan Mahat rightly summarized the whole system of Rana rule in the following words—"The Rana political system was undisguised military despotism within absolute total control over all aspects of public life".[1] In 1950 when the last of the Rana ruler was vanquished from Nepal, the country was bereft of roads and communication, schools and hospitals, infrastructural development, job opportunities and even from the basic amenities of life. More than a half of the population were denied of drinking water facilities, health care facilities, education for children and even not enough food for at least 30 per cent of population. Nepal's economy was at complete disarray with her GDP at the lowest and her people in the medieval backwardness with only two per cent literacy rate. Eighty-five per cent of her population was engaged in agriculture with primitive method of cultivation and less than one per cent was engaged in small industrial occupation.[2] The arable lands were concentrated in the hands of a few nobilities who never cultivated by themselves and rented out to the landless peasants at exorbitant rent. The population consisted of two classes of people—the richest and the poorest and the economy was overridden by feudalism. The country needed socio-economic reforms such as demolition of feudal institutions, land reforms, administrative reforms, mass mobilization and human resource development that were the pressing problems and called for immediate address as basic pre-conditions towards a sustainable economic development. In order to fulfil these urgent needs, the newly set-up Government took up First Five Year Plans since 1956-60, the implementation of which depended largely on the foreign aids which accounted for more than half of the development budget. In 2002, Nepal completed its Ninth Five Year Plan and made a steady progress towards sustainable economic growth. The priorities for development have been given to agriculture, transport and communication, tourism and industries. Agriculture remains Nepal's principal economic activity which employs 70 per cent of population and provides 37 per cent of GDP to the country. The tourism industry is expanding rapidly since 1950. Nepal's natural beauty, rich cultural heritage, diversity of sight-seeing spots and adventure opportunities have attracted large number of tourists from allover the world. In 1998 total 4,63,684 number of tourists visited Nepal. The fiscal year 1993-94 turned out to be a dream year for the economy registering a 7.9 per cent increase in GDP. The agriculture sector alone recorded an unprecedented 7.6 per cent growth rate and tourism had forged ahead to contribute 4 per cent of the GDP".[3]

The First Five Year Plan though could not achieve its goal fully, it did succeed in creating much needed public consciousness in favour of economic planning. The Second Plan of Nepal was of only three years duration with an outlay of Rs. sixty crore. The high priorities of this plan were agricultural reforms, completion of ongoing projects, transport and communication and overall improvement of administration and co-ordination among various development departments. The third Plan was for five years duration (1965-1970) with an outlay of rupees two hundred and fifty crore. The high priorities were accorded to transport and communication, power, agriculture, irrigation and development of small industries. All these development programmes involved huge amount of money which Nepal herself could ill afford to invest without foreign aids. In this context, India contributed significantly to Nepal's successful implementation of infrastructural development programmes like the construction of Tribhuvan Air

Port at Kathmandu and the Tribhuvan Rajpath connecting Kathmandu and Birganj bordering Raxaul in India which connects the two countries. The construction of major irrigation projects such as Kosi and Gandak barrages, construction of Hydro-electric projects etc. are other important development schemes by India. The longest National Highway of Nepal connecting the East to the West Nepal which was named as Mahendra Rajmarg (1024 km) was also constructed by India. This road also includes 22 numbers of bridges and innumerable culverts with its long span. The roads and communication and the power play very important role in the development of industries of a country. Nepal is endowed with the biggest water resources which has the potential to generate 83,000 MW of electricity, but it has remained untapped due to resource constraints. There is ample scope for augmenting hydro-electric energy through mutual co-operation between India and Nepal for the common benefit of both the countries.

Besides India's partnership in Nepal's economic development foreign aids came from many other countries of the world for financing Nepal's Five Year Plans, but despite all these foreign help Nepal could not progress smoothly due to political instability, frequent changes of Governments and people's movement for democracy which greatly hampered the smooth implementation of plans for economic development. Nepal suffered a great setback during the ten year long Maoist insurgency that started from 1996 to 2006 which caused death and destruction of men and materials and virtually shattered the economy of the country. It is estimated that during the period of ten years of Maoist insurgency as many as 13,000 people lost their lives. Although this period was followed by a bilateral agreement for peace with Maoist and the establishment of a coalition Government led by Shri Puspa Kamal Dahal (Prachanda) Maoist Chief through general election held in 2008 that did not last long. The new Government met with a dramatic end due to sudden resignation submitted by Sri Pushpa Kamal Dahal, (Prachanda), the Maoist Prime Minister. That pushed Nepal once again into a state of political chaos and uncertainty. The Nepalese Parliament, in an effort to form a new Government, held elections as many as sixteen times to elect a new Prime Minister, but could not succeed due to failure to obtain the required number of votes by any of the contestants. It was only on the 4th February, 2011 that Shri Jhala Nath Khanal, CPM (UML) could succeed in getting stipulated votes to be elected to the post of the Prime Minister with the support of Maoist party. Accordingly Shri Jhala Nath Khanal took the oath of office and secrecy on the 6th February, 2011 administered by Shri Ram Baran Yadav, President of Nepal.

Nepal's economy is predominantly agricultural which involves seventy per cent of manpower and accounts for forty per cent of her G.N.P. However, due to geographical conditions characterized by hilly terrains and extremely cold climatic condition, the agricultural operation is confined to comparatively small areas comprising valleys and narrow strips of gentle slopes. Unscientific and primitive method of cultivation practiced by the farmers resulted in low yield of crops. Mal distribution of land due to faulty land tenure system prevalent in Nepal ever since Prithvinarayan Shah's regime like *Birta, Jagir, Guthi, Rakam* etc. contributed to the emergence of aristocracy and feudal landlordism in the upper strata, of the society and in the lower strata the poor landless cultivators and daily wage earners. The higher class of dignified people believe that working in the field was meant for the lower caste only, and their job was only to collect rent from the tenant farmers. This attitude of the landowners of Nepal was the prime cause of deprivation, poverty and indebtedness of poor farmers and also the greatest drawback to Nepal's agrarian economy. Simultaneously, it also largely contributed to the exodus of Nepali farmers from Nepal seeking greener pastures in India and elsewhere.

In recent years tourism has become a promising industry in Nepal with the potentiality of providing large scale employment to her people. It has also become a great source of income to the state. The potential of tourism in Nepal was first realized by Government, long back in the middle of twentieth century when Sir Edmund Hillary and Tenzing Norgay climbed the Mount Everest in 1953. This great event of the century diverted the attention of the world towards the feasibility of mankind reaching the summit of the world's highest mountain peak and created a fascination in men for scaling mountain peaks. Mountaineering and trekking became the objects of passionate adventure and favourite sports, and Nepal turned to be the destination of all tourists. Some far-sighted entrepreneurs like Prabhakar Rana started the first hotel in Kathmandu named Soalti; Boris Lassanevite started Royal hotel and the hotel industry went on flourishing. The Government of Nepal established the Department of Tourism in 1957 in order to develop tourist spots in various places of Nepal to attract more tourists. The Royal Nepal Air Lines started operation since 1966 which afforded transport facility to hitherto ill-communicated sub-Himalayan country of Nepal. The Government revenue went up swiftly and by the end of 1990 Nepal received about three lakh tourists per year which pushed up the annual GDP of Nepal to four per cent. There is a bright prospect for further development of tourism in Nepal with opening-up of more tourist spots and providing better facilities to visitors.

Utilization of Nepal's mineral resources is, so far very meager and has remained unexplored and untapped. There is need for geological survey for mineral exploration with the scientific and technological co-operation from India. Nepal's enormous hydrographic potential can be tapped with the help of Indian technology for the benefit of both India and Nepal. In respect of building dams to generate power in Nepal there was a bilateral talk between the two countries during the visit of Shri Puspa Kamal Dahal, the Prime Minister of Nepal to India in September, 2008. for a mega project of 10,000 MW capacity. The issue of flood control measures on Kosi river also figured prominently in the discussion and it was decided to constitute a joint River Committee at the ministerial level to go into the basic problem involving bilateral actions and to take appropriate measures to prevent recurrence of flood in both countries.

During the three day visit of Shri S.M. Krishna, Foreign Affairs Minister of India, to Nepal on 16th January, 2010, a major agreement was reached between him and Shrimati Sujata Koirala, the Nepalese Deputy Prime Minister and Foreign Minister, giving a boost to the Indo-Nepal bilateral ties. India agreed to undertake developmental activities worth over ₹ 837 crore in Nepal under four pacts signed between the two countries, in the areas like infrastructure and power development. One of the major projects that India will undertake consists of construction of a 680 km long highway in Terai region of Nepal at the cost of ₹ 810 crore. The proposed road will run from the east to the west of Nepal across the Terai areas and provide connectivity within the regions as well as provide a better linkage between India and Nepal. This east-west highway when completed will also, to a great extent, remove Nepal's longstanding constraint of being a land-locked country. As Dr. Jagadish Pokhreal, former Vice-Chairman of National Planning Commission puts it, "we suffer from a tremendous inferiority complex", Nepal has got to shed her psyche of being squeezed between two rocks and should look beyond her political boundaries, if she really wants to prosper in trade and commerce. With better road connectivity "Nepal would be closer to Delhi than are the Indian cities of Kanpur, Lucknow and Allahabad. The markets of north-east India can more easily be serviced by the Nepal border towns of Birganj, Jogbani or Kakarvita in the east than they would be by the geographically more distant northern Indian states".[4]

Under power sector, both sides agreed that five villages of Nepal will be electrified at the cost of ₹ 6.3 crore. India is already providing 20 MW of power out of the existing power projects and further agreed to provide another 20 MW power to meet the increasing demand of Nepal. Another agreement between Nepal Stock Exchange Limited and Central Depository Services Limited of India was also signed under which India will assist Nepal in setting-up a Central Depository and clearing and settlement system at the cost of 5.75 crore. Apart from this, the two sides also signed an MoU for establishment of Nepal-Bharat Maitri Science Learning Centre in Khumaltar, Lalitpur at the cost of ₹ 15.5 crore.

The matter of reviewing of the Treaty of Peace and Friendship, 1950 which has much to do with the labour economy of Nepal, was proposed by Nepalese Foreign Minister, Shri Upendra Yadav who emphasized on the need to update certain provisions of the treaty that has become imperative with the change of time. The Government of India agreed to the proposal and decided to initiate the matter at the foreign secretaries level. Labour workforce from Nepal, both skilled and unskilled in the form of sawyers, miners, helper etc. usually come to India especially to the north-eastern

States where they are much needed, because the local labour decline to do these irksome and risky jobs. Besides this, loyalty and sincerity of Nepalese workers are always there to provide them an edge over the local workers. Under the Foroigner's (Protected Areas) Exemption Order, 1958, Clause 1(3) the subjects of Sikkim and Nationals of Nepal were exempted from the application of the order of restriction from entering into the northeastern States of India to enable them to enter into these restricted areas. But in 1976, the Ministry of Home Affairs, Government of India, New Delhi, by a Notification No. 25200/110/76-F1(1) dt. 30th July promulgated an amendment to the aforesaid Order in which the words "and Nationals of Nepal" were omitted. Since then, the district authorities in Assam and adjoining States are strictly prohibiting entry of Nepali nationals into their States without valid permit. This provision of the Order not only hampers developmental works in the north-east but also goes against the letter and spirit of the Treaty of Peace and Friendship 1950. In such situation, the Governments of India and Nepal may sit together and devise some mechanism by which the intending workmen can obtain entry permits at the border Outposts. The entry permits will not only serve the purpose to identify and distinguish the Nepalese nationals and to deport them back to Nepal in case of overstay in India, but also save the Indian Nepalis who are citizens of India from being mistaken for newcomers and get harassed by ethnic activists.

Nepal being a land-locked country her trade and commerce prospects are directly linked with India as the largest trade partner and a source of foreign investment for Nepal. India has also been the major transit providing country for Nepal. Under the Treaty of Trade and Transit, 1960, the Government of Nepal was given the right to import from or through the territory of India, arms, ammunitions or war equipments necessary for the security of Nepal. The Article II of the Treaty of Trade and Transit, 1960 is important for Nepal which states—"subject to such exceptions as may be mutually agreed upon, goods originating in either country and intended for consumption in the territory of the other shall be exempt from customs duties and other equivalent charges, as well as from quantitative restrictions". Such bilateral trade is of great significance for a country like Nepal which is land-locked and economically underdeveloped and all essential commodities, manufactured goods, medicines, textiles and machineries have to pass through India.

The principal items imported by Nepal from India included mechanical equipments, vehicles, spare parts, medicines, cotton textiles, cement, cotton thread, chemicals, electrical goods etc., while the major items of export to India are Vanaspati, tooth paste, jute goods, pulses, hides and skins, herbs, ginger, oil cakes, noodles etc. Thus, it is for the benefit of both the countries that the bilateral trade relations have to be maintained. Because of the bilateral trade facilities and transit concessions granted by India the volume of import and export between the two countries have appreciably improved ever since 1950s. In Table 9.1, the statistical data of balance of trade between India and Nepal shows a consistent increase in the volume of import and export of goods to and from Nepal.

Table 9.1: Balance of Trade between India and Nepal from 1996 to 2001

Sl. No.	*Import and Export*	*1996-1997*	*1998-1999*	*2000-2001*
1.	Nepal's Import from India	24853.3	32119.7	45364.5
2.	Nepal's Export to India	5226.2	12530.7	28864.9
3.	Trade Balance	19627.1	19589.0	16499.6
4.	Percentage of Increase	5.2%	5.7%	14.0%

Source: Not Available.

The Treaty on Trade and Transit 1960 was revised in 1996 as a result of which there has been a steady growth in bilateral trade between India and Nepal. India's merchandise trade balance has improved somewhat since 2000 with the growth of carpet and garment industries. In the fiscal year 2000-2001, exports posted a greater increase (14%) than imports (4.5%) helping bring the trade deficit down by 4 per cent from the previous year to US$749 million. Nepal's export has shown a rise more than eight times and the total bilateral trade has grown over five times since the revision of the treaty. Nepal's world-wide export has registered more than 90 per cent of increase. Nepal's import from India are—Petroleum products 29 per cent, Motor Vehicles Parts 8.3 per cent,

MS Billet 4 per cent, Medicine 4 per cent and Machinery parts 3 per cent, while her export to India are—Vanaspati 10 per cent, Processed and semi-processed food items, Toiletries, Twines, Pulses, Polyester yarn, Cardamom, and Readymade garments. The gross domestic product of Nepal has registered steady growth since 1960. Table 9.2 shows the trend of gross domestic product of Nepal at market prices estimated by the International Monetary Fund and Econ Start with figures in million of Nepalese Rupees.

Table 9.2: Trend of GDP of Nepal in 1960-2000

Year	*Gross Domestic Product in million rupees*
1960	3,870
1965	5,602
1970	8,768
1975	16,571
1980	23,350
1985	46,586
1990	1,03,415
1995	2,19,174
2000	3,79,488

Source: Not Available.

One of the important features of the revised Treaty on Trade and Transit is that the Government of India provides, on non-reciprocal basis, duty-free access to Indian markets for all Nepalese manufactured articles barring a short negative list (Cigarette, Alcohol and Cosmetics) subject to the condition that the export meet the domestic value additions requirement. This would, certainly provide an incentive to Nepalese small scale industries to produce more goods. The treaty on trade also provides for Port facilities to Nepal at Kolkata and other specific fifteen number of transit routes between Kolkata and Indo-Nepal border.

The prevalence of dual currency as legal tenders in Nepal has been a source of continuous constraints to Nepalese economy since long time. Both Nepal and Indian currency notes are circulated freely in Nepal and are converted into each other without difficulty at a certain rate of exchange. Although the Government of Nepal, as a first step to stop this practice, promulgated law declaring Nepal currency as the sole legal tender, Indian rupee continues to be used together with Nepal currency throughout Nepal especially in the southern and western border areas. As a result of this, the Rashtra Bank of Nepal has not been able to strictly control and regulate the monetary policy of the Government.

The trade and transit relations between India and Nepal has been by and large friendly and cordial besides being advantageous to both. Although some temporary differences of opinion on minor political or economic grounds have occurred from time to time, the matters have been amicably sorted out subsequently. The Indo-Nepal Treaty of Peace and Friendship 1950 which has permitted the citizens of both the countries to cross the border freely without passport or visa and "granted on reciprocal basis to the nationals of one country in the territories of other the same privileges in the matter of residence, ownership of property, participation in trade and commerce, movement and other privileges of a similar nature", has provided a strong basis for an enduring relationship between the two countries. In 1987, India showed indifference and passivity on the issue of expulsion of Nepalese settlers from neighbouring Indian states that led to expulsion of thousands of Nepali-speaking people from Meghalaya. Nepal retaliated by introducing a work permit system for Indians working in Nepal.

The relationship between India and Nepal was strained in 1989 when Nepal decoupled its rupee from Indian rupee which previously had circulated freely in Nepal. India retaliated by denying port facilities in Calcutta to Nepal thereby preventing delivery of oil supplies from Singapore and other countries. Due to this Nepal's GDP growth plummeted from 9.7 per cent in 1988 to 1.5 per cent in 1989. Nepal suffered serious economic deficiencies of imported goods such as coal, fuel, oil, medicine and spare parts.

In December 1991 during the visit to India by Nepalese Prime Minister Girija Prasad Koirala, the two countries signed new Trade and Transit Treaties and many other economic agreements. Again in April 1995 during Nepal Prime Minister Man Mohan Adhikari's visit to Delhi, he raised the question of revising the Indo-Nepal Treaty of Peace and Friendship 1950. Adhikari requested for greater economic independence for his land-locked country. In 2006, Nepal passed the Citizenship Bill that led to distribution of Nepalese citizenship to nearly four million stateless immigrants in Nepal Terai by virtue of naturalization. While Government of India welcomed the reformed Citizenship Act, certain section of Nepalese expressed deep concern. In recent years particularly after 2008 the increasing dominance of CPN-United Maoist in Nepalese politics along with larger economic aids advanced by the Chinese Government, Nepal has gradually distanced herself from India.

The visit of Indian Prime Minister Shri Narendra Modi to Nepal in August 2014 after a gap of 17 years is a definite boost to the age old relationship between India and Nepal. During that visit India provided Nepal with US$ one billion as concessional credit for economic development of Nepal. Nepal has a tremendous potentiality in her hydro-power projects. India and Nepal signed an important deal on 25 November, 2014 to build-up 900 MW hydro-power plant for the benefit of both the countries.

The original Trade and Transit treaty which was revised in 1996, became so beneficial to Nepal that it can be considered as a turning point of the trade relations between India and Nepal. Since 1996 the export of Nepal to India grew more than eleven times and bilateral trade more than seven times. The bilateral trade that was 29.8 per cent of total external trade of Nepal in the year 1995-96 increased to 66 per cent in 2012-13. The volume of trade increased from ₹ 1,755 crores in 1995-96 to ₹ 26,126.9 crores in 2012-13. The export from Nepal to India increased from ₹ 230 crores in 1995-96 to ₹ 3187.4 Crores in 2012-13 and the export from India to Nepal increased from ₹ 1525 crores in 1995-96 to ₹ 22,939.4 crores in 2012-13. The main items of export from India to Nepal were petroleum products, vehicles spare parts, machinery and parts, medicine, wires, rods, coils bars, electrical equipments etc. while the main items of export from Nepal to India were polyster yarn, textiles, jute goods threads, zinc sheets, cardamom, copper wire etc.

As regards foreign investment in Nepal, the Indian firms were the biggest investors accounting to about 40 per cent of total approved foreign direct investment. The Government of Nepal had approved till 15th, July 2013 a total of 2652 foreign investment projects with proposed FDI of ₹ 6325.50 crores. There are about

150 operating India ventures in Nepal. They are cngaged in manufacturing, services, power sector and tourism industries. Some of the largest investors include ITC, Dabur India, Hindustan Unilever, VSNL, TCIL, MTNL, State Bank of India, Punjab National Bank etc.

To do overall supervision and to look after matters relating to trade, transit, co-operation etc. there is an Inter-Governmental Committee (IGC). The Committee met in Kathmandu on 21st-22nd December, 2013 and allowed Nepal to bring imported vehicles on their own power from Kolkata port; to use Jobani-Biratnagar and Nautunawa-Bhairahawa customs points in addition to Raxaul-Birganj for importing bulk cargo from third countries. It also agreed to promoting Nepal's internal trade, including with India, the largest trading partner, at a time when Nepal has been suffering an ever increasing trade deficit.

Trade in power exchange is one of the most important trade between India and Nepal. Nepal has a tremendous potentiality in tapping and supply of power to neighbouring countries. Since 1971, India and Nepal have Power Exchange Agreement for meeting the requirement of electricity by India. Presently, there are more than twenty transmission connections of the capacity of 132 KV, 33 KV, and 11 KV which are used both for power exchange in the bordering areas and power trade. Recently an important agreement for construction of an Hydro-power project for the benefit of both India and Nepal has been reached between Shri Narendra Modi, Prime Minister of India and Shri Sushil Koirala, Prime Minister of Nepal.

There is a vast scope for extending the areas of economic co-operation between India and Nepal if only the mindset is changed from what is prevailing now between the two Governments. The time has now come to free themselves from the political psycho-complex and renew their age-old friendship to build up a stronger and wider economic nexus between the two countries. Nepal must shed her idea of being a small country sand-witched between two giant nations and redefine her new economic boundaries. Nepal has a tremendous natural potentialities in the form of hydro-power, tourism and man-power which if properly tapped in co-operation with India would greatly benefit both the countries. India has to shun her big brotherly attitude and look upon Nepal as an equal partner from both economic and political point of view.

Notes

1. Ram Sharan Mahat (2005), *In Defence of Democracy*, Adroit Publishers, p. 45.
2. Sujeev Shakya (2009), *Unleashing Nepal*, New Delhi: Penguin Books, p. 31.
3. Ram Sharan Mahat (2005), *op. cit.*, p. 58.
4. Sujeev Shakya (2009), *op. cit.*, p. 236.

10
Military Man-Power Relations

The recruitment of Gorkhas for Indian army can be termed as one of the oldest relations between India and Nepal. The Treaty of Segauli, dated 26 December, 1815, as ratified by the king of Nepal on the 4th March, 1816, is beginning of this historic relationship. The Treaty reads—"There shall be a perpetual peace and friendship between the Hon'ble East India Company and the Raja of Nepal". Ever since then, the torch of peace and friendship that was so ignited through the Treaty nearly two hundred years ago, has been burning as a steady flame of friendship and goodwill between India and Nepal even to this day, long after the British has left India. The redoubtable Gorkhas and the their Regiment in the Indian Army stand out as the living symbols of this long standing bond of friendship between the two countries.[1] The British left India more than half a century ago but the Gorkha Regiment, the legacy left behind by the British, is still serving India as they did to the British.

The history of Gorkha Regiment in the Indian army is, on its own merit, a glowing account of the outstanding bravery, loyalty and fighting spirit of the Gorkha soldiers and their supreme sacrifice of lives for the sake of India's integrity and sovereignty. This is a rare example of laying down one's life for the sake of others' country which, perhaps, has no parallel anywhere in the world. It is estimated that in the First World War the Gorkhas left their deads in France, Mesopotamia, Gallipoli and Palestine to the tune of 20,000 men while in the Second World War, the total Gorkha casualties were 23,655 of which 7544 were killed and found missing and the rest were severely wounded.[2] The Gorkhas not only lost their number, but also earned as many as eleven Victoria

Cross medals and innumerable awards for their exemplary courage and extraordinary services which is unique for one single community.

During the Indo-Nepal War 1814-16, on the very first encounter with the intrepid hill men, Sir David Octerlony, the Commander-in-Chief of the British Army was so impressed by the valor and fighting skill of the Gorkhas that he decided to enlist them in the Company's Army even before the Indo-Nepal War was concluded. He said—"The Indian soldiers of the Company would never be able to hold their own against the Nepalese in their mountain fastness". It is said that in the Gorkhas, the British found the right material around which the military dreams of the British were woven. In early 1815 while the war was still raging in the Kumaun region, Lieutenant Fredrick Young hurriedly raised an irregular Gorkha Force of 4500 strong from the Nepal army prisoners at Dehra-Dun, Nahan and Sirmur. Soon after this, another two Gorkha irregulars were raised which together with the first battalion formed the nucleus of the future Gorkha Regiments under British Indian Army. John Pemble, rightly asserted when he said—"The Gorkha Rifles was the legacy of the Nepal War".[3]

Whenever, the occasions served them, the Gorkhas displayed their mettle, courage and fighting spirit and successfully proved worthy of the salt with their inherent loyalty, élan and grit. The Recruitment of Gorkhas went ahead swiftly though clandestinely; more and more battalions were raised and the number of the Gorkha soldiers multiplied despite restrictions imposed by the Nepal Durbar against Gorkha recruitment. "The *Durbar* is, and always has been averse to its subjects entering the British service, and orders have long existed to prevent their doing so without the Ministers' previous permission."[4] Eventually in 1885 an Agreement of Mutual Concession was signed between India and Nepal which, for the first time, enabled the Government of India to recruit Gorkha young men officially in stipulated number in exchange of equal number of arms to be supplied to Nepal.[5] Recruitment Depots were set-up at Gorakhpur and Darjeeling and the recruiting system was reorganized on a sound footing. With the easy availability of Gorkha recruits, the British stepped up recruitment process and the Gorkha regiments grew up from strength to strength.

The First World War brought enormous pressure on the Government of India's military man power necessitating large scale recruitment of soldiers to reinforce the ever expanding war fronts. In order to cope with this requirement Chandra Shamsher Jang Bahadur Rana, Prime Minister of Nepal came out of his way to help India in her desperate war efforts. He allowed massive recruitment of Gorkha young men that drained out Nepal of its best able population. It is said that the agricultural operation of the little sub-Himalayan country almost came to halt during war period due to absence of male population. Acknowledging the great contribution of Nepal to British Sir Francis Tuker said—"Gorkha's selfless devotion to British causes which can hardly be matched by any race to another in the whole history of the world".

The Gorkha soldiers shed great amount of their blood during the First World War by fighting heroically in the foreign countries like Galipolli, Mesopotamia, France and Egypt where they earned a great many Gallantry Awards. Chandra Shamsher, the Nepalese Prime Minister was never tired of standing by India's side for the sake of her defence and internal peace. He wrote to the Viceroy of India—"In case the peace of India be threatened from outside and any assistance from us be needed for, then your Excellency and your Government may rely upon the Nepal Government ... and myself for rendering such help as is possible for us to give".

The Second World War witnessed yet another spurt in the requirement of additional manpower for strengthening of Indian Army to meet the emergent situation. Yuddha Shamsher, the Prime Minister of Nepal responded to the call magnificently with both men and material. The Gorkha regiments were quickly expanded by fresh recruitment which reached all time high from existing 20 battalions to 45 battalions. During the war period almost all the units of the Gorkha regiments took part in the war in various countries like France, Germany, Italy, Greece, North Africa, Palestine, Burma and Malaya and displayed extra-ordinary bravery and dash in fighting. The Japanese brought the war close to the door-steps of Imphal and Kohima of Assam threatening the security of India. The Gorkha soldiers fought bravely and gave their precious lives rather than allow the Japanese to set their feet on the Indian soil. According to an estimate, the Gorkhas lost 7,544 lives with

23,655 of them found missing and wounded—a sacrifice by one single community which, perhaps, has no parallel in the military history of the world. The Gorkhas also earned as many as 11 Victoria Crosses, 2734 medals of various high grades and numerous decorations which taken together, was adjudged as the highest number by a single community. Words of admiration and praise were spontaneously poured out from both civil and military quarters, such as :

> "The best soldiers in Asia, perhaps the best foot soldiers in modern history", or "These are the stuff of which military dreams are made", and also "The bravest of the braves".

India's independence in 1947 saw the Gorkha regiments divided into two halves under the Tripartite Agreement of July 1947 concluded between India, Nepal and Great Britain. Out of the existing twenty-seven Gorkha battalions eight battalions consisting of four Gorkha Rifles *viz.*, 2nd, 6th, 7th and 10th went to Great Britain to serve the British while the remaining nineteen battalions comprising six Gorkha Rifles *viz.*, the 1st, 3rd, 4th, 5th, 8th and 9th Gorkha Rifles remained with India to form part of Indian Army. Initially, Jawaharlal Nehru was reluctant to part with the Gorkha regiments in favour of the British. Field Marshal Montgomery wrote in his memoirs that Nehru raised many objections and did not agree to spare Gorkhas till the evening of 24th June, 1947. It was ultimately on the insistence of the Nepal Government that the division could be made possible. According to the Tripartite Agreement, Nepal allowed the recruitment of Gorkhas to continue for future. This privilege was, however confined to India and Great Britain only and no other country. Although China and Pakistan were applying pressures on Nepal for similar facilities of Gorkha recruitment, or if not for termination of the Tripartite agreement, the Government of Nepal remained firm on her commitment till to this day. The only restriction imposed by Nepal was that the Gorkhas must not be used against Hindus or against unarmed people in times of civil commotion and uprising. A significant part of the agreement was that Great

Britain was allowed to recruit Gorkhas only after India's requirement has been fully satisfied. India was also permitted to raise or expand up to twenty Gorkha battalions in case of her need. Thus, India was given the preference over Great Britain of extra facility to expand or raise more Gorkha battalions without asking for it. The Gorkhas served India well and impressed their Indian officers equally as they did to the British with their loyalty, valour and fighting prowess. General Karriappa was so much impressed by their bravery that he said—"If a man, not a Gorkha, says that he does not fear death then he is a liar". Field Marshal, Sam Manekshaw remarked—"The Gorkha's rich tradition and record of honour and awards are the source of great inspiration to our army".

Immediately after independence India faced a host of serious problems both from external and internal sources which persisted nearly two decades. The invasion of Kashmir by Pakistan in 1948, Chinese aggression of 1962, the Indo-Pak War of 1965, the Bangladesh War of 1971 and many other serious exigencies visited India one after another staking her very sovereignty and integrity at peril. Internally, the North-East region became restive with insurgent activities. The Nagas and the Mizos took up arms against the Government demanding secession from India. During these difficult and confusing moments, the Gorkhas played a crucial role in defending India from outside enemies and keeping peace and order inside the country. They fought against the external aggressors with their blood and pushed them out of Indian soil.

On the night of 27/28 June, 1948, Major Kaptan Singh Rana of 2/3 Gorkha Rifles led an attack on Pirkanthi, a strategic post occupied by Pakistani force, approximately forty miles from Baramula. Pirkanthi posed a potential threat to Srinagar from Pakistani army and therefore, it was imperative to capture this post. Kaptan Singh's leading platoon reached within 70/80 yards of the enemy post when there was stiff opposition from the Pakistani army with heavy firing. Major Kaptan Singh rushed forward with his men without regards to his personal safety. Although the enemy inflicted nearly 80 per cent casualties on his platoon they advanced forward towards the Point No. 10930 inflicting heavy casualties to the enemy. L. Naik Purna Bahadur Thapa rushed forward under heavy shower of LMG guns and threw a grenade in the enemy bunker killing two enemy LMG crews and wounding a few others. Rifleman Jas Bahadur Thapa crawled forward with the intention of throwing grenades into the enemy post, but he came under a heavy shower of enemy guns and was seriously wounded. Purna Bahadur Thapa also died in the action, but their personal gallantry enabled the platoon of Major Kaptan Singh Thapa to capture the Prikanthi post. Major Kaptan Singh Rana, L. Naik Purna Bahadur Thapa and Rifleman Jas Bahadur Thapa were awarded *Vir Chakras* posthumously.

Gorkhas at Siachen Border

On April 13, 1948, Siachen was declared an 'active war zone' and since then India and Pakistan must have lost nearly 2500 soldiers out of which more than 90 per cent of the casualties must have occurred due to extreme cold, and high altitude hazards rather than by enemy bullets. Located at an altitude of 18,000 to 20,000 feet on the extreme north-western fringe of Indian sub-continent covered snow all the year round human life at Siachen glacier is a battle in itself. At this "highest battle field" of the world our Jawans are constantly exposed to high velocity blizzards, frost-bite, snow blindness and hypertension. This is not a war with enemy, but more than that, it is a constant battle for survival against nature. Our Gorkha Jawans are there faithfully performing their toughest duties ever since the first Siachen firing began. For, they are the kind of stuff whose physical endurance has surpassed all wraths of nature and mental toughness has overcome the fear for life. In the words of Ralf Turner :

> "Once more I see you in your bivouacs or about your fire, on forced marches, or in trenches, now shivering with wet and cold, now scorched by pitiless burning sun, uncomplaining you endure hunger and thirst and wounds, and at the last your unwavering lines disappear in smoke and wrath of battle".

The morale of the Gorkha boys is ever high in the desolate, frozen Karakoram ranges. They are there ever smiling and whistling, as they do, and reverberating the icy stillness of the bleak mountain with the sound of their music and dance. They have fought many a battle too against Pakistani soldiers and protected Indian borders. Indian defence experts argue that Siachen is vital to our country's security as it happens to be a strategic place to defend Jammu & Kashmir from Pakistan and China. Geo-politically, Siachen assumes a great strategic importance having been situated at a point where the lands of India, China and Pakistan meet together.

In the small hours of 23rd September, 1984 Pakistani troops attacked Indian post with heavy artillery and rockets. The LMG detachment of 3/4th Gorkha Rifles under the command of Hom Bahadur Thapa and his Jawans fought with courage for more than an hour and succeeded in repulsing the enemy inflicting heavy casualties. Again on the night of 24 September, the enemy with overwhelming number mounted a sudden attack on the post with heavy missile and artilleries. Naik Hom Bahadur jumped out of his trench, despite his severe injuries and in an astounding show of elan charged the enemy with his LMG killing and wounding many Pakistani soldiers until he fell unconscious due to heavy loss of blood. He was removed from the scene and given medical treatment. Later he was awarded Vir Chakra for his exemplary courage.

The Chinese Aggression of 1962

In the morning of 20th October, 1962, the Chinese troops descended from Thag La ridge in overwhelming number and mounted a massive attack supported by field artillery and morters and easily overran the Indian posts. Simultaneously with this, the Chinese forces crossed the McMahon Line in other sectors also and launched offensives against Indian posts located in NEFA areas. The Gorkhas of the 9th G.R. and Assam Rifles bore the brunt of first attacks unprepared. At Khenzemane, the Chinese attacked three Indian posts at 04.00 hours of 20th October with heavy bombardment by field guns and mortars. The Gorkhas fought valiantly for nearly two hours, but the overwhelmingly superior number of the Chinese troops blew away Indian post. Hav. Som Bahadur and twenty others went down fighting.

On 16 November, the Chinese launched another attack on Indian post in the Walong sector. The Chinese swooped on A Company of 4-Sikh under heavy barrage of artillery, mortar and machinegun fire. Within half an hour, the Sikh position was overrun and the enemy advanced towards D Company of the 3/3rd Gorkha Rifles. Subedar Kharka Bahadur commander of the forward platoon and his men fought back valiantly killing 12 and wounding at least 15 Chinese. The enemy retreated quickly. At 06.30 hours, the Chinese attacked second time more vigorously. The gallant Gorkhas pushed them back for the second time inflicting heavy casualties. Seeing that the stubborn Gorkhas would not give them an inch, the Chinese went behind the D Company and launched a rear attack. Naik Keshar Bahadur Gurung picked up his LMG and moved immediately to a vantage point towards the left where he effectively engaged the enemy throughout the day, until he received a mortal shot in his neck and lay dead. Havaldar Chandra Bahadur Pun, then took over the LMG and kept the enemy at bay by continuous firing from close range until the last man of his company was out of the enemy cordon. Thus, Hav. Chandra Bahadur Pun broke the enemy cordon and saved his men from a certain carnage, but he himself was wounded seriously and killed.

Simultaneously with the NEFA sector, the Chinese struck war in the Kashmir sector also. Three battalions of 9th Gorkha Rifles who were posted along the peaks in Ladakh bore the brunt of the first Chinese attack on 20th October, 1962. Major Dhansing Thapa was commanding one of the forward posts at Sirjap when the Chinese mounted a massive offensive with machine guns, mortars and grenades. Major Dhansing Thapa put-up a stiff resistance wreaking a tough fight, though far inferior in number and weapon. He moved from trench to trench commanding his Jawans to push forward in complete disregard of his own safety. However, they could not hold on to themselves for long against the heavy showering of mortar and grenades of the enemy. Almost all his men were pinned down by Chinese artillery and he himself received severe injuries. Major Dhansing Thapa was awarded India's highest gallantry award, the *Param Vir Chakra* for his exemplary show of fighting skill and commanding prowess.

The Bangladesh War, 1971

The Gorkhas played a significant role in the Bangladesh War in December, 1971. The 5/5 Gorkha Rifles marched from Dawki in Khasi Hills along Jaintiapur-Sylhet road and captured Chandghat. The 1/3 Gorkha Rifles advanced from Jessore sector and captured Boyra post. Another battalion 4/5 Gorkha Rifles fought heroically in the Sylhet sector and succeeded in capturing Pakistani post at Fenchuganj and marched forward to Sylhet town which also surrendered hearing the name of Gorkha Palton and evacuated their post. Another column of 2/5 Gorkhas advanced *via* Nawabganj and seized Bhaduria and Hathbangi pushing back the enemy. The 5/11 Gorkha Rifles attacked Pakistani post at Ichamati river which was strongly held by the Beluch regiment of Pakistan army. The Gorkhas fought a pitched battle and compelled the enemy to beat a retreat with heavy casualty. Thus, the Indian army wrested a crushing defeat at every front over the Pakistan army resulting in the inglorious surrender by Pakistani Commander LT. General A.A.K. Niazi to General Jagjit Singh Arora, G.O.C-in-C, Eastern Command on the 16 December, 1971 with more than 90,000 Pakistani troops laying down their arms.

The Kargil War of 1999

During the winter months of 1999 when patrolling by Indian troops was less frequent due to extreme cold in the high mountain region, the Pakistani troops, in a calculated move to grab the strategic Kargil hills crossed the LOC and established a number of permanent bunkers. The Indian intelligence and the border security organization were blissfully ignorant about this for a number of months. On the 14th May, 1999 the nation was shocked to learn about it when the Pakistani intruders captured an Indian patrolling party of five Indian soldiers including one Lieutenant Saurabh Kalia and killed them in a most barbaric way after they were meted out inhuman treatment in captivity in blatant violation of Geneva Convention. Later on their mutilated bodies were returned back to Indian army. It also came to light that the intruders were not Kashmiri militants as claimed by Islamabad but they were foreign mercenaries from Afghanistan mixed with Pakistani army regulars.

They had built three storied *pucca* bunkers equipped with power generator around Kargil several kilometers inside the line of control. Trenches had been dug and many posts built-up connecting them with roads on their side of the LOC. They had stored ammunitions including shoulder-fired surface to air stinger missiles and stored provisions that would last for several months. Such a meticulous arrangement made by the invaders proved beyond doubt that the intrusion had taken place months before without a shred of knowledge of the Indian side. On the 27th May, 1999 an Indian MIG 21 was shot down well within Indian side of the LOC by Pakistani shoulder to air stinger and Flight Lieutenant K. Nachiketa was captured.

All these developments made the situation extremely emergent and provocative to Indian army. However, the enemy positions were very difficult to tackle by land force. The topography of the enemy position gave them extra logistic advantage. The Pakistani posts being located on top of high mountain ranging between 15,000 to 18,000 feet above it was logistically impossible to dislodge them. The Tiger hill located only four kilometers away from the LOC was one of the most strategic posts held by the enemy which had a dominating command over the Shrinagar-Leh High way, the life-line of Indian defence. The Tiger hill rose steeply ending in a conical shape with no spur or ridgelines on either sides which rendered climbing most difficult. Even a small force of 25 to 30 men sitting atop the peak could hold more than a Brigade – said Col. A.S. Chebrewal of the 8th Mountain Division. Pakistani plan was to occupy the advantage points on the top of the high ridges overlooking Shrinagar-Leh road, to snap communication system and to capture Siachen region. Their plan was, however, frustrated by powerful Indian air strikes which proved to be effective encounter which Pakistani army had never thought of. The Indian Air Force combat jets and helicopter gun-ships launched their sorties and air strikes over the enemy posts in Kargil and Drass sectors pounding and destroying the enemy hide-outs not sparing their stores and provisions. While doing so extreme care and restraint was taken to see that not a single bomb was dropped on the other side of the LOC. Side by side with air strikes Indian land force started artillery shelling from below and advancing towards the enemy posts. Heavy fighting continued in all sectors. Indian jawans fought heroically inflicting heavy casualties on the invaders. On June 8, 1999, after a ficrce gun battle in Kargil sector Indian troops achieved a major success by recapturing two main features in Batalik sub-sector. The troops gunned down thirteen Pakistani infiltrators and pushed the remainders back to the close of the LOC. India lost three jawans in this encounter. The intruders were dislodged from the Tiger hills and Tololing sectors also but they shifted to new positions in Kaksur and Batalik sectors making it difficult to flush out completely without crossing the LOC. General V.N. Sarma (Retired) said that unless the intruders were encircled from the other side of the LOC it would mean a continuous operation involving heavy casualties. Another military expert opined that India was fighting a war in which the time, place and scope of operation were being decided by Pakistan. The issuc of crossing the LOC hanged on indecision until 24th June, 1999, when Atal Bihari Vajpayee, Prime Minister of India finally set the speculation at rest by announcing that the sanctity of the Line of Control would be respected. Inspite of the nefarious intention of Pakistan, the Indian policy of restraint by maintaining the sanctity of the LOC and her ever readiness to promote good neighbourly relationship with Pakistan paid a rich dividend. The international community took the side of India as one body and censured Pakistan for its ill-conceived political agenda. Pakistan was isolated from the international comity of nations. British expressed deep concern over the infiltration of foreign mercenaries in Kargil and urged India and Pakistan to de-escalate the situation. A ten member ASEAN (Association of the South East Asian countries) backed India's stand on the Kargil issue and asked both India and Pakistan to resolve the dispute through dialogue. The US Secretary of State Madeliene Albright told a crowded Press Conference in Singapore that Pakistan should withdraw from Kargil and stop further terrorism. Even China, Pakistan's ally failed to appreciate Nawaz Sharif's action and asked him to resolve the dispute through peaceful means.

On 17 June, 1999 Indian Air Forcc, further intensified its attack on the intruders position in Kargil and recaptured Tololing peak that was strongly held by the enemy. In the operation Major Ajay

Singh Jasrotia and a *jawan* laid down their lives after fighting bravely and killing eight Pakistani troops and wounding nine others. A major success was achieved on 20th June, 1999 when Indian *jawans* recaptured peak No. 5140 under the able leadership of Captain Bikram Batra of 13th Jammu-Kashmir Rifles. Gallant Bikram Batra, however, lost his life in subsequent encounter for which he was awarded posthumously the country's highest gallantry award of *Param Vir Chakra*.

The 11th Gorkha Rifles played an important role in Kargil war operation, as they did on earlier occasion. This was the second time that the Gorkhas fought against the Pakistani forces in these inhospitable snow capped mountains of Kargil. It reminded them how in 1948 the Gorkha boys stormed upon the Pathan tribesmen and Pakistani regulars along Kargil borders with *khukries* and bayonets wreaking a carnage and pushing the enemy back until they become demoralized and flee the battle ground. It was on 26th June, 1948 that the 2/3rd Gorkha Rifles under the command of Major K.S. Rana launched a decisive attack on the Pakistani post at Pirkanthi. This time around although their target was very steep and difficult to climb and they were almost swept away by the enemy shelling the Gorkhas, disregard of their life risk rushed forward inflicting heavy casualties to the enemy. They lost two men of their side viz., Lance Naik Purna Bahadur Thapa and Rifleman Jas Bahadur Thapa, but succeeded in capturing the enemy post.

Recounting his experience Rifleman A. Gurung says—on the 10th June, 1999 we headed for the Peak No. 5040 which was the immediate target of our assault. As we started climbing the peak we came under heavy enemy shelling from the top. Our position was so vulnerable that our opponents from the top could count our heads. Undaunted, we pushed forward and gave roaring reply with our M.M.Gs guarding ourselves against rocks and bushes whatever we find at hand. I shot four Pakistani dead and before I could refill my M.M.G. for the next round I was hit by a morter in my leg and was bleeding profusely while I saw Major Tripathy by my side hit by a bullet on his head. The next moment there was darkness in my eyes, my head whirled and I fell unconscious until I woke up to find myself in the army hospital.

When fierce fighting was ravaging in the Kargil sector two Gorkha soldiers of 4/5 Gorkha regiment Ram Bahadur Gurung and Jim Bahadur Thapa lost their lives together with seven others in a train bomb blast at New Jalpaiguri on 22nd June,1999. The train was carrying Indian troops to Kargil and it was an act of sabotage by Pakistani ISI (Inter Service Intelligence) against the movement of Indian soldiers to Kargil. Rifleman Vijoy Gurung who was seriously injured in the blast was fighting a grim battle for life in Calcutta hospital when he said—"I do not regret, for I am a Gorkha soldier destined to die. I still wish to join the Kagil war and kill Pakistani intruders after getting well."

During 'Operation Vijoy' in Kargil the Gorkha soldiers of the 11th Gorkha Regiment and the 2nd Nagaland Regiment played crucial part in the fight and showed extreme courage, skill and determination. They also suffered the maximum casualties. The Gorkhas sacrificed as many as twenty-two precious live of which (to specify regiment-wise) eight killed from 11th Gorkha Regiment, six from Nagaland Regiment, five from 4th and three from the 3rd Gorkha Rifles. It may be made clear at this juncture that all the twenty-two Gorkhas who laid down their lives in the operation were the sons of Indian Nepalis settled in India and none from Nepal. Most of the parents were third or fourth generation Indian Nepalis who retired from Indian army. Undoubtedly, it is a unique contribution for a single community to sacrifice so many lives for the sake of the country in one operation. The following paragraphs highlight, in brief, on the saga of valour and sacrifice of the young Gorkha jawans who gave their lives for the country.

Havildar Man Bahadur Rai of 6/11 Gorkha Rifles together with his Gorkha jawans launched a gallant and determined offensive on the Pakistani intruders on the 12th June, 1999, and inflicted heavy casualties to the enemy. During the course of fighting Man Bahadur Rai rushed forward leading his men against heavy enemy shelling and in complete disregard of his personal safety when he received a fatal injury and succumbed to it. His mortal remain was brought to Sukia Pokhari, Darjeeling, his home town and cremated on 18th June, 1999 with full military honour. His widowed wife Lolita Rai proudly said—"I am a daughter of Vir Gorkha, I will not cry, I'll rather send my only son to the war to avenge his father's death.

Earlier on the 15th May, 1999 another Gorkha *jawan* Suniljong Mahat of 1/11 Gorkha Rifles became a martyr after fighting bravely in Kargil sector. He comes of a traditional army family. His grand father Major Nakul Mahat served in the Jammu-Kashmir Regiment from 1921 to 1961 and after retirement settled at Kangra in Himachal Pradesh. He had eleven sons all of whom served in the Indian army. Suniljong's father was the tenth son who is now working in Lucknow after retirement from army.

In the same encounter in Kargil sector another brave son of a brave father laid down is life for the country. His name was Mekh Bahadur Gurung of 1/11 Gorkha Rifles. His father Ram Bahadur Gurung was in the Indian army and fought at various theatres of war during Chinese aggression in 1962 and Bangladesh war of 1971 and earned many a laural. This brave hearted ex-serviceman was proud of his son who died in the battle ground fighting bravely. Rifleman Mekh Bahadur was born and brought-up in the military ambience at Dehra Dun army cantonment and received education from the 58 GTC Junior High School.

Two young boys Rifleman Linkon Pradhan of Sukia Pokhari, Darjeeling and Arun Kumar Rai of Sonada, Darjeeling joined army in the 1/11 Gorkha Rifles together in 1999 and received training together. They were hardly twenty years of age when they fought their last battle of life at Kargil with courage and determination. Rifleman Linkon Pradhan was making a desperate attempt to climbed the hill top braving against shower of enemy bullets, but was hit by a gun shot on his head and fell dead. His friend Rifleman Arun Kumar Rai was killed on the 3rd July, 1999 in a similar attempt to repulse the enemy from their position. In the tragic death of these two young soldiers their wives Smt. Kavita Pradhan and Smt. Vijoya Rai were left as widows at a very prime of their life.

In another encounter with Pakistani intruders Rifleman Ramesh Thapa of 2/3 Gorkha Rifles fought heroically and gave his life in the Drass sector on the 3rd July, 1999. His dead body was brought to his village Haripur Kanwali, Dehra Dun and cremated with full military honour. The public of Haripur named one of their village roads as Shaheed Ramesh Thapa road in the honour of this brave martyr.

The most crucial battle of this series was, however, fought in the Moskoh valley and Tiger hill in the first week of July, 1999 in which Indian jawans gave a decisive blow to the Pakistani troops and pushed them back to the Line of Control. The casualties on both sides were colossal. The Gorkhas alone lost as many as seven *jawans* at various places of fighting. In one of these encounters two companies of 1/11 Gorkha Rifles advanced towards the peak No. 4812 on second July under the command of Col. Lalit Rai. As they reached about 800 metres short of the peak the Pakistani forces greeted them with shower of heavy shelling. Undaunted by this the Gorkhas pressed forward in their counter attack. The Commanding Officer took the lead with six bodyguards one of whom was Havilder Gyan Bahadur Tamang. As they got at a point barely 200 metres away from their target the Pakistani forces intensified firing of which a splinter pierced the neck of Havildre Gyan Bahadur Tamang. Not caring for the injury and his personal safety he maintained close guard with his Commander and in the process killing Pakstani soldiers with his LMG. Soon he found himself soaked in blood and too weak to fight. So, he jumped down five metres below to find a safer place. Hurriedly, he tore out his vest and tied-up the injured neck so as to stop heavy flow of blood and then he jumped out of his hiding and sprayed bullets to the enemy killing three Pakistani invaders.

On the night of 6th July, 1999 a fierce fighting took place at Moskoh valley between Second Nagaland Regiment and Pakistani troops. The redoubtable Gorkhas and Naga jawans of this regiment under the able leadership of their Commander launched a massive attack on the enemy undaunted by the logistic disadvantage they had to face. Heavy shelling from both sides continued throughout the night when the Indian troops inflicted heavy casualties to Pakistanis compelling them to retreat back to near LOC. In this encounter Indian side lost eight *jawans* which include three Gorkhas. Rifleman Sanjoy Gurung showed extreme courage and skill when he continued to fire through his LMG killing Pakistani soldiers despite bullet injuries received by him and until he became exhausted and fell dead When the sad news of Sanjoy Gurung's death was broken to his father Hav. Meher Singh Gurung he reacted calmly saying—This was expected to happen one day. While in military service I have seen many deaths from close quarters. One son of mine has given his life for the country, I am ready to sacrifice all the three sons who are now in the army.

Rifleman Ratan Kumar Pradhan was another Gorkha who fell to enemy bullets during the Kargil operation. He belonged to Second Nagaland Regiment and fought valiantly in close company with Sanjoy Gurung. The third Gorkha *jawan* who met with the same fate was Rajesh Gurung. He also belonged to the same Second Nagaland Regiment which played an important role in the Kargil war of 1999. His mortal remain was brought to his village Chandmari, Dehra Dun when his father, ex-serviceman Shyam Singh Gurung received the coffin with sprightly military salute. Shyam Singh Gurung himself was a hero of many such battles in Bangladesh in 1971 and Jammu & Kashmir in 1965 and had not forgotten the horrors of war. He said—At this moment my blood boils-up and longs to join Kargil war to avenge the death of my son. The public of Dehra Dun dedicated a road in the name of Rajesh Gurung whose mother Basanti Devi Gurung lights a lamp by the side of this road every evening in her son's loving memory.

The Second Nagaland Regiment, the youngest regiment of the Indian army (raised in 1964) bore the brunt of the Operation Vijoy and suffered the highest casualty in terms of man and materials. Hav. Mohan Pun Magar, Naik Hari Bahadur Ghale and Rifleman Suresh Chhetri of this regiment immortalized their names and upheld the tradition of their regiment by fighting bravely and sacrificing their lives for the motherland. Naik Hari Bahadur Ghale fell to the enemy bullet while engaged in heavy gun battle in Moshkoh valley on the 6th July, 1999. Hav. Mohan Pun Magar was killed on the 7th July in the Moshkoh valley while Suresh Chhetri went down fighting in the Tiger hills sector on the 7th July together with seven other Indian jawans. Smt. Manju Chhetri, 22 year old wife of martyr Suresh Chhetri , when asked said,—I am pregnant and I wish I have a son so that I may send him to army to follow the foot-steps of his father. A brave wife of a brave Gorkha soldier. In a condolence massage to her the Union Minister for Defence, Mr. George Fernandez wrote—"Your husband Suresh Chhetri laid down his life for the country like a brave soldier".

Naik Krishna Bahadur Thapa of the 3/4th Gorkha Rifles was killed in the Operation Vijoy on the 11th July, 1999 while fighting in the Drass sector. His father Captain Mohan Singh Thapa was a retired army officer of Dehra Dun who said that he was proud of his son to lay down his life for the country.

Another young Gorkha soldier who laid down his life for mother India was Rifleman Phurba Tamang of Kalingpong. He had joined 4/4 Gorkha Rifles only in 1992 and had fought the war for the first time. He left behind his young wife Sunita Tamang and a nine month old daughter when he went down fighting in the Batalik sector on the 23rd August, 1999.

The saga of valour and sacrifice will not be complete if we do not mention the names of the following brave Gorkha soldiers who took part in various sectors of Kargil war at different times and laid down their precious lives. They are—Rifleman Birendra Thapa of 5/3 GR, Rifleman Ashish Thapa (24 years), Rifleman Manish Thapa (22 years), Rifleman Deepraj Pradhan (26 years), Rifleman Dibakar Tamang (25 years), Rifleman Kritagna Singh Rana, and Rifleman Dal Bahadur Pun.

Thus, the Gorkhas played a crucial role in the Kargil war of 1999. By the end of June, 1999 the Indian army had retaken almost all the important positions and expelled the invaders from Indian territories. Behind this spectacular success was, undoubtedly, the saga of extreme courage and supreme sacrifice of the Gorkha and Indian jawans. The Pakistani intruders who had so strongly fortified themselves on the hill tops could not have been dislodged so easily within a short span two months, had it not been for the valour and skill of these redoubtable soldiers. More than 400 *jawans* of the Indian army laid down their lives of which 22 were Gorkhas, which is a unique contribution to India for one community alone.

Today Gorkhas are zealously guarding the borders of India against intrusion of external enemies like the Pakistanis and the Chinese from the west and the north. The Gorkhas are there at the Siachen glaciers in the extreme north-west frontiers : they are there along the McMahon lines in Arunachal Pradesh, and they are also there along the Line of Control in Jammu & Kashmir indefatigably defending Indian borders. Our borders are assuredly safe in the hands of the redoubtable Gorkhas.

Gorkhas in the Indian National Army (INA)

The Gorkha's participation in the INA or the Azad Hind Fouj is one of the significant annals in the history of India's freedom movement which, unfortunately, has not received due attention of India's historians. A host of noted historians have dealt with a wide parameters of the Indian National army including that of its great leader Subhas Chandra Bose, but they have very conveniently chosen to refrain from dealing with the legendary role played by the Gorkha soldiers who joined the INA and fought against the British army to liberate India. Many movies and electronic visuals have also projected on the role played by the Indian soldiers in the Azad Hind Fouj but very little or nothing at all has been highlighted about the Gorkhas who made supreme sacrifices by their lives for the sake of the country's freedom. Some writers like Field Marshall William Slim (*Defeated into Victory*, 1956) and Arthur Campbell (*The Siez: A Story From Kohima*,1956) have given a volume of information about the Second World War in Burma, but they have omitted to mention anything about the Gorkhas who changed sides and joined their enemy, the Japanese. Peter Harclerode and David Raynolds (Gurkhas, 2003) who have written details about the many reverses suffered by British and Indian Army in the hands of the Japanese troops have mentioned that only twenty-six Gorkhas changed the side while, in reality, not less than twenty thousand Gorkhas had joined the INA. Byron Farwell, a British historian (*The Gurkhas*,1984) has squarely denied any Gorkha having joined the INA except one Gorkha line boy named Durga Singh Lama who is said to have been captured by the British troops and hanged to death. Thus, the history has been twisted conveniently to suit their purpose of concealing events detrimental to their interests.

On 15 February, 1942 Singapore fell to the Japanese and the next day the British army laid down their arms and surrendered at Singapore. On 17 February 45,000 Indian prisoners of war (POW) joined the INA under the leadership of Captain Mohan Singh, an Indian army officer captured earlier by Japanese troops. There were approximately 20,000 Gorkha soldiers among the above 45,000 Indian army who surrendered to Japanese as POWs. Most of these Gorkha POWs were the sons of retired Gorkha soldiers who had settled down permanently at Dehradun, Nainital, Bhaksu, Delhi, Darjeeling, Nalapani etc. They were educated and bred in Indian environment. They loved India as their mother land and were inspired by nationalistic ideas. For this reason they came forward willingly to join the INA. The inspiring address of Captain Mohan Singh and Pritam Singh at Ferrar ground on 17 was well received by the Gorkhas who joined the INA instantly.

As INA soldiers the Gorkhas played a crucial role with their classic fighting spirit, grit and valour. Their physical hardiness and climatic endurance helped them to push forward through the thick jungles and mountain fastness of Burma. Their versatility in the technique of guerilla fighting added extra capability to Gorkhas which was much appreciated even by Netaji Subhas Chandra Bose.

Most of the Gorkhas were enlisted in the Bahadur Group of the INA which, as a striking force of the INA was responsible to take the lead in the offensives. It was the Bahadur Group which took the leading role in attacking and breaking the British Indian column while advancing towards Imphal and Kohima. It was this Bahadur Group again which suffered the heavest casualties. Naik Man Bahadur Thapa of the 1st Bahadur Group was killed in action during the offensive in the Arakan. Havildar Sital Bahadur of the 1st Bahadur Group was killed in a hand to hand fight against the British force near Ramakori, Burma in August 1944. Captain Sher Bahadur Bhandari who belonged to Durga Malla's 2/1 Gorkha Rifles and joined INA together with him, was seriously injured during the fight near Rangoon and died later in Burma Hospital. He was also in the Bahadur Group. Thus, we find in record as many as twenty-five Gorkha soldiers including Durga Malla who laid down their lives fighting against the British force. (A list of these INA soldiers is given at Appendix IX) These were only a few Gorkha soldiers whose names were recorded by Dr. P.N. Chopra, in his book—*Who is Who of Indian Martyrs*, Vol. I, 1969, but there were many more others of the INA Gorkhas who were killed in encounter, maimed and missing whose names are either not known or not recorded. There were also a good number of Gorkha soldiers who acquitted themselves well in the war and received Azad Hind Fouj awards and medals for their fighting spirits and show of extra-ordinary bravery and absolute contempt for danger.

The Gorkha soldiers, fighting side by side with the Japanese troops advanced through the thick of battle against the British army and finally set their feet on the Indian soil at Kohima on 6 April, 1944. Another column of INA advanced towards Imphal but eventually, before they reached Imphal the Japanese troops had to retreat back due to logistic adversities. The Gorkhas, in their effort to live up to the high ideals of their great leader Netaji, displayed extreme bravery and laid down their lives in hundreds. Two valiant Gorkhas—Major Durga Malla and Captain Dal Bahadur Thapa were captured while on duty by the British troops. They were taken to Delhi jail and after brief trial were hanged to death.

Maintenance of Internal Peace and Security

Apart from defending Indian borders from external aggressions, the Gorkhas have played commendable role in maintenance of internal peace and security of India. The task of quelling internal rebellions and helping the civil authorities in maintaining peace and tranquility is very essential for the growth and development of the country. India being a multi-racial, multi-religious, multi-lingual and multi-cultural country internal clashes and conflicts arising out of any of the aforesaid grounds can occur at any time with large scale violence, murder and arson. This apart, regional acts of insurgency on political grounds are also frequently wreaked by armed outfits with the name and style of Naxalites, ULFA, HNLC, MNF, NSCN etc. On many occasions the civil Police and the Para-military forces who are meant for maintenance of law and order fail to contain the situations for which the civil authorities have to call in the army to restore peace and tranquility. This part of their duty is, however, entirely different in nature from what the soldiers are trained to do in the war. It is a kind of task which calls for a great deal of restraint in action, caution and tactfulness in every step of operation. The first and foremost consideration that should prevail upon them is the minimum use of force and the least destruction of life and property. In the discharge of such duties the Gorkhas have invariably shown great deal of restraint and coolness even under grave provocative situations. The following incident is a classic example of this fact:

> On 14th March, 1961, India dispatched a contingent of 5650 men to Katanga province of Congo as part of United Nations Peace Keeping Force (UNPKF). This included a detachment of 3/1, 2/5 and 5/5 Gorkha Rifles. In December 1961, a mob violence of extreme form took place at Elizabethvile and other places. Tshombe, the leader of the secessionist movement took out a huge procession of men, women and children who turned violent, hurled stones at the soldiers on duty, crossed barbed wire barricade and spitted, they even urinated on the army bunkers, but restraint, on the part of the soldiers, was the order of the day. The Gorkhas remaincd absolutely calm and unprovoked; not a single round of fire was shot, nor a *lathi* was raised, although several of them sustained stone injuries.

In April 1985, the Gorkhas exhibited yet another outstanding example of restraint during anti-reservation agitation in Ahmedabad. The most notorious and worst affected part of Kalupur-Dariapur was allotted to 2/9 Gorkha Rifles for law and order duty. The Gorkhas were faced with a tough and tricky situation. As the mob turned violent, the Gorkhas were *gheraoed* by thousands of clamouring and lamenting women and children defying curfew orders and hurling filthiest abuses at them. It was very tough time for the peace-keepers to disperse the surging mob. The Gorkhas, however, once again managed to bring the situation under control without a *lathi* being raised, which otherwise would have gone out of control with a little provocation or show of authority on the part of the Gorkhas.

Immediately after independence serious problems of internal peace and security arose in the North-East following emergence of separatist movement which took the form of full-scale insurgency with guerrilla trained armed outfits that unleashed reign of terror upon the loyal villagers. The Gorkhas of Assam Rifles and 8th Gorkha Rifles immediately took up combined operations to flush out the hostile Naga hideouts. Difficult terrain and thick jungles of Nagaland and the guerrilla warfare tactics adopted by the insurgents did not dampen the spirit of the redoubtable Gorkhas. In one major operation, the 4/8 Gorkha Rifles raided insurgent hideouts and killed one hostile Naga and wounded seven of them besides capturing large quantities of arms and ammunitions. In another encounter on the night of 7-8th June, 1957, they killed thirteen hostiles including a self-styled Major and injured 17 others. One of the biggest operations was carried out at Injoana area in February 1961 where 26 hostiles were killed and one LMG, one Sten gun, eight rifles including Japanese rifles were captured.

In 1960s, the Mizo secessionist movement under the banner of Mizo National Front (MNF) swept over the length and breadth of the district. Spearheaded by a firebrand leader, named Laldenga, a retired Army Officer, the Mizo National Front raised a military force entitled Mizo National Army (MNA) of 5000 strong, trained and fully armed with sophisticated weapons and capable of striking even a well organized military force of the Government. On the night of 28th February, 1966, the Mizo National Army made a sudden and simultaneous attack on the Assam Rifles Posts at Aizawl, Lunglei and Champhai, obviously with a preconceived plan to capture Assam Rifles establishment, cripple the administrative machineries and to loot government treasuries. At Aizawl they snapped all communications, broke into the government treasury and took away Rs. 20,000 when the armed constabulary guarding the treasury surrendered without resistance. At Champhai, the Assam Rifles Post was overrun killing two sentries and the government treasury and armory were looted. At Lunglei, the Assam Rifles men put-up a stiff resistance and held their position for four days against the massive attack of the insurgents. But on the fifth day as their ammunitions and water ran out, they surrendered. On March 8, the 2/11 Gorkha Rifles arrived at Champhai and in a series of counter-attacks the Gorkhas succeeded in breaking into the barricade of the secessionist and recaptured Champhai inflicting heavy casualties to the insurgents.[6]

After the Government of Assam declared the whole of Mizoram district as 'Disturbed Area' under the Armed Forces (Assam and

Manipur) Special Powers Act, 1958, on the 2nd of March,1967 the Gorkhas of Assam Rifles together with other Jawans and the Battalion of Gorkha regiment carried out combing operations, cleared many hideouts of the insurgents, captured haul of arms and ammunitions, killed and apprehended many insurgents.

In Punjab, the Gorkhas played a significant role during the peak of disturbances by Akali extremists who unleashed a reign of terror by senseless killings and wreaking various acts of violence during 1984. The State Police having totally failed to maintain the semblance of peace and security, army was called in on June 2, in Punjab and Chandigarh to assist the Civil Administration. On June 22nd the President of India promulgated an Ordinance, intensifying the provisions of Internal Security Act. Sant Bindranwale operating from the safe sanctuary of the Golden Temple of Amritsar established secret nexus with foreign powers including Pakistan and smuggled large quantities of lethal weapons into India and stockpiled them inside Golden Temple complex, reportedly to strike a coup for creation of Khalistan. Under such compelling situation, the army was ordered to enter into Golden Temple complex to flush out the extremists from their hideouts. Keeping in view of the religious sentiment attached to Golden Temple where entry of army was considered outrageous to the feeling of the Sikh community, the operation needed to be carried out with utmost restraint, caution and fairness. In this 'Operation Blue Star' 2/5 Gorkha Rifles took part in collaboration with other Indian army and accomplished their job with traditional 'drill book discipline' by capturing great amount of lethal weapons including highly sophisticated foreign arms and arresting over 4000 terrorists.

Discharge of Impartial Duty

Strict adherence to impartiality in dealing with communal riots is another important quality which must be present in the police or army vested with law and order duty. This is a prominent feature of Gorkha character which has been widely recognized by Government. The following extract of Sir Geoffrey De Montemorency's speech in the Punjab Legislative Council on July 18, 1927 bears witness to this fact:

> "The experience of Hindu-Muslim riots in Amritsar and our efforts in posting additional police to that city taught us that in such circumstances Gorkha policemen were extremely useful. They were efficient in patrolling purpose and likewise were considered by the inhabitants generally to be impartial. They neither favoured Hindus nor the Mohammadans".

Stephen, P. Cohen, Military journalist, was of the same opinion when he remarked as follows:[7]

> "It was always regarded as dangerous to use troops of one class or religion in quelling a riot by the same class. For this reason Gurkhas with few ties in India except Dehradun were extremely useful in civilian riot control".

In the wake of India's independence in 1947, Hindu-Muslim riot spread like wild fire throughout the country. The state police and armed forces not only failed to keep peace and order but openly connived with the frenzied mob belonging to their own communities and religions. The country was swept over by hysteria, confusion and insecurity when Hindus killed Muslims and the Muslims killed the Hindus. In such a terrible time, the Gorkha soldiers stood firm like rocks performing their duties with utmost sincerity and impartiality. In Calcutta, the 1/3 and 3/8 Gorkha Rifles performed commendable job by saving minority pockets of Muslim population; in Bihar the 4/10 Gorkha Rifles evacuated 15,000 refugees and saved them from genocide; in Allahabad 2/1 Gorkha Rifles took charge of the riot torn city and managed to put down the carnage while in Punjab 2/9 Gorkha Rifles was instrumental in saving a Muslim refugee laden train from being blasted with powerful bomb on its way from Ambala to Lahore. Had it not been for the timely and alert action of the Gorkhas, the train and its Muslim occupants would have been completely massacred.

Dera Baba Nanak (North Punjab, now in Pakistan) witnessed an extreme form of murder, arson and looting. Both Hindus and Muslims slaughtered each other when the Sikhs took the side of Hindus. Neither Hindu nor Sikh, nor Muslim security personnel could be relied upon in their patrolling duties as each one of them joined his own community. The Gorkhas alone stood impartial and firm as disciplined and dutiful soldiers.[8]

Economy of Remittance

The remittances received from India by the retired Gorkha pensioners in Nepal by way of their pension and gratuity constitute a great source of economic booster of the Government of Nepal. Nepal's economy has considerably prospered through the remittances received from the retired Gorkha soldiers as well as the non-resident Nepalese who come to India for livelihood. Of late, the Nepalese diaspora has become one of the major revenue earning industries of Nepal. The migration of Nepalese for livelihood has spread far and wide covering, at least, thirty-two countries of the world involving nearly 70 million people. Out of those countries, India happens to be the largest country to attract Nepalese workers. Migration has become the way of life of the Nepalese, everyone looking for a better life in foreign country. According to an estimate, at least twenty-five per cent of Nepal's population was outside the country at any point of time.[9]

More than ten per cent of the GDP of Nepal consists of remittances received from the Nepalese migrants.[10] Within a period of five years, the remittance shot up from ₹ 90.7 million in 1974-75 to ₹ 216.8 million in 1980-81. Then it tripled to ₹ 676.8 million by the close of 1980s. Surprising to say, Nepal, a small country, stood as the fifth largest nation among the remittance receiving countries of the world, by the end of 2007, with an annual remittance of 1.6 billion US Dollar.[11] India alone sent ₹ 370.6 crore during the period 1999-2002. The pension disbursing system between India and Nepal was simplified and made easier after independence so that the ex-servicemen living in Nepal get their pension without much difficulty.

Welfare Measures for Gorkha Ex-servicemen

The Government of India have magnificently reciprocated the benefit of the military man-power it received from Nepal by extending a number of welfare measures for the Gorkha ex-servicemen who return back to Nepal after their retirement. This has come their way both as a token of love and gratitude to the Gorkha ex-soldiers who made supreme sacrifice with their blood for the security, integrity and sovereignty of India. This is also being done as an abundant measure of social security of the retired soldiers and their families which is normally provided to all its ex-servicemen in India. The Government of India have established District Soldiers Boards (D.S.B.) in Nepal for the welfare of the Gorkha ex-servicemen who go back to settle in Nepal after retirement. According to an estimate, there are over 80,000 Gorkha Ex-servicemen settled in various parts of Nepal. It is the concern of the Government of India that these Gorkha ex-servicemen, their families and dependents get all possible help and assistance in respect of payment of pension, medical care, education of children, supply of drinking water and many other facilities. For this purpose, an organization named "India Ex-servicemen Welfare Organisation" (IEWON) has been functioning directly under the supervision and patronization of the Indian Embassy in Nepal. Among the major welfare measures rendered by the above organization, the following deserves mention here.

Medical Care

Health care facility to the ex-servicemen at their old age is an essential part of social security measure of contemporary world. As a person grows old, many old age related sickness visit him, besides this, soldiers who are rendered maimed and physically handicapped in war require special care even after retirement. Government of India have established two Medical Centres at Pokhara and Dharan each managed by two doctors and necessary medical staff to cater to the health care needs of the ex-servicemen and their families. These Medical Centres are well-equipped with X-Ray, laboratories, Electro-Cardiography and other diagnostic facilities. For specialized treatment, a number of medical teams comprising doctors specialized in Eye, Dentistry, Cardiology etc. go round the rural areas for the treatment of the ex-servicemen.

Drinking Water Facilities

In order to provide pure and potable water to the families of Ex-servicemen Government of India has provided water connection through HDP and CGI pipes in the interior villages with concentration of ex-servicemen. The implementation of such projects is carried out with the active co-operation of the village people. According to an estimate, more than 877 water supply projects have already bee completed.

Education Scholarship

Government of India is giving education scholarships to the wards of those ex-servicemen who died in 1962, 1965 and 1971 wars in India including those who lost their lives in the major operations such as Operation Pawan, Operation Vijay and Operation Meghdoot etc. So far 183 such scholarships have been awarded.

Financial Assistance to Schools

In the areas where large number of children of the ex-servicemen go for study, financial aids are extended for construction, repairing and extension of school buildings. They are also given grants for purchase of books, school equipments, sports materials etc. A sum of ₹ eight lakh is spent annually for this purpose.

Pension Payment Facilities

Pension disbursement to the Gorkha ex-servicemen living in Nepal has always been of greatest concern of the Defence Ministry of the Government of India. Prior to independence the British had established a few Pension Disbursement Centres in the border areas where the Gorkha ex-servicemen and the widow family pensioners had to go to receive their pensions. Now, after independence, the responsibility of pension disbursement has been taken over by the Indian Embassy in Kathmandu. In view of the fact that the Gorkha pensioners do not have to travel all the way to border Treasuries to receive their pension and that they can get pension without delay, the Indian Embassy conducts as many as 32 Seasonal Pension

Payment Camps annually in the remote places of Nepal. Besides, there are Military Pension Branches located at Pokhara, Dharan and Kathmandu which cater to pension disbursement for both ex-army and civil pensioners who retired from India. Table 10.1 shows the volume of pension amount disbursed by Government of India annually in Nepal.

Table 10.1: Volume of Pension Amount by GoI Annually in Nepal of 1994-2002

Years	*₹ (in Crores)*
1994-95	175.00
1995-96	199.00
1996-97	249.50
1997-98	206.07
1998-99	297.00
1999-2002	370.60

Source: Defence Ministry, GoI.

Conclusion

The age-old alliance between India and Nepal for supply of military manpower continues for ever sustaining and trailing behind it a glorious history of nearly two hundred years of friendship that has almost passed into tradition. The cost of this friendship to Nepal in terms of the loss of human lives is staggering which cannot be measured by any standard. The loss might, for some, seem to have been compensated by remittances that Nepal received by way of pay and pension of the retired Gorkhas but the loss of human lives, mental agony, orphanization and material deprivation suffered by the families of the soldiers concerned are something beyond earthly indemnification. Nevertheless, the Government of Nepal remains steadfast in fulfilling the terms and conditions of the Tripartite Agreement of 1947 despite political pressures from China and Pakistan to terminate or modify the agreement. Their contention is that Nepal being a neighbour country to them both (China and Pakistan) it is morally unfair on the part of Nepal to help India with military manpower to be used against them. China wants that in case Nepal cannot stop supplying Gorkha recruits to India she should allow the same privilege to China also as her next-door neighbour. But Nepal is ever steadfast in its stand as incorporated in the Tripartite agreement of July, 1947. Even if she stops supplying Gorkha recruits to India, at any point of time, there would be no dearth of Gorkha recruits in India, in so far as the sons of Indian Gorkhas who settled in India will be more than enough to replenish the existing Gorkha regiments. Nearly twenty-five per cent of the present roll in the Gorkha regiments are already filled by the sons of Indian Gorkhas and it can, reasonably, be hoped that they will definitely prove to be a better staff for Indian Army with their better education, knowledge of Indian languages and quicker adaptability to the changing war technology.

After India's independence the remaining six Gorkha regiments including one more newly raised the 11th Gorkha Rifles fought many a battle for the defence of Indian borders in Kashmir, Ladakh, Siachen, Arunachal Pradesh and Bangladesh and laid down their precious lives. At Kargil in 1999 alone, at least twenty-two Gorkha young men lost their lives. This is no mean a contribution towards India's integrity and sovereignty by a single community.[11]

Notes

1. K.K. Muktan (2002), *The Legendary Gorkhas*, Guwahati: Spectrum Publications.
2. H.S. Bhatia (1957), *Military History of India*.
3. John Pemble (1971), *The Invasion of Nepal*, Oxford: Clarendon Press, p. 348.
4. Ramsay to Secretary to the Government of India, in the Foreign Department, Simla, No. 18 dated June 15, 1866.
5. K.K. Muktan, *op. cit.*, Guwahati.
6. Major Gen. D.K. Palit (1984), *Sentinels of North East*, New Delhi.
7. Stephen, P. Cohen (1971), *The Indian Army—Its Contribution to the Development of the Nation*, Bombay: University of California Press, p. 284.
8. Byron Farwell (1984), *The Gurkhas*, Alen Lane, p. 284.
9. Shakya, Sujeev (2009), *Unleashing Nepal*, New Delhi: Penguin Books.
10. *Ibid.*
11. *Ibid.*

11
Matrimonial Relations

India and Nepal have a very long tradition of matrimonial alliances. History of Nepal and India are replete with interesting accounts of matrimonial relations between the princes and rulers of the two countries ever since prehistoric times. The great Epic of *Ramayana* describes about the king of Janakpur of Nepal having given his beautiful daughter Sita on marriage to Shri Ram Chandra, the prince of Ayodhya in India. Today Janakpur, the ancient capital of king Janaka is an important city of Tarai in Nepal. Here stands a magnificent Janaki temple said to have been constructed by an Indian prince about one hundred years ago at an expenditure of ₹ nine lakhs. Hearsay goes that because of the huge cost of construction involved in that temple it is called 'Naulakha' temple even to this day. Nearly 2200 years ago emperor Ashoka visited Nepal to glorify Lord Buddha. The pillars erected by him at Patan and Kirtipur, both in Nepal are the silent witnesses to this historical event. During these days emperor Ashoka's daughter Charumati and Nepali prince Devpal had tied a nuptial knot in this beautiful city of Kathmandu. This significant event of Nepalese history leads one to believe that the sub-Himalayan kingdom of Nepal, in those days, must have been a prosperous and powerful country to match the high dignity and honour of the prince of the great Mauryan empire of India.

According to history of Nepal, a vanquished Lichchavi prince of Vaishali (present Bihar) entered Nepal around about 100-160 A.D. overthrew the Kiratas who were settled there and established a Lichchavi kingdom. One of the Lichchavi kings named Sivadeva-II married the grand daughter of Adityasena, the accredited emperor of Magadha.[1] The kingdom of Magadha was, undoubtedly, a powerful state in northern India and its rulers claimed undisputed sway over the whole territory lying between the Ganga and the Himalayas. The founding of Vikram Era is traditionally associated with the king Vikramaditya of Magadha. It is believed that Vikramaditya defeated the Shakas or Scythians who were becoming powerful in India. In order to commemorate this victory over the Scythians, king Vikramaditya is said to have introduced the Era of Vikram Samvat in fifty-eight B.C. In Nepal Vikram Samvat calendar, is used in all official and non-official purposes which indicates that the Gupta empire had its political boundary spread as far as Nepalese territory.

It is found in the history that matrimonial alliances between two countries or royal families were often made on political and diplomatic reasons rather than on ethno-cultural affinity. Instances are galore where treaties were concluded between two belligerent countries and heavy tributes were paid by the countries losing the battle in order to re-establish lasting peace and friendship. Many times such treaties involved giving royal princess in marriage together with gold and jewelleries to the king winning the battle. It was, perhaps, on such dipolmatic occasion that Kumaradevi, a Lichchavi princess was given in marriage to Chandragupta-I, the founder of Gupta dynasty. For, this marriage took place after the battle between Chandragupta and the Lichchhavi King Vrishadeva.[2] The history of Assam states that towards the 7th century A.D. Pragjyotishpura, modern city of Guwahati, Asom was ruled by the dynasty of Salastambha, the great Chief of the Mlechchhas or Kirata. He was accredited "as a great king" by the copper plate of Harjjaravarman. Harsa, the king of this famous dynasty is said to have given his daughter Rajyamati in marriage to Jayadeva II, the king of Nepal.[3] It is to be noted that Nepal was a country with its name and fame well known to all parts of India during ancient period of history. As regards the identity of the Nepalese king Jayadeva-II, E.A. Gait has not mentioned any account of his book.[4] According to the chronological list of the kings of Nepal as alluded to by Lt. Colonel E. Vansittart we may infer that he might be one of the kings of the Thakur dynasty founded by Amsuvarman in 635 A.D. Later in the 16th century A.D. the Koch dynasty rose in power in the north-east India under the leadership of Viswa Singha, the founder of the Koch dynasty. The Koch kings used to maintain records of the major events of their kingdom in a book called *Darrang Raj-Vamshavali*. It is recorded in the *Raj-Vamshavali* that Viswa Singha had eighteen wives from different countries like Gova, Kashmir, Tippera etc. and one of them was Ratnakanti, a princess from Nepal. Ratnakanti Devi was the daughter of Malla king of Kantipur. It is stated that Viawa Singha's son Naranarayan, the greatest king of the Koch dynasty was born out of Ratnakanti's womb, the Nepalese princess (D. Nath).

The process of matrimonial relations between the royal families of Nepal and the Indian kings has continued from the prehistoric period dcwn to the contemporary times despite the vast changes that have taken place in political arena as well as in their royal status. After India's independence, the numerous native states of India merged with Indian dominion and the native kings lost their royal status, while in Nepal the Rana rule ended in 1950 yielding place to democratic pattern of government in the name of the king of Nepal as the titular head. However, the royal families of Nepal are still maintaining the matrimonial alliances with the erstwhile princely States of India like, Gwaliar, Kapurthala, Mayurbhanj, Jodhpur, Kashipur etc. To give a few instances, Shri Pashupati Shamsher Rana, the former Minister of Nepal married Usharaji Scindia, the daughter of late Vijairaji Scindia, the mother of late Madhav Rao Scindia, former Union Minister of India. Madhav Rao Scindia himself married a daughter of Rana family. Mention may be made here that Miss Devyani Scindia whom the Crown Prince of Nepal, late Dwipendra Vir Vikram Shah wanted to marry and failing which he had to take the extreme and ghastly steps to kill his father King Birendra Vir Vikram Shah, his mother, Queen Aisharya Rajya Lakshmi and six other members of the royal family on the 1st June, 2001,was none other than the daughter of Usharaji Scindia and the niece of late Madhav Rao Scindia. Dr. Karan Singh, the former Union Minister of India married Yasho Rajyalakshmi, the grand daughter of General Mohan Shamsher Jangbahadur Rana, the Prime Minister of Nepal. Yasho Rajyalakshmi is also the cousin sister of Pashupati Shamsher Rana of Nepal. The king,Tribhuvan Vir Vikram Shah of Nepal had two wives and both were the daughters of the king of Kashipur State. All the three sisters of the king Mahendra Vir Vikram Shah were married to the princes of

Indian native States like Poonch, Sikar and Mayurbhanj. Late king Birendra Vir Vikram Shah of Nepal was directly related to the Maharaja of Jodhpur and also the Maharaja of Mayurbhanj. Further, Hemlata, the wife of Maharaja Gaja Singh of Jodhpur and the Rajkumari of Poonch are the nieces of king Mahendra Vir Vikram Shah and the aunties of late king Birendra Vir Vikram Shah of Nepal besides all these matrimonial relations the royal families of Nepal have many other blood relations with their counterparts in India.

It looks as if it is a taboo on the part of the royal families of Nepal to make a matrimonial alliance with the commoner or other subjects of their own kingdom. As far as possible they would prefer marrying from the Rana Lords family of Nepal itself and if not they would look outside towards India. This is one of the reasons why the people of Nepal considered the royal Shah family and the Rana family as the alien rulers. The royal Shah family and the Rana family both being the ruling classes of Nepal there could be no socio-political embargo attached to the marriage between them. The Ranas on their part welcomed the matrimonial ties with the royal families in so far as it served the interest of the Ranas in more than one way. Firstly, it brightened the prospect of the Ranas in sharing the throne of Nepal with the royal families; secondly, it raised the social status of the Ranas *vis-à-vis* the Indian princeses, thirdly, it prevented the king from going against the Rana Prime Minister's totalitarian designs and lastly, it enabled the daughters of Ranas, on being the royal wives, to put wedges into the affairs of the Nepal Kingdom. Thus, the matrimonial alliance between the Ranas and the royal families of Nepal proceeded headlong right from the days of Jang Bahadur Rana whose son Jagat Jung was married to the eldest daughter of King Surendra Bir Bikram Shah. This was followed by the marriage between the second daughter of King Surendra Bir Bikram Shah and Jung Bahadur's second son Jit Jung in 1855. Politically more consequential was the marriage between the Crown Prince Trailokya Bir Bikram Shah with one of the daughters of Jung Bahadur which enabled his first grand-son Prithvi Bir Bikram Shah to occupy the throne of Nepal on May 17, 1881.

For the people of Nepal, however, it made no difference whether the Shahs or the Ranas became their rulers, neither of them were considered to be their well wishers. Both of them were outsiders who came to rule Nepal from India. That was the reason why both of them were eventually eliminated from the affairs of the Nepalese governance. It may be remembered that after the overthrowing of the Rana regime in 1950, the king Mahendra Bir Vikram Shah attempted to suppress the democratic rights of the people by promulgating a new constitution in 1960 that envisaged a party-less Panchayati System of Government. This system gave absolute power to the king as the head of the state with sole authority over the Government including the Council of Ministers and the democratically elected Parliament of Nepal. The people of Nepal had again to fight against the king to restore their democratic rights. There was a large scale protests and anti-monarchical demonstrations launched by different political parties and student communities demanding multi-party system of Government which continued for a long time and cost several precious lives. Eventually, after three decades of hard struggle, the people achieved victory, and multi-party system of government was re-established in Nepal in 1991.

Another attempt to usurp the people's democratic rights was made by king Gyanendra in 2005 in the wake of Maoist insurgency when the king dissolved the democratically elected cabinet and assumed to himself all the powers of the Government. This, however was, withdrawn by himself in 2006 and the Parliament was re-instated back to its power. Finally, the centuries old and obsolete monarchy was destined to go. The Nepalese Parliament, in a historic resolution adopted on the 28th May, 2008, abolished the Nepalese monarchy and declared Nepal to be a Soveriegn Democratic Republic. With this the 240 years long, monarchical Government in Nepal was abolished and together with that the only 'Hindu Kingdom in the World' came to the end.

Notes

1. Raghunath Singh (1950), *Jagrata Nepal* (Hindi).
2. Ram Rahul (1978), *The Himalaya as a Frontier*, New Delhi: Vikas Publishing House.
3. E.A. Gait (1967), *History of Assam*, Calcutta.

12
Diasporic Relations

The term 'diaspora' is originated from the Greek word which means wide dispersal of nations into different parts of the world for temporary or permanent settlement. Originally, this term was exclusively used to signify the Jews who were scattered all-over the Asiatic and European countries. Today, the social scientists and historians use it in a generic sense to denote all peoples or communities who migrate from one country to another for eking out livelihood. Implicit in the aforesaid assumption is that the migrants may live in the foreign country on temporary basis or settle down permanently as citizens of the adopted country, but he must maintain his ethnic and cultural identity of his original home in tact.

Migration of people from one country to another is a global phenomenon and history is replete with stories of human movements allover the world from ancient times till date. India has a very long history of migration across different countries of the world. It starts before the beginning of the Christian era, or even earlier than that, when the Indian saints and seers went out to far reaching countries like Shri Lanka, Indonesia and Nepal to spread the message of Lord Buddha and also the movement of the ancient maritime adventurists, and then in the nineteenth century the indentured labours who left India for foreign countries. The British took Indians as indentured labours to far-flung parts of British empire in the nineteenth century—Fiji, Mauritius, Guyana, Trinidad, Surinam, Malayasia, South Africa, Sri Lanka etc. to settle there permanently. In recent years the large scale migration of Indian workers into the Gulf countries and lastly the movement of technically educated Indian youths to the western countries for higher salaries and better economic prospects are some of the classic examples of human movement across the world. It is estimated that roughly three million Indian workers are engaged in the Gulf countries of Bahrain, Iraq, Kuwait, Saudi Arabia and UAE. All together, nearly twenty-one million Indian people are staying in more than 135 countries of the world.

The diasporic relations between India and Nepal is very old which is bolstered by common language, tradition, history and culture and facilitated by geographical proximity. The open border policy followed by both countries and also the privileges offered to the nationals of one country to settle down and carry out trade, commerce and other economic activities in other's country, under Article 7 of the Indo-Nepal Peace and Friendship Treaty, 1950 have immensely contributed to the diasporic movement into each other's country. According to an estimate nearly four million people of Indian origin are residing in Nepal, while on the other hand, approximately six million people of Nepalese origin are presently settled in various parts of India. In other words, at least 16.7 per cent of the total population of Nepal is composed of the people of Indian origin, whereas, 0.75 per cent of India's population consists of the people of Nepalese origin. Speaking in terms of ratio, Nepal has one Indian for every six Nepalese, while India has one Nepali for every 200 Indians. The vast majority of the immigrants are permanently settled down in their respective countries of domicile for generations as citizens by swearing allegiance to the constitutions of each other's country.

There are currently about four to five million Nepalese of Indian origin living in Nepal. They are settled mostly in the Terai region of Nepal. The immigration of Indian people started since nineteenth century and it continues till recent times. The Government of Nepal encouraged the Indians living in Bihar to settle down and do cultivation in the Terai region of Nepal where Nepalese from the hills dare not to come down due to fear of malaria and hot climate of the place. The Indian immigrants who moved into Terai were mostly landless tenants from the Indian State of Bihar. They were primarily agriculturists and also do animal husbandry and other minor occupations. They settled down in Terai in large number and turned the fertile land into a granary of Nepal. They are mostly Hindus and Muslims. The Government of Nepal passed the Citizenship Bill in 2006 and converted more than four million stateless Bihari immigrants into Nepalese citizens by virtue of naturalization. The Government of India welcomed the reformed Citizenship Act while certain section of Nepalese leaders expressed deep concern.

The Madheshis belong to a different ethnic group. They are the natives of Madhesh, which means Madhya-desha, i.e., the plains lying between Nepal and India, such as Mithila, Jhapa, Morang, Sunsari, Kailali, Kanchanpur etc. Madhesh contains 22 districts out of the total 75 districts of Nepal and covers 17 per cent of Nepal's geographical area and it is a home to 35.9 per cent of total population of Nepal. The Madheshis are considered as indigenous people whose prehistoric ancestors were indigenous to the ancient Bideha, Mithila, Awadh and Shakya kingdoms. Many of these groups are the descendants of king Janaka, father of Sita and king Suddhodhana, father of Buddha. Dr. Ram Baran Yadav, Ex-President of Nepal and Shri Paramananda Jha, Ex-Vice President of Nepal are inhabitants of Madhesh. The term 'Madheshi' was coined by the Nepasese living in the hills. It must be noted that the term Madheshi also includes Indian Nepali people who migrated into Madhesh from Indian States of Bihar and Uttar Pradesh and became Madheshis by naturalization in 2006 according to the controversial Citizenship Act of Nepal.

The people of Indian origin inhabiting the Tarai regions of Nepal are comparatively more advanced and enterprising than the indigenous Nepalese living in the northern hill areas of Nepal. Terai, with the exception of Kathmandu valley, is considered as the most literate region of Nepal. Due to proximity to India and open border policy followed by the Government, most of the Terai people are educated in India and groomed up in Indian style of life and culture. Being educationally and socially advanced and politically better organized, they are capable of putting pressures on the Government and getting their grievances fulfilled through political movements. In 2015 the Government of Nepal promulgated its new constitution but the Madheshis, Janajatis and Tharus felt they were being left out in the new constitution. These groups then blocked the border points deliberately worsening the embargo by not allowing vehicles carrying essential commodities from India to pass from check-points. The Government of Nepal, after having met the Madheshi parties in several dialogues, had to accommodate their demands. Citizenship has been an emotive issue among the immigrant Madheshis as they often marry Indians from the border districts of Bihar and Uttar Pradesh. According to Nepali citizenship rules the spouses of Nepali citizen become 'naturalised Nepali citizen', however, there is a discriminatory provision regarding the offsprings of such marriages. Children of a Nepali male marrying a foreigner are 'Nepali by descent' whereas if a Nepali woman marries a foreigner their children are 'naturalised Nepalis'which bars them from important constitutional position. This is one of the issues for which the Medheshis are in loggerhead with the Government of Nepal. It must, however, be admitted that the credit of converting the once most backward and malaria infested Terai into a prosperous economic bastion of Nepal goes to these people who originally hailed from the Gangetic plains of Bihar. They were mostly hard working landless farmers belonging to both Hindus and Muslims.

Of late the Indian overseas diaspora has become so wide spread around the world that the sun is said never to set in the Indian diaspora. Dr. L.M. Singvi, the Head of the High Level Team for the overseas Indian affairs, rightly remarked—"the empire of minds of children of mother India spread all over the continents including the icy reaches of Antarctica on which the sun truly cannot set."[1] It is estimated that the approximate number of overseas Indians is twenty-two million, as in 2005 covering thirty-five countries across the world. The term overseas includes two groups of people of Indian origin; those who have permanently settled in foreign country by adopting the citizenship of the countries of their domicile and the other group, those who possess Indian pass ports for reasonably long periods of time.

Nepalese Diaspora in India

India has been historically playing the host country to the people from Nepal ever since time immemorial. India and Nepal are two ancient countries connected to each other geographically, historically and culturally. Numerous evidences are extant which reveal that there had been a steady flow of people from Nepal into India from prehistoric period to modern times. Ever since the age of the Lord Buddha and the Emperor Ashoka till present day there has been continuous movement of people both ways, while after the advent of the British the process has been made more organized and accelerated one. The reasons for this movement are, undoubtedly, innumerable and varied. The homogeneity of ethnicity, language and culture and the long shared history between the two countries were the immediate causes that helped the two peoples come closer to each other. No two countries are there in the world which are so closely related as India and Nepal. The movement of people from Nepal to India and *vice-versa* have taken place for many reasons such as—pilgrimage, trade, matrimonial alliances, roving saints and seers, and of course for economic opportunities. Common border, short distance, shared history and culture and geo-climatic affinities were other factors responsible for the movement of Nepalese into India. In an interview with Journalist Bholanath Chetterjee on 29th June 1979 late Bisheshwar Prasad Koirala, the first Prime Minister of Nepal said—

> "We Nepalese come to India for various reasons – namely, for medical treatment, for learning education. We have between us matrimonial relations and socio-cultural relations too. Besides, we are victims of common geo-climatic vagaries—If there is drought in India, there would be drought in Nepal too; if there is heavy rainfall in our hill region that would cause flood in India. In this way we are bundled together and hence, we have to either swim together or drown together."

The Earliest Link between India and Nepal

The old historical records reveal that India had a close political, religious and ethno-cultural relations with Nepal ever since prehistoric times. Geographically, politically and culturally Nepal remained an integral part of ancient India for a considerable period of time. The Allahabad pillar inscription of Samudragupta bears testimony to the fact that Kamrupa, Nepal, Kiritipura etc. were the vassal states of the Mauryan empire. References to Nepal are found in Kautilya's *Arthashastra*. The ancient Indo-Mongoloid race called the "Kiratas" which constitutes the larger portion of present Nepal's population were originally the aborigines of the North East India. According to noted historian, Suniti Kumar Chatterjee the indigenous tribes of Nepal, such as the Limbu, Rai, Tamang, Newar, Gurung, Magar etc. are all descendants of the ancient Kiratas. The testimonies extant in ancient Indian literatures like *Mahabharata, Ramayana* and *Puranas* leave no doubt about the existence of the Kiratas around eastern Himalayas, Assam, Bengal and north Bihar . The present indigenous tribes of the North-East, like—Garo, Boro, Kachari, Tripuri, Koch, Hajong etc. who live around the hills and plains of the Brahmaputra valley and speak Tibeto-Burman language, are also the descendants of the ancient Kiratas. According to *Tantric* literature, Ghataka the ruler of ancient Kamrupa with its capital at Pragjyotisha was a Kirata king who was defeated and slain by Naraka.[2] In *Mahabharata* there is a mention of Bhagadatta, the Mlechchha king of Kamrupa who raised one *Akshouhini* of soldiers consisting of Kiratas and Cinas from the Himalayas and took part in the epic war of Kurukshetra as an ally of Duryodhana. Janakpur, the birth place of Sita; Viratnagar, the capital of epic king Virat and Lumbini, the birth place of Lord Buddha are all in Nepal. Lord Buddha, though born in Nepal moved around different places in India and gave messages of middle path. Charumati, one of the daughters of Emperor Ashoka, married the prince of Nepal and settled down there. Thus, there is no end to such legends and stories which speak about the ancient bond of history, religion and culture between Nepal and India. The Pashupatinath temple of Kathmandu and the Vishwanath temple of Baranasi stand out as the ancient cultural link between India and Nepal which draw seers and sages from both countries ever since prehistoric times till today.

Movement during Medieval Period

Coming down to medieval period, we have credible records of the participation by Nepalese soldiers in Indian wars as written by eminent historians like Romila Thapar and D.R. Regmi in their monumental books. They have eluded to that on the death of Harsh Vardhan in 647 A.D. his throne had been usurped by one Arunaswa, a Gupta prince who misbehaved and molested a Chinese political ambassador named Wang Huen Tse who arrived India to pay tribute to Harsh Vardhan. The Chinese Ambassador, with a view to take revenge raised a strong army of 7000 Nepalese soldiers with the help of Bhaskarvarman, king of Kamrupa and inflicted befitting punishment to the usurper.

Reliable historical records are available about matrimonial alliances between the royal families of Nepal and those of Kamrupa. The daughter of Harsha Deva, the king of medieval Kamrupa was married to Jayadeva II, king of Nepal. The great Epic of *Ramayana* describes about the king of Janakpur of Nepal having given his beautiful daughter Sita on marriage to Shri Ramchandra, the prince of Ayodhya in India. Today Janakpur, the ancient capital of king Janaka is an important city of Tarai Nepal. One of the Lichchhavi kings named Sivadeva II of Nepal married the grand daughter of Adityasena, the accredited emperor of Magadha. In sixteenth century A.D., Biswa Singh, the founder of Koch kingdom, married Ratnakanti, the daughter of Nepal's king Ratnamalla. It is said that the Koch king brought from Nepal to his kingdom, a number of Brahmin priests, wood work artisans, stone and metal sculptors and a host of other workers. The royal matrimonial alliances, as referred to above, undoubtedly promoted lasting peace and friendship, augmented trade relations between two countries resulting in free movement of people into one another's country.

The deep faith and devotion of the Nepalese to the mythological places of worship is another factor which has ever drawn chains of devout Nepalese to different places of pilgrimage in India. Renowned places of worship like Haridwar, Vadrinath, Kedarnath, Kanshi, Goya, Kamakhya, Parashuram Kunda etc. have ever been the cherished destinations of the pious people of Nepal. The *Yogini Tantra* is an important compendium of pilgrimages which provides valuable guidance to *Hindu Sadhus* and *Sannyasis* of India and Nepal. Worship of Kamakhya Devi of Guwahati, is an irresistible urge of every Hindu Nepali. This is because according to Hindu mythological text when *Sati* Parvati died of vexation at the discourtesy meted out to her husband Siva by her father Daksha, Siva overcome by extreme grief wandered about the world carrying the dead body of his beloved on his head when various parts of *Sati's* body fell off in fifty-one different places. It is said that the Kamakhya Pith of Nilachal hill at Kamrupa and the Gujyeswari Pith of eastern Nepal where *Sati* Parvati's private parts fell assumed great religious importance. The Parashuram Kunda of Sadiya, Assam has been a significant place of worship for the Nepalese. It is a cherished desire of the pious Nepalese to take a dip in the Parashuram Kunda which, they believe, would wash off their sins and provide them salvation from earthly bondages. Large number of Nepalese including Royal and Lords families come to visit Parashuram Kunda and Kamakhya Dham of Assam. The king of Nepal is reported to have appointed a Lalmohariya Panda (priest) at Kamakhya Dham, Gawahati in 1881 for the purpose of performing *puja* exclusively for the devotees from Nepal. Ever since then the institution of Lalmohariya Panda has continued to exist at Kamakhya Dham, Guwahati by way of inheritance.

Similarly, the Himalayas have been the abode of Hindu Gods and Goddesses which have attracted the *Rishis*, *Sadhus* and *Sannyasis* of India ever since time immemorial. The Greeks found the Olympus mountain as the abode of their Gods, so also the Indians found in the wilderness of Himalayas, the existence of their gods and goddess. Both the Greeks and the Indians cooked up a maze of mythology and legends out of them and linked them up with their cultural history in a manner difficult to separate one from the other. For the Hindus, the great Himalaya holds a deep religious significance that conjures up a profound reverence and awe in their minds. Man has always seen in the nature and in her beauteous forms, an eternal truth, beauty and purpose in life—*satyam, shivam, sundaram*. The Himalaya is a holy place, an abode of Gods and Goddesses and at the same time, a sacred land of meditation and spiritual attainment for Indian saints and sages. The *Skand Purana* writes—

> "He who thinks of Himalaya, though he should not behold him, is greater than he who performs all worship in Kasi. In a hundred ages of Gods, I could not tell thee of the

glories of Himalaya. As the dew is dried up by the morning sun, so are the sins of mankind by the sight of Himalayas."

'Himalaya', a Sanskrit word meaning 'abode of snow'—"the very utterance of the word carries with it some inexplicable thrills – the thrills that pass from the mind to some deeper plane of consciousness" For a poet it is an object of high soaring imagination. Kalidas, the great classical poet, compared Himalayas with the great beam of a weighing balance that is meant for measuring the globe.

Migration during Modern Period

We have credible evidences of migration and settlement of Nepalese in the North-East during the last quarter of 16th century A.D. Dr. Tirthanath Sarma, former President of Asom Sahitya Sobha, alluded to that the Nepalese came to Assam during or little before the initial period of Neo-Vaishnavite movement. The establishment of *Satras*, (Vaishnavite monasteries), in Assam started during the middle of 16th century which was actively patronized by both Koch and the Ahom kings. Dr. Sarma revealed that during that time there was a person who was deeply involved in the process of setting up and development of *Satras*, and he was a Nepali Brahmin, Rati Kanta Upadhyaya by name. He was a devout follower of Srimanta Sankardev and he founded and acted as *Satradhikar* of two *Satras*, one at Tiyak of Sibsagar district and another at Nowgoan. These two *Satras* are known as Nepali *Satras* even to this day. Dr. Tirthanath Sarma quipped that a host of the Assamese Gokhains of today including the three time Secretary of the Asom Sahitya Sobha, Prof. Jyotindranath Goswami were the descendants of this Nepali Satradhikar of 16th century of which they are blissfully unaware.[3] It is very likely that a handful of Nepalese who came to Assam in those days might have gradually assimilated with the emerging Asamiya society, abandoned their past Nepali identity and became pure Assamese.

The large scale and organized migration of Nepalese into India, however, took place from early nineteenth century when the East India Company started recruiting Gorkha sepoys for Indian army immediately after the Treaty of Segawly in 1815. During the Indo-Nepal war the British, for the first time, realized the valor and fighting spirit of the Nepalese army under the command of Amarsingh Thapa and Vir Balabhadra Singh. The British General, David Ochterlony who commanded the British army in the Anglo-Nepal war was so much impressed by the bravery, toughness and skill of the Nepalese that he frankly declared during the war—"The Indian soldiers of the Company would never be able to hold their own against the Nepalese in their mountain fastness." Another British officer expressed his fear, saying—"In the war, dreadful to say, we have had number on our side, and the skill and bravery on the side of our enemy".[4] Thus, in the Gorkhas the British found the right material for Indian army which they were looking for, in the run-up of their colonial expansion. The British went headlong with the recruitment of Gorkhas and constituting separate units of Gorkha battalions, strictly officered by Englishmen with a view to keeping their martial quality unadulterated. Lieutenant Frederik Youngn hurriedly raised an irregular Gorkha Force of 4500 strong from the prisoner of war camps at Dehra-Dun, Nahan and Sirmoor. It was named as Sirmoor Rifles after the place name from which most of the men came, later to become the 2nd Gorkha Rifles. Another battalion was raised, simultaneously, before the operation against Malaun started to which General Ochterlony gave the name '*Nasiri*',—meaning friendly battalion so as to distinguish it from the bulk of enemy Gorkha soldiers. A few months later a third battalion was raised with the name Kumoun battalion by the men who had been defeated at Almora.

The First World War brought enormous pressure upon the British military manpower, requiring immediate expansion of Indian army to meet the situation. The Gorkhas who had already proved their mettle in successive wars in Burma and Afghanistan, were the right choice for the proposed reinforcement of Indian army. Chandra Shamsher Jang Bahadur Rana, the Prime Minister of Nepal, came out of his way to help the British Government with Gorkha recruits. He sent over 55,000 young Gorkhas to be part of the Indian army and another 18,000 Nepali soldiers to take-up garrison duties in India. The exodus of Nepalese young population from Nepal was so massive, it is said, that the agricultural operation of the small Himalayan kingdom almost came to a grinding halt during the period of war.

The Second World War witnessed yet another boost in Gorkha recruitment. Yuddha Shamsher Jang Bahadur Rana, the Prime Minister of Nepal responded to the war efforts magnificently with supply of Gorkha young men in tens of thousands. The Gorkha regiments of Indian army expanded all time high pushing the total strength from twenty battalions to fifty-five, composed of ten Gorkha Regiments. At the close of the war, obviously, all of them did not return to Nepal. In the First World War as many as 20,000 were killed while in the Second World War 32,640 were killed, maimed and found missing. Out of the rest who returned back, many of them settled down in India after retirement. Ever since 1864 the British Government of India started providing Regimental Homes for the families of Gorkha soldiers stationed at Dehradoon, Dharamshala, Almorah and Bakloh. Such steps were taken, ostensibly, with the intention that if the Gorkha Sepoys were allowed to bring their families to India, in the long run, part of the recruits needed could be obtained from their children and the Government would be less dependent on Nepal for future requirement of recruits. This scheme was carried out vigorously; Gorkha Regimental Homes were established all over India wherever Gorkha Rifles were stationed. Gorkha soldiers married in Nepal were liberally granted travel expenses for bringing their families, schools were established for education of their children, the future recruits to Indian army, and other amenities like hospitals, clubs, *dhobis, hajams* etc. were also provided. The retired Gorkhas who wanted to settle down in India with their families were allotted lands in the vicinity of the Regimental Centres. The retired Gorkhas were also given employment in civil and military offices as Peons, Choukidars, Darwans and Babarchis for earning their lively-hood. Soon, clusters of Gorkha communities grew-up around the Regimental Centres with temples, shops, bazaars and other infractructures. This is what may be called the genesis of the Nepalese diaspora in India.

Side-by-side with the recruitment to Indian army, large number of Gorkha young boys were also enlisted in other para-military forces like Cachar Levy, Assam Rifles, State Police Constabularies etc. ever since 1835, the year of raising Cachar Levy. The Gorkha boys with their loyalty, hardihood and courage were preferred to the local tribes like Assamese, Manipuris, Kukis and they were liberally recruited in all the semi-military organizations. From 1870 onwards the Gorkhas began to dominate the rolls of all Frontier Police of Assam, their percentage reaching fifty of the total strength.[5] This adversely affected the supply of Gorkha recruits to the regular Indian army and consequently, in 1887 the Government of India prohibited enlistment of Gorkhas of martial class (Magars, Gurungs Tamangs, and Limbus) in para-military forces. This, however, did not hinder the process of Gorkhas recruitment since other Gorkha boys belonging to non-martial class were forthcoming in plenty.

Towards the middle of the nineteenth century when a fairly large number of Gorkhas retired from Indian army as well as other para-military organizations had settled down in various parts of India like Dehradoon, Dharamshala, Darjeeling, Shillong, Kohima, Manipur, Aijawl, and the foothills of NEFA (North-East Frontier Agency) of Assam, a third stream of civilian migrants started flowing out of Nepal. These Nepali migrants settled down in the vicinity of the previously settled Gorkha communities, mostly in the Assam region and took to farming and cattle rearing. In Assam land for cultivation was plentiful and vast areas of grazing reserves for cattle rearing were opened by the Government on payment of grazing fee along the southern bank of Brahmaputra *char* land or *chapari*, (dereliction of river). The local tribal and Assamese people were slothful, self-content and unwilling to do hard work while the Government was acutely starving for revenue to meet the cost of administration and military establishment required for the consolidation of British rule in Assam and maintenance of peace in adjoining hill districts. Waste lands covered with thick jungles were surveyed, land revenue assessed and settlements were given liberally to Nepali immigrants. Major H. Vetch, Deputy Commissioner, Darrang wrote to J.M. Mills— "In a country so abounding with waste land as Assam and with so scanty a population, Government may well part with a portion on any terms if thereby settlers be induced to come into the country." Hard working and enterprising Nepali farmers who had never owned a shred of land in Nepal had the best of time to come down from

Nepal and grab the opportunity. They occupied waste land to their choice and working capacity, cleared the jungle and cultivated all varieties of crops locally grown there. The land area possessed by Nepali immigrants increased swiftly from 17,000 acres in 1913-14 to 28,000 acres in 1919-20.[6] In Darrang, Lakhimpur and Sibsagar districts sugarcane cultivation was the main crop grown by the Nepalis and large areas were brought under this cultivatioin. Even today some places in those areas are named as Kuiherbari (*Kuiher*=sugarcane, *bari*=cultivated field). The flow of Nepalese immigrants continued ever on and their population increased from 88,306 in 1931 to 3,49,116 in 1971, according to Assam Census Reports. Simultaneously, in 1939-40 the total land occupied and cultivated by Nepalese rose to 1,04,773 acres.[7]

Rearing of cattle and production of milk and milk products was absolute monopoly of the Nepalis who kept large *Bathans* (cattle farms) in Nagaland, Manipur, Khasi-Jaintia Hills, Garo Hills and almost all the districts of Assam. The official record of cattle farming business by the Nepalis in Assam goes back to 1892 when the number of tax paying buffloes was registered at 13,025 and the number of cows 462 for which grazing tax amounting to ₹ 6772 was paid. They are, however, believed to have started cattle rearing much earlier than that, at least from 1860s coinciding with the Gorkha presence in Assam Light Infantry.[8] The grazing fees were realized at the rate of 8 *annas* per head for buffalow and 4 *annas* per other horned cattle which were raised from time-to-time. As the time passed by, the revenue from this source swiftly increased from ₹ 1,83,000 in 1916-17 to ₹ 3,41,000 in 1920-21 and simultaneously, the number of cattle also increased substantially from 42,000 in 1915 to 86,325 in 1920.[9]

Migration became the way of life of the Nepalese, every one looking for a better life in foreign country. According to an estimate, at least twenty-five percent of Nepal's population was outside the country at any point of time.[10] Given the advantage of similar language, culture and tradition and free border crossing without passport and visa, India was the first preference for the Nepalese workers. Besides recruitment in Indian army and working as cattle rearers, or cultivators, they were ready to take up any works like, Chaprasi, choukidars, porters and even menial jobs in hotels and restaurants. In 1952-54 census of Nepal around 1,57,000 Nepali workers were found to be working in India.[11] This figure is supposed to be including the floating population who came to India for temporary stay.

Nepal's economy was considerably improved through the remittances received from the non-resident Nepalis. Within a period of five years the remittance shot up from ₹ 90.7 million in 1974-75 to ₹ 216.8 million in 1980-81. Then it tripled to ₹ 676.8 million by the close of 1980s. Surprising to say, Nepal, a small country, stood as the fifth largest among the remittance receiving countries of the world, by the end of 2007, with an annual remittance of 1.6 billion US Dollar.[12] India alone sent Rs.370.6 crores during the period 1999-2002. The pension disbursing system between India and Nepal was simplified and made easier after independence so that the ex-servicemen living in Nepal get their pension without much difficulty. Now, they need not have to travel all the way from remote villages to Indo-Nepal border Treasuries to receive pension. The Indian Embassy at Kathmandu conducts as many as 32 seasonal pension payment camps annually spreading interior areas from where the pensioners can draw their pension without much problem.

As the Government of Nepal enjoys a huge financial benefit out of the remittances received from her people working in foreign countries, logically it becomes a responsibility on the part of the Government of Nepal to look after the interest of those non-resident Nepalese. Unfortunately, the Government of Nepal, so far, does not seem to have done what is expected of it for the Nepalese living outside Nepal. The Nepalese nationals working in the Gulf countries are facing racial discrimination of the worst kind. In Saudi Arabia they are subjected to trafficking, ill-treatment and non-payment of wages. In United Arab Emirates there are more than 1.25 lakh Nepalese labour working in inhuman condition. In Qatar 70,000 Nepalese are ill-treated and cheated by their employers. The Nepalese Embassies there have not been helpful to them.

Large number of Nepalese working in the middle east countries very frequently fall prey to the attacks of terrorist organizations such as Al-Qaida, Muzahidin, Taliban etc. On 20th June, 2016 a bus carrying a group of Nepali Security Guards working for the Canadian Embassy in Kabul was blasted by the Talibans killing twenty-four of them at the spot. This wave of violence came in retaliation to the Washington announcement of the expansion air strikes against Taliban.

India is the largest Nepalese diaspora with more than six million Nepalis population. There exists a Nepalese Embassy in Delhi to keep liaison between the two Governments. But it has no programme or a policy of action for the welfare of the non-residential Nepalese. They are working all over Indian cities and towns as security guards, choukidars, hotel boys, domestic helps etc. in inhuman conditions facing racial discrimination, ill-treatment, trafficking and non-payment of salaries, but there is no one to help them out or to speak a word on their behalf. Large number of Nepali daughters are brought to Indian cities with the promise to provide jobs in beauty parlours and they are engaged in massage centres or forced into slave trade. Sex trafficking with Nepali women in India is rampant which has been causing great concern among the Nepalis living in India. The Government of Nepal should either take adequate measures for their safety, security and human dignity or stop exporting slavery to India and abroad.

The Indian Nepalis who are permanently settled in India are often victimized by the local insurgents thinking them to be the new comers from Nepal. They are frequently facing ethnic violence, arson, looting and even murder in the name of Nepalese nationals or foreigners. The political leaders from Northeast India have been demanding for the amendment of the Clause Seven of the Indo-Nepal Peace treaty of 1950 which allows Nepali nationals free passage into India. The Government of Nepal is well aware of the problem arising out of Nepali refugees thrown out from India and their rehabilitation. Shri Puspa Kamal Dahal (Prachanda) the former Prime Minister of Nepal, during his visit to India had raised this issue and proposed to review certain Clauses of the treaty which have become irritant to both sides. But this major issue relating to the safety and security of the Nepalis living permanently in the North-East India has been left pending till today.

Realising the importance of NRI's involvement in the process of India's development the Government of India has established a separate Ministry for looking into the affairs of the overseas Indians. The Government has also extended certain basic rights to the NRIs, such as, acquiring, holding and transferring immovable properties in India, admission of children in educational institutions of India under special NRI quota including medical and engineering colleges, IITs, IIMs etc. Since the year 2003 the Government of India has started organizing Pravasi Bharatiya Divas every year in New Delhi in which thousands of NRIs participate for discussions on common problems and their future course of action with regard to Indian relations. On this occasion eminent overseas Indians are honoured with Pravasi Bharatiya Samman (PBS) awards. So far the recipients of this award are—Sir, Aniroodh Jugnauth, the Prime Minister of Mausitius, Mr. Ujjal Dosangh, former Premier of British Columbia, Canada, Lord Novnit Dholakia, Member of House of Lords in 1977, Mr. S.S. Ramphal, Former Secretary General of Commonwealth, Mr. Bharat Jagdeo, President of the Republic of Guyana, Lord Meghnath Desai, Member of the House of Lords, Mr. Basdeo Pandey, former Prime Minister of Trinidad and many more. Undoubtedly, Dr. Ram Boran Yadav, President and Shri Paramananda Jha, Vice-President of Nepal are also eligible for this award as Pravasi Bharatiya.

On the 9th January, 2004, the Government of India took-up a major step by passing a Bill to grant Dual Citizenship to the people of Indian origin residing in sixteen countries. This will enable all the overseas Indians, who have migrated after January 26, 1950 and have taken the citizenship of the countries of their domicile, to adopt Indian citizenship subject to the laws prevailing in their adopted countries. They will be able to enjoy in India, all the privileges of an Indian citizen except the right of voting. Compared to all these privileges, the Government of Nepal, so far, has done very little to those living outside Nepal although Nepalese diaspora, especially in India, is considerably large and time honoured. Considering the interdependence and neighbourly good relationship existing between India and Nepal it is only desirable that there is some kind of arrangement between the two Governments which may provide their people living in either countries some impetus to keep in touch with the place of their origin.

As the labour industry of Nepal expanded to international level, Nepal's economy was considerably improved through the remittances received from the non-resident Nepalis. Within a period of five, years the remittance shot-up from ₹ 90.7 million in 1974-75 to ₹ 216.8 million in 1980-81. Then it tripled to ₹ 676.8 million by the close of 1980s. Surprising to say, Nepal, a small country, stood as the fifth largest among the remittance receiving countries of the world, by the end of 2007, with an annual remittance of 1.6 Billion US Dollar.[13] India alone sent ₹ 370.6 crores during the period 1999-2002. The pension disbursing system between India and Nepal was simplified and made easier after independence so that the ex-servicemen living in Nepal get their pension without much difficulty. Now, they need not have to travel all the way from remote villages to Indo-Nepal border Treasuries to receive pension. The Indian Embassy at Kathmandu conducts as many as 32 seasonal pension payment camps annually spreading interior areas from where the pensioners can draw their pension without much problem.

Notes

1. S. Chandrashekharan (2007), "Indians Abroad", in *Manorama,* p. 582.
2. E.A. Gait, *A History of Assam.*
3. Bisnulal Upadhyaya (2004), *Khan Mihali* (Assamese), p. 36.
4. K.K. Muktan (2002), *The Legendary Gorkhas*, Spectrum Publications, Guwahiti, p. 45.
5. K.K. Muktan, *op. cit.*, Guwahati.
6. *Report on the Land Revenue Administration of Assam*, 1919-1920.
7. *Report on the Land Revenue Administration of Assam*, Valley Division, 1939-40.
8. *Progress Report on Forest Administration*, 1892-93.
9. Tejimala Gurung – Human Movement and the Colonial State : The Nepalis of the North-East India under British Empire, in *The Nepalis in North-East India*, Ed. A.C. Sinha and T.B. Subba, 2003, New Delhi: Indus Publications.
10. Sujeev Shakya (2009), *Unleashing Nepal*, New Delhi: Penguin Books Ltd., p. 156.
11. *Ibid.*
12. *Ibid.*
13. *Ibid.*, p. 161.

13

Indian Nepalese Participation in the Freedom Movement of India

In the wake of Mahatma Gandhi's freedom movement during 1920s when the mass people of India joined hands together the Indian Nepalis living in different parts of the country could not remain aloof. Initially, the elite section of the Nepalis from Darjeeling, Calcutta, Banaras and Dehradun spearheaded the cause of nationalist movement through separate organizations such as—the Hillmen Association of Darjeeling formed in 1921, the Gorkha Association of Calcutta formed in 1926 and the All India Gorkha League established in 1921 at Dehradun. Through the platforms of these organizations the leaders of Indian Nepalis took the cudgels of arousing national awareness among them. Side by side with the activities of these socio-political organizations the press also took its own role to educate people by publication of various news magazines and periodicals in Nepali language. The pioneers among them were the *Gorkha Sathi* from Calcutta (1911), the *Gorkhali* and *Janma-bhumi* from Banaras (1914 and 1921 respectively), the Tarun Gorkha from Dehradun (1927). The Nepali periodicals, besides writing on social and cultural aspects, published articles on Mahatma Gandhi's doctrine of non-violence and non-co-operation and *Swadeshi* movement and instilled feeling of nationalism among the Gorkhas. The British government was, however, extremely careful to see that the seed of nationalism did not grow among the Indian Gorkhas, who produced the Gorkha recruits for Indian army. British wanted that the Gorkha young boys should not be adulterated by political ideologies which might erode their loyalty to the Crown and therefore, they kept strict vigilance on them. One Nepali periodical named *Gorkhali* was proscribed by Government of India in 1922 under Indian Vernacular Press Act, 1910 on the suspicion that it disseminated nationalist ideas among the Indian Nepalis. Another Nepali news- magazine was ordered to deposit security for maintenance of good behaviour under the same Press Act, as a result of which it ceased to publish at all. Strict confidential instructions were issued by the Government of India, from time to time, to all Deputy Commissioners and Superintendents of Police to keep close watch on the political activities of Indian Nepalis and to prevent them from indulging in politics Government, clandestine political activities continued to be carried out by elite Nepali young men infiltrating political ideas into the areas of Nepalis concentration. The echoes of Mahatma Gandhi's clarion call for non-co-operation movement, found their ways into the hills and plains of India. In Darjeeling a good number of Nepalis joined the Indian National Congress and took active part in *Satyagraha* movement under the guidance of Nepali leaders like Dal Bahadur Giri, Jonbir Sapkota and Prithiman Lama. Mahatma Gandhi's visit to Darjeeling in 1921 brought about a new enthusiasm among the Nepalis who met him personally and became influenced by him (S.K. Singh, *Tribal Movement in India*, p. 342). A political leader Bhagat Bir Tamang was arrested and severely beaten by police for his active participation in the non-co-operation movement and put in prison where he died in 1923. He was the first political martyr among the Nepalis in India.

In Calcutta, the hub of the Revolutionary group of national activists, Nepali youths coming from various parts of India and Nepal for study were inspired by the firebrand leaders like Aurobindo Ghose, Bhupendranath Dutta, Rash Behari Bose, Prafulla Chaki etc. who wanted to wrest freedom from the hands of the British by violent means. They believed in armed conflict against the British Government with the help of Indian soldiers working the Indian army. For this purpose a group of Gorkhas under the leadership of Khadak Bahadur Bist, a law student of Calcutta University and General Secretary of Calcutta Gorkha League, had established secret nexus with army cantonment to enlist support of Gorkha soldiers. In June 1930 while engaged in this clandestine work Khadak Bahadur and Dhanapati Singh a Gorkha soldier were arrested and jailed. Later, Dhanapati Singh was dismissed from his military service as an exemplary punishment. Another Gorkha soldier Prithiman Thapa deserted his service and joined the revolutionary group of Bengal and continued to carry on secret political activities. Khadak Bahadur Bist was arrested in May 1930 for attempting to loot the Government salt depot at Dharsana together with 13 others, 150 miles from Bombay and was imprisoned at Sabarmati jail with his thirteen Nepali associates. After his release from Sabarmati jail he continued his political activities of secretly enticing Gorkha soldiers for revolutionary works. Khadak Bahadur Bist was a close associate of Sachindra Sanyal, revolutionary leader of Bengal who mentioned in his autobiography that contacts were established with the Indian soldiers of the Army Cantonments of North India from where many Gorkha soldiers agreed to join the revolutionary party. Later on, Khadak Bahadur was once again arrested and the police recovered from his possession many incriminating documents including a list of Gorkha soldiers willing to join freedom movement. Since 1943 Khadak Bahadur Bist was found missing from his home and since that time he has never been seen nor his where about is known. His missing from this country is still a mystery.

The Indian Nepalis were also inspired by the political leaders of Nepal who crossed over to India for political asylum during their anti-Rana activities of 1920s. One Krishna Prasad Koirala came to settle in Benaras after he was exiled by the Rana Government. Together with him came his two sons – Matrika Prasad Koirala and Biseswar Prasad Koirala who were to become the two leading protagonists in Nepalese politics in course of time. In 1950s after the autocratic Rana Government was overthrown both the brothers were elected as the Prime Ministers of Nepal one after another. In 1920-21 Krishna Prasad Koirala together with Ramkrishnalal Shrestha, Ram Chandra Adhikari and many other Gorkhas of Benaras actively participated in *Swadeshi* movement and burnt foreign clothes. It was said that the heap of the imported garments burnt by the Gorkhas at Maidagil ground of Benaras was the biggest of all the heaps of cloths burnt by other communities (B.L. Upadhyaya, 2004, *Khanmihali*, p. 126). At that time Matrika

Prasad and Bisheshwar Prasad were students of High English school and they were shifted to Rashtriya Vidyalaya so as to comply with the call of the *Swadeshi* movement which decided to boycott English language, Foreign goods, honorary offices under the Government and membership of Legislative Council (L.P. Sarma, *Indian National Movement*, p. 98). Ramkrishnalal Shrestha was the President of the Benaras City Congress and Krishna Prasad Koirala and other Gorkhas of Benaras were members.

Later on Krishna Prasad Koirala and his family moved to Pratapgarh in the district of Bhagalpur in Bihar and settled down there. There he continued his political career and became the member of the Bhagalpur district Congress Committee and the President of the Pratapgarh Thana Congress Committee. As the time passed, his son Matrika Prasad Koirala became an active member of the Indian National Congress. In 1926 he came to Assam to attend the All India Congress Conference held at Pandu as a delegate. He became the General Secretary of Patna District Congress Committee and also held the office of the Joint Secretary of Bihar Provincial Committee for launching movement against the Simon Commission. The Congress had decided to boycott the Simon Commission in 1927 which was constituted by the British government with seven members of the British Parliament with Sir John Simon as its Chairman, all white members, without a single member from India. It was for this reason that the Congress leaders decided to boycott the Simon Commission.

His brother, Bisheshwar Prasad Koirala also took active part in Indian politics and suffered imprisonment for four years at different jails in India. He met Dr. Rajendra Prasad (Later the President of India) as a co-prisoner at Bankipur jail in 1930 and later on he was shifted to Hazaribag jail where he met Jagjivan Ram, who became the Defence Minister and Deputy Prime Minister of India after India became independent in Janta Party Government. During these days of political turmoil he established very intimate relations with the top socialist leaders of India like Jaiprakash Narayan, Dr. Ram Manohar Lohia, Acharya Kripalini etc. His father, Ram Krishna Koirala at his old age returned back to Nepal only to be arrested on the charge of harboring Indian political leaders who fled to Nepal during Quit India movement in 1942.

He was put behind the bars where he breathed his last. At this time Bisheshwar Prasad Koirala was in Hazaribag jail in India and was not allowed to visit his bereaved mother and family in Nepal.

The freedom movement of India proved as a training ground for the Nepalese leaders to learn politics against the autocratic Rana rulers in Nepal. They not only learnt the techniques of political movement from the veteran leaders of India like Mahatma Gandhi, Jaiprakash Narayan, Dr. Ram Manohar Lohia etc., but also continued to receive constant guidance and inspirations from them during the civil movement in Nepal. To cite an instance, in 1935 a group of elite Nepalese young men, under the leadership of Pandit Sukraraj Shastri formed an association named Nepali Praja Parishad. A delegation of this organisation consisting of Sukraraj Shastri, Gangalal and Dharma Bhakta met Mahatma Gandhi and Dr. Ram Manohar Lohia in India and after receiving necessary guidance and blessings from Mahatma Gandhi they returned back to Nepal. But no sooner had they set their feet on the soil of Nepal than they were arrested and put in jail by the Nepalese Government. The intelligence network of the Nepalese Government was in close liaison with its counterpart in the Government of British India which passed quick information about the whereabouts of these Nepalese leaders. By the first October,1940, Narashamsher Rana, the Director-General of Police arrested nearly 500 Nepalese insurgents under the charges of conspiracy for waging war against the Rana Government and put them into the prison cell. After a brief trial Yudh Shamsher Rana, the Prime Minister of Nepal pronounced the final judgement of the case in the *Singha Darbar* before a jam-packed audience which included top Civil and Military officials. According to the judgement order : Sukraraj Shastri, Dasarath Chand, Dharma Bhakta, Gangalal and Subba Puran Chandra were found guilty of treason and conspiracy against the Government and awarded death sentences with appropriation of their properties; Tek Prasad Upadhyaya, Ram Hari and Sankar Prasad Sarma were awarded life imprisonment, appropriation of properties and ex-communication. The other twenty-six accused persons were awarded imprisonment of various lengths and severities while the rest of the arrested persons were acquitted. This historic event sent the message of shock and terror down the hills and valleys of Nepal. After a period of two months, on the fateful day came of 30th January, 1941,—early morning, the above named five gallant patriots of Nepal were executed in open public view. With this ended the anti-Rana movement of Nepal never to resurrect again in the soil of the Himalayan kingdom for a considerable time. This historic day of 30th January,1941 will be remembered forever by the people of Nepal as a *Black Day* in the annals of democratic movement in Nepal.

The exemplary role played by the Nepalese political leaders in the freedom movement of India had a direct impact on the Indian Gorkhas. The clarion call of *Swadashi* movement given by Swami Dayananda Saraswati and the *Satyagraha* movement of Mahatma Gandhi reached the nooks and corners of the country. The Nepalis who had been living for generations in the hills and plains of the North-East responded magnificently to the call and joined hands together with other local Indians. Their real political movement was, however, triggered by an incident that took place in 1920 when, on one fateful day a group of Forest officials, accompanied by armed police arrived at the scene, and set fire on the cattle sheds and dwelling houses of Nepali graziers of Kajiranga numbering hundred and one families. Within minutes, their dwelling houses and cattle sheds, including their house-hold goods and wearing apparels turned into heaps of ashes. No prior notice was served nor a reasonable time was allowed to them to salvage their household goods. These Nepali graziers had been living there peacefully for more than fifty years paying grazing fees to the Government at stipulated rates per head of cattle. Such an unjust and inhuman act of the British Government mortally hurt the sentiment of the loyal and peaceful Gorkhas. They became disillusioned and rebellious and looked for a course of action that would provide them with collective security. Finally, they decided to come under the banner of the political organization under the leadership of Babu Chhabilal Upadhyaya, Chandranath Sarma, Ramlal Upadhyaya, Bogiram Saikia, Hari Prasad Upadhyaya etc.

A historic meeting of the 'Assam Association' held at Jorhat on 17th April, 1921 marked the turning point of the political history of Assam. The meeting was presided over by Babu Chhabilal Upadhyaya which adopted historic decision to merge the 'Assam

Association' with All India Congress Committee and to launch the non-cooperation movement of Mahatma Gandhi in a stronger and wider parameter. The meeting also decided to bring the Nepalis of Assam under the fold of the Congress and to take-up the issue of Kajiranga eviction of graziers with the Government of Assam. The Nepalis joined the National Congress under the leadership of Babu Chhabilal Upadhyaya, and Assamese leaders like Tarunram Phukan, Nabin Chandra Bardoloi, Dr. Hem Chandra Baruah, Amiya Kumar Das, Kuladhar Chaliha, Gopinath Bordoloi etc.

The Nepalis actively took part in the non-cooperation movement of 1921 protesting against the repressive measures taken by government and the heinous killing of innocent people at Jalianwalla Bagh on 13 April,1919. They boycotted foreign clothes, used home woven clothes, helped collection of Tilak Swaraj Fund, boycott of offices, schools and colleges. Babu Chhabilal Upadhyaya was a real Gandhian leader with *Khadi kurta* and knee-length *dhoti*. He took the leadership of the Nepali community of Assam during non-co-operation movement of Mahatma Gandhi in 1921. He was arrested and imprisoned in Tezpur jail for six months for taking part in non-co-operation movement. His younger brother, Hari Prasad Upadhyaya was also imprisoned for the same offence for three months.

Dalbir Singh Lohar was another Nepali leader from Dibrugarh, Assam who started his political career as Congress volunteer as early as he was a school student. In 1930 he suffered imprisonment for three months for joining the agitation against the Cunninghum Circular, a political issue raised by the National Congress. During the period of Civil Disobedience movement in 1930 he was arrested for the second time and was detained in Dibrugarh jail for two months. Dalbir Singh Lohar was known for his close association with Labour Union as its leader. He was the President of the Dibrugarh Circle Tea Workers' Union and also the Vice-President of the Assam Branch of the Indian National Trade Union Congress (INTUC). He also held the responsible office of the All Assam State Transport Workers' Association. He was elected as member of the Assam Legislative Assembly from Soikhowa constituency of Dibrugarh district during the first general election held in 1952.

Bhakta Bahadur Pradhan of Dibrugarh joined Congress in 1934. He was an active leader of the Assam Oil Company Labour Union. He met Jawaharlal Nehru for the first time when he visited Dibrugarh and was greatly influenced by his speech, delivered at the Jubilee Field, Dibrugarh. He lost his service as Motor Mechanic and Fitter in the Assam Oil Company for his involvement in the Labour Union strike. In December,1940 Bhakta Bahadur Pradhan was expelled from Assam by an order of the Governor of Assam. He was ordered to leave Assam within 72 hours and was prohibited from entering the districts of Lakhimpur, Sibsagar, Darrang and Kamrup under sub-rule (1) Clause (C) of Rule 26 of the Defence of India Rules. This was done "with a view to preventing him from acting in a manner prejudicial to the defence of British India and maintenance of public order." In 1942 he was imprisoned at Dibrugarh jail for one year for taking part in the freedom movement. After India became independent he was awarded "*Tamrapatra*" by the Chief Minister of Assam as a token of gratitude for the sacrifice made by him in bringing freedom to India.

During Quit India Movement of 1942 all the top leaders of India were arrested including Mahatma Gandhi and members of the Congress Working Committee. The Indian National Congress was declared an illegal organization. But the people took-up the challenge. Through out the length and breadth of the country a mass movement was organized boycotting government offices, closing schools and colleges and taking out demonstrations demanding the British to quit India. The Nepalis of Assam participated in the movement in large number. They resorted to *hartals*, processions and mass meetings. The Government banned them all and imposed restriction of assembly of more than five persons under Section of 144 Civil Procedure Code. The public meetings, and processions were forcibly dispersed, and *lathi* charged. The Nepalis held meetings defying the restriction as a result of which they suffered imprisonment in different jails of Assam. Among those who were imprisoned were, Babu Chhabilal Upadhyaya, Dalbir Singh Lohar, Bhakta Bahadur Pradhan, Ramlal Upadhyaya, Bishnulal Upadhyaya, Jainarayan Upadhyaya, Kashinath Luitel, Homnath Guragain etc. More than three hundred young Gorkha volunteers were recruited in '*Santisena*' and '*Mrityu*

Bahini' who joined processions leading to police stations shouting slogans like, *'Bande Mataram', 'Inqilab Jindabad', 'Karenge yaa Marenge'* etc. On many occasions the police prevented the processionists from entering into police station compound, snatched National Congress Flags and *lathi*-charged on the crowd and sometimes opened fires. In one such event at Gohapur (Assam) a minor school girl named Kanaklata died out of police firing.

Dehradun, the hive of enlightened Gorkha ex-servicemen, was quick to be involved into the freedom movement of India from its very early stage. Being the part of erstwhile Nepalese territory till the Treaty of Sigouli (1816), Dehradun contained a good number of original Nepalese from Terai besides the ex-servicemen of British creation. At a later stage, some non-privileged Rana families migrated to Dehradun and around the neighbouring districts in order to settle down in business. From the early beginning of the twentieth century the Nepalis of Dehradun evinced keen interest in the Arya Samaj movement led by Swami Dayananda Saraswati whose doctrine of *Swaraja, Swabhasa* and *Swadharma* attracted the Nepalis. This concept of *Swaraja* which means 'Self-rule' was converted into the political theme later on by C.R. Das and Pt. Motilal Nehru who formed another political party called Congress-Khilafat Swaraj Party. In 1924 when Gandhiji was released from imprisonment he gave his silent consent to the working of the Swarajists and both parties worked together side by side with the common goal of India's freedom.

Madan Singh Gorkha was the first person to spearhead the cause of Arya Samaj movement who played a leading role as the Secretary and later as President of Dehradun Arya Samaj from 1902 to 1907. Through this organization they came under the influence of great National leader like Lala Lajpat Rai who sowed the seed of socio-religious and political awarness among the Nepalis of Dehradun. In 1921 they formed all India Gorkha league which was initially led and dominated by Gorkha ex-servicemen and in course of time the organization covered the whole of India. Thakur Chandan Singh, the firebrand President of the Gorkha League was an ex-serviceman who took part in the First World War and earned laurels for bravery. He belonged to Class 'C' of non-privileged Rana family and was the son-in-law of Khadak

Shamsher, the brother of Chandra Shamsher, the Prime Minister of Nepal. More specifically, Gorkha League had majority of its members from among the 11000 and odd disgruntled ex-army personnel whose names were struck off from the army roll as a measure of peace time retrenchment after the end of the First World War and who bore deep grudge against the British government. They voiced their demands, among other, were to refrain from using the Gorkha soldiers in suppressing the Indian freedom movement and to stop classifying Gorkha soldiers into separate Gorkha Battalions on the basis of caste. It may be noted that the British Government followed the policy of classifying Gorkha soldiers into matrial and non-martial groups and organizing separate Gorkha battalions based on castes with a view to breed disunity and ill-feeling among them. This act of the British government was not acceptable to the Gorkha soldiers at large.

Gopal Singh Thapa a retired personnel of the Survey of India and a dedicated social worker of Dehradun, sacrificed everything of his life in the freedom movement. He was imprisoned several times and his pension on which his family depended was confiscated by the British Government. He established "*Tapovan*" at Nalapani with all his heart and soul which is presently under the charge of the Arya Samaj. Another staunch Congress worker Dhruba Singh Thapa suffered severe police atrocities, got his house and property confiscated, lost his wife while in prison and after his release from jail, he spent the rest of his life in abject poverty sharing a room in the Congress office.

In 1930s when the Civil Disobedience movement launched by Mahatma Gandhi swept the country the Nepalis of Dehradun, Nalapani and Delhi rose to the occasion and rallied under the banner of the Indian National Congress. Nepali leaders like Dhruba Singh Thapa, Riths Singh, Hukum Singh, Dal Bahadur Thapa, Lalbir Newar etc. Other with other Gorkha men, women and children held picketings and demonstrations and courted arrest. While in prison, living together with Pandit Nehru they were so much influenced that after their release from jail they changed the name of their village from Grant No. 8 to Nehrugram as a mark of their love and esteem to their great leader. During mass picketing of Government offices and Government institutions in Delhi by

Mahatma Gandhi in 1930 Khadga Bahadur Bist and Dhruba Singh Thapa together with thirty other Nepali associates suffered imprisonment. Again in the historic Dharapani movement fifty numbers of Nepalis were arrested and lodged in jail.

References

Sarma, L.P., *Indian National Movement*, p. 98.
Singh, S.K., *Tribal Movement in India*, p. 342.
Upadhyaya, B.L. (2004), *Khanmihali*, p. 126.

14
Nepal Earthquake and India's Help

April 25, 2015 will be remembered as the Blackest Day in the history of Nepal. On this day at 11:15 AM, an earthquake of the magnitude of 7.8 Richter scale struck Nepal which killed 8669 people, destroyed lakhs of dwelling houses and rendered millions of people homeless. This earthquake was said to be the worst of its kind since the great earthquake of 1934 and its aftershocks were counted more than 250 times stretching for months together and adding to its toll an appalling death and destruction. The Indian Meteorological Department (IMD) evaluated its magnitude to be 7.9 Richter scale while the United States Geological Survey (USGS) too, first placed it at 7.9, but later corrected to be 7.8 Richter scale. Though the tremor recorded was two decimal points less than what makes it a "great earthquake", its impact was devastating because it was a shallow earthquake with a depth of 15 km. only. The tremor was felt in most parts of northern India, Bangladesh, Tibet and Pakistan. A number of houses were destroyed and many people were killed in northern Bihar adjoining areas with Nepal. In Nepal the intensity was so great and extensive that it levelled down entire villages in both the upper mountain areas on the north and the Terai regions on the south. At Barpak village which was the epicentre of the quake all the 1200 houses were totally erased by the quake. In Kathmandu regions, hundreds of historical buildings, monuments and heritage sites were turned into rubbles. It looked as if the very clock of Nepalese civilization was pushed back to more than a couple of centuries. The age old *pagoda* temples in the *Darbar* Square of the Malla Kings with all their grandeur and exquisite artistic workmanship were left in ruins by the unprecedented tremors. Gone was the renowned wooden temple of Kasthmandapa that gave Kathmandu its name. The Hanuman Dhoka Darbar Square at Kathmandu, the temple palaces in Patan and Bhaktapur were all raged down to earth making them completely untraceable. It was, however, a miracle that the temple of Pashupatinath remained unaffected; not a single wall was cracked. It may be due to some divine power or the expertise of ancient architecture. The iconic nine-storey Dharhara Tower constructed by Bhimsen Thapa, the legendary Nepalese Army General, crumbled down to ground burying alive a number of tourists who had been climbing on it. This monument was erected as a Victory Tower of the Gorkhas against the British during Anglo-Nepal War (1814-16). In the great earthquake of 1934 this tower had partly collapsed and was rebuilt by the Government of Nepal to mark the bravery of the Nepalese army in the battle of Nalapani in which the British General Gillespie was killed. In fact, this was the glorious period in the Nepalese history when the Gorkhas *fouj* of Prithvinarayan Shah rose to the zenith in military strength and succeeded in extending their kingdom from the river Mechi on the east to the river Kali on the west.

In the mass destruction of the ancient buildings and monuments the very history of medieval Nepal was completely obliterated. The impact of the quake was so huge that the Mount Everest shifted three centimeters south-west by the tremor of 7.8 Richter scale. It did not, however, change the height of the world's tallest peak of some 29,000 feet. There was an extensive damage caused to the topography of the whole mountain terrain. Massive destructions were caused to the hydro-electrical installations, roads and bridges, irrigation dams, hotels and tourist spots which caused an irreparable damage to the basic economic infrastructure of Nepal. No less than anything else was the deep seated fear psychosis, paranoia and a sense of total hopelessness that prevailed in the minds of the people at large. They became totally frustrated with the Government and their faith on the corrupt politicians almost exhausted. Recovery of Nepal from this colossal break down will, of course, be extremely painful and difficult if not impossible and will take a long time which might stretch to half a century or more. The work of rehabilitation of the homeless people is, however, urgent in view of the fast approaching monsoon within the next one month.

Indian Help in Rescue and Relief Works

Nepal was in desperate need of help from the neighbour countries. The work of rescuing the people trapped in the debris, giving medical help to the injured and providing food and shelter to the homeless was so colossal that it was well-nigh impossible for Nepal alone to cope with it. India came out of its way to Nepal's rescue. Shri Narendra Modi, the Prime Minister of India, ordered immediate rushing of NDRF (National Disaster Relief Force) teams to Nepal with food, medicine and all necessary relief materials. He tweeted—"Nepal's pain is our pain", India is ready to "wipe out the tears of every Nepali—and hold their hands and stand with them". The Operation Maitri got under way—Indian army personnel swung into action. Within a matter of four hours they landed in Kathmandu with helicopters loaded with food, medicine and other relief materials and started rescue operation. Some one from India cracked a joke—Sushil Koirala, Prime Minister of Nepal came to know of the earthquake only from Narendra Modi. The Indian Embassy in Kathmandu too buzzed into action—"Within 7 hours of the earthquake", the Embassy spoke to media, "7000 officers of the NDRF were despatched to Nepal to rescue the earthquake victims". There were also medical teams with doctors and medicine deputed to Nepal who reached the affected areas in time. They started rescue and relief operation in tandem with local voluntary organizations like—Clubs and civil volunteers of Nepal. The Indian army teams were mostly consisted of the Gorkha regiments who had the extra advantage of language and familiarity with the terrain that helped them function more efficiently in their rescue operation and in dealing with the victims. The army also requisitioned the services of 30,000 Gorkha Ex-servicemen residing in Nepal. Army field hospitals were established at the convenient places where injured and sick victims were brought from villages by army choppers were treated. The Indian pilots managed to reach helicopters to interior places with great courage and skill and dropped food packets, blankets, medicines and camp materials. Roads were blocked by land-slides at most places and the bridges were destroyed. Major General, J.S. Sandhu said—Army Engineering teams joined in clearing debris in the areas such as

Bhaktapur and Borpak so that relief materials could be moved to affected places. They cleared roads buried in rubbles and evacuated people from building on the verge of collapse. As many as forty helicopters of the Indian Air Force were deployed for three weeks in the rescue and relief operation in Nepal.

Besides India there were other countries also who sent contingents for rescue works, but India's rescue teams and consignment of relief materials were the largest of all. The U.N. Officials who supervised the work in the field lauded India and China's operations to be the best. Indian Government also detailed on duty the Power Grid Corporation of India and the Indian Oil Corporation who pitched their camps in Nepal. The India Government run Telecommunication Organization, BSNL (Bharat Sanchar Nigam Limited) announced that all inter-state telephone calls would be charged at local rates so as to facilitate communication between the earthquake affected people of Nepal with the rest of the world at concessional rates. The Indian External Affairs Ministry set-up 24 Control Rooms to help out Indians who were stranded in Nepal or fell victim to earthquake for their relief and rescue through Indian Embassy at Kathmandu.

The country of Nepal, as we all know, had just survived from a decade long bloody civil war and had been gradually progressing towards the formation of a federal democratic government after concluding in 2007 a Seven-Party alliance with the combating Maoist insurgents. The work of preparation and adoption of a constitution acceptable to all was passing through a rough weather for quite some time as a few political parties were strongly dissenting on certain major issues. At such inopportune time, the strike by devastating earthquake was not only unfortunate but also shocking on the part of Nepal.

After completion of relief operation, the main work of reconstruction and rehabilitation of Nepal would be a tremendous task which would be a long time programme of the Government of Nepal. The task would, undoubtedly, involve huge amount of men, materials and money that would be an uphill task for a country like Nepal. More than 3.5 million people were estimated to be rehabilitated and provided food and other necessities of life in order to provide monetary help to Nepal in her reconstruction programme a global meeting was organized at Kathmandu on 25th June, 2015 at the behest of the United Nations. This meeting was attended by 260 countries of the world who expressed their sympathy and solidarity with Nepal and promised to advanced monetary helps for the re-building up of damaged housing infrastructure of Nepal. Smt. Sushma Swaraj, India's Minister for External Affairs attended the meeting and promised ₹ 100 Crore monetary help from India. Mr. Sushil Koirala, Prime Minister of Nepal expressed deep gratitude and thanks to the world community for the valuable help and co-operation advanced to his country at her distress.

For India, Nepal has a special gratitude and thanks. A few words need be spoken in order to explain this statement. The recent help and co-operation given by Indian Government to Nepal is nothing new considering their close relationship and the history of give and take. India and Nepal, the two ancient countries, have been trailing a long and unique relationship—a relationship of shared history, language, culture; a bond of sacrifice of lives for each others freedom, sovereignty and integrity. Both the countries suffered a prolonged political domination by foreign country—India was under the British rule while Nepal was ruled by autocratic Ranas. The people of both the countries fought hard for freedom hand in hand. During the freedom struggle of India, a group of young Nepali political leaders came to India, took active part in Indian freedom movement and suffered imprisonment. India too played a significant role in helping Nepal out of the autocratic rule of the Ranas. This reciprocal bond of friendship and co-operation has ever continued and in the recent past after the establishment of popular Government in Nepal, the political ties between the two countries have become even deeper and broader—politically, socially and economically. Thus, Mr. Modi's good gesture and all out help to Nepal during the recent earthquake is time honoured, reciprocal and a step in the right direction.

A Lesson to Learn

The lesson that the earthquake has left behind must be learnt by every nation, especially India with more than 58.6 per cent of the country's landmass being very prone to earthquake (according to *Vulnerability Atlas of India, 2006*). Over the last couple of decades India has faced the brunt of many high intensity earthquakes which have taken huge toll of human lives and destroyed properties. To cite a few instances—the Latur earthquake of 1993 in Marathwada region of Maharashtra that claimed 7,928 lives and injured 30,000 people, the Gujarat earthquake of 2001 which took 13,805 lives and 6.3 million affected and the Sikkim earthquake of 2011 which killed and rendered homeless many people. In absence of earthquake management plans, the disaster becomes a man made tragedy. There is a saying—earthquake does not kill but buildings do. And men are responsible for constructing multi-storied buildings, unplanned and mushroom growth of cities and towns. Rules and bye-laws like National Building Code of India, 2005 were formulated, the Disaster Management Act, 2005 was passed. But these statutes have remained mostly in papers, no proper implementation of the laws and rules have been done. We have never been serious about anything even though they have vital bearing in our lives. As development takes place industries grow, which in its turn, help growth of urban areas. Unplanned urbanization, illegal construction of high-rise buildings, rampant growth of slums, environmental degradation, climate change all combined together to build-up a potential human tragedy. Earthquake, flood, fire havoc and epidemic strike without warning. One disaster leads to another kind of disaster and, more often than not, the aftermath turns to be more devastative than the original disaster. The densely populated pockets of Indian cities are the veritable human traps which have no open space where people can take shelter in case of earthquake. The Bureau of Indian Standards (BIS), after consultation with the scientific research reports of various agencies and the data supplied by the Meteorological Department of India has divided India into four seismic zones—Zone II, III, IV and Zone V. Out of these zones, Zone V is rated as the most seismically active zone, and Zone II the least active. The Zone V comprises the entire North East region, parts of Jammu & Kashmir. But, unfortunately, the State Governments of these respective zones do not seem to have come up with adequate disaster management measures to minimize human casualties.

Japan and New Zealand are the two most earthquake prone countries where building codes are strictly enforced and each building is rated according to its earthquake-resistance capability. In India every State Government should formulate building bye-laws according to the earthquake prone zone prepared by the Bureau of Indian Standard (BIS) and strictly implement them. The Government and the people should be more serious in adopting preventive measures. Precaution is the best policy; if the lesson from the past human tragedies are seriously taken and the steps to avert these situations are strictly adhered to we can surely avert earthquake tragedies to a great extent in the days to come.

Epilogue

India and Nepal have a long history of trance-migration and settlement of their peoples into each other's country involving very large population. This to-and-fro movement of human population between India and Nepal has been primarily motivated by geographical proximity, similarity of language, cultural and religious affinities and the last but not least, better job opportunities. The Indo-Nepal Treaty of Peace and Friendship, 1950 has been the legal provision which has facilitated the nationals of the two countries to enter into each other's country and carry out trade and commerce. According to an estimate nearly four million people of Indian origin are residing in Nepal, mostly in Terai region bordering Bihar, while approximately six million people of Nepalese origin are permanently settled in various parts of India, such as the North-Eastern states, Northern Bengal, Sikkim, Bihar, Uttar Pradesh, Uttarakhand, Himachal Pradesh etc. Demographically speaking, nearly 16.7 per cent of the total population of Nepal is composed of Indians, while 0.57 per cent of the total population of India is constituted by the people of Nepalese origin. Looking in terms of ratio we find that Nepal has one Indian for every six Nepalese, whereas India has one Nepali for every two hundred Indians. These immigrants, with the exception of some floating population, have permanently settled down in each other's adopted countries as citizens by swearing allegiance to the constitutions of respective countries while their children and grand children have automatically become the citizens by birth.

The people of Indian origin inhabiting the Terai regions of Nepal are comparatively more advanced and enterprising than the indigenous Nepalese living in the northern hill areas of Nepal. Terai, with the exception of Kathmandu valley, is considered as the most literate region of Nepal. Due to proximity to India and open border policy followed by the Government, most of the Terai people are educated in India and groomed up in Indian style of life and culture. Being educationally and socially advanced and politically better organized, they are capable of putting pressures on the Government and getting their grievances fulfilled through political movements. It must, however, be admitted that the credit of converting the once most backward and malaria infested Terai into a prosperous economic bastion of Nepal goes to these people who originally hailed from the Gangetic plains of Bihar.[1] They were mostly hard working landless farmers belonging to both Hindus and Muslims. The Government of Nepal encouraged these people to immigrate into Terai because the Nepalese living in the hills did never like to settle down in the Terai for fear of *aulo* (malaria) and the hot climate of the region. The apathetic Rana Government had no concern about the territory, except revenue interest, and hence left it to the mercy of the land-hungry Deswalis from Bihar.

Over the years the Madheshis of Terai, whom the Ranas had kept isolated and deprived of their civic rights, remarkably grew up in population and became advanced in education with considerable number of elite middle class who polarized themselves into strong political and social forces. In recent years, the Terai Sadbhavana Party formed by Gajendra Narayan Singh came up as one of the powerful political parties working among the Madheshis to safeguard their rights and interests since its inception in 1983. The Madheshi Peoples Rights Forum, led by Upendra Yadav, is another strong political organization which is working for the civil rights of the Madheshis. These organizations and many other NGOs and Voluntary associations are spearheading the cause of socio-political and economic emancipation of the people living in Terai region. The political strength of the Madheshis can very well be understood from the elections held on 21st July, 2008 in which the Nepal Assembly elected two of their leaders Dr. Ram Baran Yadav as the President and Shri Paramananda Jha as the Vice-President of Nepal. Their major demands are, removal of discrimination against the Madheshis in respect of job reservation and other privileges, Government policy to keep the borders open (this issue emerged out of Harka Gurung's call for an end to the open border with India in 1983), and demand for raising a separate Madheshi battalion in Nepal Army. Recognition of Hindi as a second official language of Nepal and adoption of liberal policy on granting citizenship to recent immigrants are also among the major demands of the Sadbhavana Party. Mention may be made here that the Government of Nepal conceded the demand of the Madheshis in 2006 and passed the Citizenship Bill that allowed Nepalese citizenship to nearly four million stateless immigrants in Terai region by virtue of naturalization. The Government of India welcomed the reformed Citizenship Act, 2006 while certain sections of Nepalese leaders expressed deep concern. Linguistically, the people of Terai region, by and large, are more comfortable with Hindi than Nepali although they are in Nepal for generations. Their children receive education through the medium of Hindi. Other languages spoken in Terai region are Tharu, Avadhi, Bhojpuri and Maithili. Significantly, the election results of 2008 in Nepal show that Madhesis are in a leading position in Nepal politics with 20 per cent representation in the House of Representatives of the last coalition Government. Even more astounding political development of Nepal is the fact that the two highest offices of the Nepal Government *viz.*, the President and the Vice-President of Nepal were occupied by the Madheshis. The former Prime Minister, Mr. Madhav Kumar Nepal also comes from the same ethnic group although bears a longer family background in Nepal and was a veteran leader of the Nepali Congress for quite a number of years. The appointment of Dr. Ram Baran Yadav as the President and Shri Paramananda Jha as the Vice-President of Nepal is, undoubtedly a new dimension in the Indo-Nepal relations which, it is hoped, will help in bringing the two countries and the peoples closer to each other.

On the other hand, the condition about the Nepalis or the Gorkhas living in India is completely different from that of Madheshis of Nepal. They are underdeveloped, backward and deprived group of people compared to their Indian counterparts in Nepal. They are educationally backward, economically weak and politically neglected. They live primarily in the rural and remote areas and earn their livelihood doing hard labour in agriculture, animal husbandry (dairy farming) and petty Government and private services. Although the total population of Nepalis living in India is fairly big (estimated roughly six million) as per official record it is only 14,11,835—1971 census. The Nepalis population being scattered around distant parts of India they are socially scattered, culturally isolated and politically unorganized. Over and above these factors, their economic and educational backwardness stand out staggeringly as the major disabling factors for their development and progress. Want of strong political leadership and absence of proactive middle class base which constitute the much needed catalyst for the progress of any community, are the basic causes that account for the backwardness of the Indian Nepalis. Government's apathy and restricted opportunities in trades, business and jobs especially in the hill states of North-East have come as the major obstacles on the way of their progress.

The history and origin of the Indian Nepalis in India can be traced from early nineteenth century when, immediately after the Treaty of Segauli in 1815, the British Government of India started recruitment of Gorkha Sepoys for Indian Army. According to E.A. Gait, colonial historian, the Gorkha soldiers penetrated into Assam as early as 1817, nine years prior to British annexation of Assam, ostensibly to drive out the marauding Burmese.[2] Many of these Gorkha Sepoys when retired from service preferred to remain in India as the British Government provided them with employment in other civil offices as Choukidars, Chaprasis, Peons etc. "A Nepali used to get the benefit of preference over others including the indigenous population for certain jobs".[3] The British encouraged Gorkha population to grow up in India with the view that the children of these Indian Gorkhas could be recruited in Indian Army. For the demand for Gorkha recruits was very great while their supply from Nepal was extremely restricted. The Nepalese Durbar was strictly against the idea of its subject joining Indian army. It looked at every activity of the East India Company with suspicion and distrust and stood firm in its close door policy to the British. There was a popular saying among the Nepalese—"With the British comes the muskets, and with the Bible comes the bayonet" To cope with this situation, the Government of India established Gorkha Regimental Homes at several Army Head Quarters in 1864 to provide accommodation to the families of the Gorkha soldiers and encouraged the Gorkha soldiers married in Nepal to bring their families to live in India by granting them travel expenses.[4] Lands were settled to the ex-service men in the vicinity of the Regimental Homes, where schools and hospitals were established for the Gorkha families. With the passage of time many other para-military forces like state constabulary, Assam Rifles, Central Reserve Police Force, Border Security Force, etc. were raised in various parts of India in which large number of Gorkhas were recruited. Together with the Gorkha recruits there came from Nepal civilian Nepalese seeking self-employment in rural occupation like agriculture, cattle rearing and petty jobs. Behind this large scale migration of civil population from Nepal, there were certain strong push factors which are responsible for a large number of Nepalese to seek their livelihood outside Nepal. These factors were: (1) increasing fragmentation of landholdings; (2) heavy exploitation of landless tenants by the landlords due to faulty land tenure system; (3) Indebtedness; (4) ecological crisis through deforestation; (5) rising population and unemployment; (6) poverty and hunger of common people; and (7) oppression of the Rana rulers. Together with these push factors from Nepal there were also certain pull factors from India which propelled the Nepalese migration into India and especially into Assam. These pull factors were : (1) the colonial patronage; (2) wide scope for job opportunities in Indian army, paramilitary forces, state constabularies, office peons, choukidars, *darwans*, etc.; (3) abundance of land in the hills and plains; and (4) wide scope for cultivation and cattle rearing. Because of the aforesaid reasons Nepalis population in India and especially in the North-East region increased rapidly. In 1872, Nepali population in Brahmaputra Valley was 983 (W.W. Hunter, *A Statistical Account of Assam*). In 1881 Nepali settlers in Surma Valley was 499; in Brahmaputra Valley it was 2521; in the Hill Tracts was 1465 (Alexader Mackenzie). According to an estimate, during the period of thirty years, from 1901 to 1931, the Nepalis population in Assam increased from 21,000 to 88,000.

The Nepalis population continued to grow during the post-colonial period too. The following Table gives state-wise estimated figures of Nepalese population in India in 1961.

Sl. No.	*States*	*Population*
1.	Andhra Pradesh	1,283
2.	Assam	2,15,213
3.	Bihar	29,289
4.	Gujarat	2,657
5.	Himachal Pradesh	9,984
6.	Jammu & Kashmir	613
7.	Kerala	276
8.	Madhya Pradesh	7,670
9.	Maharashtra	12,002
10.	Manipur	13,572
11.	Meghalaya	1,682
12.	Karnataka	715
13.	Nagaland	10,400
14.	Orissa	1,878
15.	Punjab	11,680
16.	Rajasthan	1,820
17.	Sikkim	44,319
18.	Tamil Nadu	1,325
19.	Uttar Pradesh	68,118
20.	West Bengal	5,24,284
21.	Goa, Daman & Diu	8
22.	Andaman & Nicobar	164
23.	Pondicherry	51
24.	Delhi	3,397
25.	North East Fr. Province	10,610
26.	Dadra & Nagar Haveli	4

Source : Census of India, 1961.

The population figures mentioned above cannot be accepted as true because of the fact that: (1) the method of enumeration and tabulation of census figures during 1960s was not scientifically perfect and possibilities of errors were many; (2) the census enumerators did not cover interior and inaccessible areas where the Nepalis normally inhabit; and (3) many Nepalis returned their language to the enumerators as other than Nepali for fear of taking them to be foreigners. Especially in Assam the illiterate Nepalis were instructed by political parties to return their mother tongue as Assamese.

The Article 7 of the Indo-Nepal Treaty of Peace and Friendship, 1950 granted the nationals of one country in the territories of the other, the same privileges in the matter of residence, ownership of property, participation in trade and commerce, movement and other privileges of a similar nature. To this day the people of one country can enter into the country of other without any restriction and stay as long as one desired or could legally carry out any trade or occupation. No passport or visa is required to cross the border. Thus, the friendship between the two countries is unique and time honoured which no other two countries in the world possess. This open border policy adopted by India and Nepal is not a recent arrangement; it had been there ever since the British rule when the peoples from the two countries could, as a matter of right, cross each other's borders freely and settle down in their adopted countries at their will. This practice, over the ages, has eventually resulted in large scale inter-migration and settlement of people in both countries.

The Indian Nepalis, who have permanently settled down in India over the last couple of centuries, have adopted India as their home-land and followed the culture and language of their neighbours with a sense of close affiliation, no matter wherever they live. They adapted the language and customs of whichever India community they come in contact. They have socially and politically integrated themselves and joined hands with the sons of the soil in every social and political movement including the freedom movement of India and suffered imprisonments as well as martyrdom. Monirul Hussain writes—"The Nepalis of earlier generation had impressive records of fighting for India's independence in Assam."* The elite section of Nepalis of Darjeeling, Calcutta, Banaras and Dehradun took active part for the cause of nationalist movement by forming their own political organizations like the Hillmen Association of Darjeeling, the Gorkha Association of Calcutta and the All India Gorkha League of Dehradun etc. Shaheed Bhagat Bir Tamang of Karseong who joined non-co-operation movement and died in Darjeeling jail in 1923 became the first political martyr among the Nepalis. Gopal Singh Thapa of Dehradun sacrificed everything of his life in freedom movement. He was imprisoned several times and his pension was confiscated by the British Government.

In the wake of India's struggle for freedom during 1920s when the people of India, irrespective of caste, creed and religion joined hands together under the leadership of Mahatma Gandhi the civilian Gorkha living in different parts of India could not remain aloof. The Nepalis of Assam rose to the occasion under the able leadership of Chhabilal Upadhyaya, Bhakta Bahadur Pradhan, Dalbir Singh Lohar, Bisnulal Upadhyaya etc. and actively participated in the *Satyagraha* and Civil Disobedience Movement and suffered imprisonment. During 'Quit India' movement of 1942 they suffered imprisonment several times.

The Gorkha's participation in the Indian National Army (Azad Hind Fouz) is one of the significant events in the annals of India's Freedom Movement. Under the inspiring leadership of Subhas Chandra Bose a large number of Gorkha soldiers captured by the Japanese in Malaya and Singapore joined Indian National Army in 1942. The Gorkhas played a crucial role with their renowned fighting spirit, and their versatility in the technique of guerrilla warfare added extra capability to the Azad Hind Fouz which was much appreciated even by Netaji Subhas Bose himself. They fought grim battles against the British army in the jungles of Arakan and laid down their lives for India's freedom. Two of them, *viz*. Major Durga Singh Thapa and captain Dal Bahadur Thapa were captured by the British army, brought to Delhi jail and hanged to death after a brief trial at Delhi Red Fort. The names of twenty-five valiant Gorkhas, out of many, who went down fighting in Burma war are mentioned as martyrs by Dr. P.N. Chopra in his book entitled, *Who is Who of Indian Martyrs,* Vol. I, 1969.

The contribution of the Gorkha soldiers for India's sovereignty and integrity is monumental which is writ large with their blood on the pages of Indian military history. Today, the Gorkha Jawans are defending Indo-Chinese borders along the McMahon line in the North-East; they are there on the North-West frontiers resolutely protecting Jammu & Kashmir. They are also there in Siachen glacier, the world's highest battlefield, where extreme cold, high velocity blizzards and dreadful avalanches have rendered human survival extremely difficult. India is ever safe in the hands of loyal and redoubtable Gorkhas.

The Nepalis of Assam joined hands with the local Asamiyas and raised their voices against the Grouping Scheme proposed by the Cabinet Mission of 1946.[5] They also fought for the official recognition of Asamiya language as the medium of instruction up to graduate level at par with English". They have identified themselves with their Indian neighbours in their daily socio-cultural inter-course; they speak local languages and dress themselves like their local counterparts of the hills and the plains wherever they live. To quote Prof. A.C. Sinha, "Most of these residents (Gorkhas) have adapted themselves to the local conditions in such a way that they are counted among the indigenous people with all the benefits even though they have their own communities and their own way of life, speak their language, maintain their own traditions. But the Nepalis have a great capacity to assimilate themselves with the hill communities. They adopt the language of their neighbourhood, contract marital alliances, and turn out to be an inseparable part of the local economy".[6] This is especially true about the Gorkhas living in the North-Eastern states where the ethno-political consciousness among the local communities is menacingly high.

It is, however, tragic to say that despite all these contributions made by them, the Nepalis living in the North-Eastern States are not treated kindly by their Indian neighbours. They are looked upon as unwanted intruders into their homes, as foreigners and are victimized in various ways, threatened, assaulted, killed and, at times, uprooted from their hearths and homes. The political turmoil that rocked Assam during 1979-84 under the aegis of All Assam Students Union (AASU) and Assam Gana Sangram Parishad (AGSP) recorded some of the worst ethnic violence in Indian history. As per Official report submitted by the Government of Assam to the Centre, the agitation took a toll of 3059 lives only within the period of six months, from January to June 1983, which includes a large number of Nepalis.[7] Earlier in February, 1983 over 1200 people, mostly women and children were butchered to death at Nellie about 70 km. east of Guwahati in Nawgoan district.[8] It may be mentioned here that the Assam Movement and mayhem started in the middle of 1979 and continued till the Assam Accord was concluded in 1985.

The foreign national issue of Assam found an echo in Manipur with Shri Daben Singh, President, State Students Co-ordination Committee, demanding immediate deletion of names of foreigners from voter lists and then deportation from Manipur.[9] In another incident, about 500 homesteads were set ablaze at Sagolmang, 25 km from Imphal on the night of 1st May, 1980 rendering homeless over 2500 people, mostly Nepalis. A group of 300 persons armed with firearms and other lethal weapons from nearby areas swooped on the village and went on committing arson which left 18 cattle and many other domestic animals charred to death.[10] The Revolutionary Communist Party of India (RCPI) in a booklet (7-8 pages) published by the party demanded immediate action to stop the unabated flow of Nepalese nationals into Assam.

The ethnic violence perpetrated by the Khasi Students Union (KSU) against the Gorkhas of Meghalaya in 1987 sent the greatest shock to the Nepalis who lived there for generations in close cultural assimilation and friendship. Many of them were indiscriminately assaulted and killed, their dwelling houses, cattle sheds and school buildings were set on fire and forced them to flee their homes for Nepal. Approximately 12,000 Khutiwala Nepalis (cattle rearers) fled away leaving behind their cattle or selling them at throw-away prices. According to an official source, more than 6600 persons took shelter in the Government run Relief Camps for more than four months.[11]

Apart from the atrocities perpetrated by political organizations and communal forces, there was a gross miscarriage of justice meted out to the innocent Nepalis by the Government officials vested with legal powers and authorities. As for example, in 1971 as many as 4500 eligible Nepali voters' names were deleted from Electoral rolls of Dibrugarh Lok Sabha constituency depriving them of their fundamental right of franchise.[12] On being raised the issue by Shri B.L. Upadhyaya, MLA in the Assam Legislative Assembly through Assembly Question No. 988, Shri Mahendramohan Choudhury, the Chief Minister of Assam had assured the Hon'ble MLA that a special commission will be deputed to enquire about the matter and an appropriate action will be taken soon. But nothing had really been done in the long-run. On another occasion, on 16th October, 1979, Shri R.N. Mathur, Superintendent of Police, district Lakhimpur, Assam served notices to twenty Nepali families of Bihpuria village to leave India within a period of two weeks from the date of the notice and not to re-enter India again.[13] The news created a sensation, fear psychosis and a sense of insecurity among the Indian Nepalis at large. A deputation of the Assam Gorkha Sammelan, consisting of four MLAs, waited upon the Chief Minister of Assam and the Leader of the Assam Legislature Party, Shri Sarat Chandra Sinha who expressed surprise at the uncalled for action of the concerned officer. The Chief Minister immediately darted a wireless message instructing the Superintendent of Police to stop action on the matter until further orders and assured the delegation of all necessary action. Sensing a sign of omen in store, the Officer hurriedly called back all the copies of the notices issued by him from the villagers. Now the question is, whether a Superintendent of Police is competent enough to call for proof of citizenship of a person who is a permanent resident of Assam and if not satisfied, to deport such persons from India on his own accord? Secondly, whether the provisions of the Foreigners Act, 1946 read with Government of India, Ministry of Home Affairs notification No. 1/7/61-F III dt. 23.3.61 and No. 1/32/62-III-F III dt. 15.3.62, as quoted by the said Superintendent of Police in his Quit India notice, already served, are applicable in case of such Nepalis? (copy of the Quit India notice is at Appendix 4 of this book). If the answers to these questions are in the negative what action is warranted against such errant, if not politically motivated, officer?

The Foreigners (Protected Areas) Exemption Orders, 1958 exempts the nationals of Sikkim and Nepal from the restriction to enter into protected areas of North-East region. But this facility given to the Nepalese nationals was withdrawn by the Notification No. 25022/110/76-F1(11) Government of India, Ministry of Home Affairs, New Delhi, 30th July, 1976 which reads—"2. In clause (a) of the first proviso to Paragraph 3 of the Foreigners (Restricted Areas) Order 1963, the words for, "Nationals of Nepal" shall be omitted".[14] Since that time the State Governments of Assam and adjoining States are strictly vigilant on the nationals of Nepal not allowing them to enter into Assam. On 14th July, 1978, the Assam Police arrested 144 Nepalese nationals consisting of sawyers and helpers booked by some timber contractors at Guwahati Railway station and put them in the judicial custody (Jail hajat) for a couple of months without trial until their deportation to Nepal. In this way reports are seen in the newspapers when, on many occasions the Assam Police, local NGOs and the Railway Police intercept Nepalese nationals at different places and Railway Stations like Fakiragram, Bongaigoan, Kokrajhar, Rangia, Guwahati etc. and strip them off their money, wrist watches, mobile sets etc. not even sparing the ornaments worn by women-folk on the plea of fine imposed on them for their offences and then they are sent back to Nepal.[15] This Restricted Area Order of the Government of India is obviously repugnant to the Article 7 of the Peace and Friendship Treaty of 1950 which allows people of both countries (India and Nepal) to cross into each others' border and carry on any occupation or settle down in each others' territory permanently. Here the question that arises is, if the Indian citizens are entering any part of Nepal and living peacefully for generations under the provisions of this Treaty without any restriction why the Nepalese nationals are prohibited from entering the North-East areas. Nevertheless, the Indian Nepalis living permanently in India are not against this restriction imposed against the Nepalese nationals, as their presence arouses unpleasant ethnic sentiments among the local Indians and implicates the Indian Nepalis who are in peace and amity with them. The *Assam Gorkha Sammelan*, the only representative body of the Indian Nepalis living in the North-East, welcomed the restriction and even urged upon the Government of India to abrogate the Article 7 of the Treaty of Peace and Friendship, 1950 and to introduce some sort of Permit system which will help identification and deportation of newcomers. In this connection a delegation consisting of eight leaders of the Assam Gorkha Sammelan including four MLAs, met the Prime Minister of India, Mrs. Indira Gandhi on the 1st February, 1980 and submitted a Memorandum to her indicating all the problems faced by the Indian Nepalis living in the North-East as Indian citizens and urging upon her to look into them at an early date.[16] They clearly mentioned in the memorandum that the Indian Nepalese "welcome the Restricted Area Permit system introduced by Government of India with effect from 30th July, 1976 and that should be the deadline to distinguish the Indian Nepalis from the nationals of Nepal".[17] It is not clear as to what compelled the Government of Nepal and India to remain silent spectators while the people of both the countries are clamouring for immediate abrogation of the Article 7 of the Peace and Friendship Treaty, 1950. The local Indians of Assam, the hill tribes of Meghalaya, Nagaland, Mizoram, Arunachal Pradesh, all demand that the free and unrestricted entry of Nepalese citizens into their territories should be stopped forthwith by amending the provisions of the Treaty. The Indian Nepalis who are permanently settled in India also support their demand because of the fact that they are often victimized by the local insurgents thinking them to be the newcomers from Nepal. Majority of the political leaders from Nepal are also in favour of amendment of the Clause Seven of the Peace treaty. The Government of Nepal is well aware of the problem arising out of Nepali refugees thrown out from India and their rehabilitation. Shri Puspa Kamal Dahal (Prachanda), the former Prime Minister of Nepal, during his visit to India had raised this issue and proposed to review certain Clauses of the treaty which have become iritant to both sides. It will, therefore, be in the interest of both the Governments and the people of Nepal and India if the existing open border system is stopped and the practice of free entry into each other's territory is strictly regulated. This will remove the prevailing animosity and hatred especially against the Nepalis living permanently in the North-East India and will bring about an atmosphere of peace and harmony.

Under the facts and circumstances stated above, the Indian Nepalis face certain predicaments, which are experienced in various degrees in various parts of India. The following are those predicaments according to Dr. T.B. Subba, Professor, Anthropology Department, NEHU.[18]

"*One*, the foremost predicament is the fear of eviction.... This fear is based on the past experience of their eviction from states like Manipur, Mizoram, Nagaland, Assam and Meghalaya".

"*Two*, one of the main reasons why they fear eviction is their political status in the region as 'foreigner'. Most of them are bona fide citizens of the country with voting rights and with ownership of immovable properties. But politically they are categorized as foreigners and treated at par with the immigrants from Bangladesh".

"*Three*, on account of the open border between Nepal and India even the descendants of those Nepalis who got settled in India in early nineteenth century and are very much of Indian origin may be suspected to have just come from Nepal".

"*Four*, the Nepalis in the region have been experiencing a loss of their identity". In other words, they are in search of an identity which will show that they are bona fide citizens of India, as they actually are and they are not the Nepalese nationals who can be termed as foreigners. Attempts are being made to adopt new nomenclatures in lieu of the term 'Nepali' so as to distinguish themselves from the newcomer Nepalese nationals like, Gorkhas, Gorkhalis, Bharpalis (short form of Bharatiya Nepalis), Bhargolis (short form of Bharatiya Gorkhalis) or simply Nepalis (instead of Nepalese, the people of Nepal). But these nomenclatures are not going to help them, as long as a Nepali is Nepali in the eyes of their Indian neighbours. The ultimate solution lies only in the suitable measures to be undertaken by the Governments of India and Nepal to stop unauthorized infiltration of Nepalese into the North-East without valid permit.

There is an urgent need to improve the relations between India and Nepal through frequent meetings and dialogues between the two Governments and by effecting necessary amendments and adjustments of the existing bilateral agreements. So long the two Governments are viewing each other's position only through political and economic prisms, completely losing sight of the socio-cultural dimensions, which, are vital for strengthening the ties between them. It is, therefore, through the dynamics of the socio-cultural relations that the peoples of the two countries can build up a strong and lasting bond of friendship and brotherhood. This is a unique advantage which no other two countries of the world have except India and Nepal. This is also a major plus point that India possess over China which has no cultural relations whatsoever with Nepal nor with India. Therefore, the principle of "keeping equidistance with China and India" as some of the political leaders of Nepal seem to propound does not sound correct and fair. In an interview with Bhola Chatterjee, Press Reporter of the *Ananda Bazar Patrika*, on 29th June, 1979, Biseswar Prasad Koirala, the first elected Prime Minister of Nepal, said—

> "So far as India and Nepal's relations are concerned, we are in the same boat and if there is a leakage in it, we must, in our collective interest, plug it....We are related to each other in many ways, socially, culturally and matrimonially. Besides all these, we have geographical constraints too; If Nepal gets no rain, India also suffers from drought, if our hill regions get heavy rains, they cause floods in India....The Indians are one of the greatest nations and biggest powers among the South-East Asian countries; I would like to remind my Indian friends that they must possess big hearts towards us, the smaller neighbouring nations".[19]

Late Biseswar Prasad Koirala was a great friend of India who joined Indian freedom movement and suffered imprisonment together with Indian political leaders. Today our leaders from India and Nepal must honour the sentiments expressed by their forebears and maintain the same cordial relations with a spirit of love and sacrifice. On many occasions former leaders of Nepal seem to have expressed their resentments about the 'Big Brother' attitude of India towards Nepal. Shri M.P. Koirala, former Prime Minister of Nepal, in his book entitled—'A Role in Revolution', has revealed how Nehru shepherded Nepal's transition to democracy and became involved as mediator between Koirala brothers and the king. He wrote not only about his own perception of the relations between the two countries but frankly spoken how successive Indian Ambassadors to Nepal behaved as if they were New Delhi's Viceroys. Nehru also prevented Nepal from establishing diplomatic relations with other countries and even prevailed on Chinese Prime Minister, Chou Enlai not to send an Ambassador to Kathmandu, warning him that if he did the United States would follow suit.[20]

We cannot take for granted that Nepal would always be close to India, nor can we blame Nepal for taking the side of China. Sand-witched between two giant nations, who are at daggers drawn, Nepal a small country must be careful and cautious in her foreign policy. Dr. Jagadish Pokhreal, former Vice-Chairman of National Planning Commission said—"We suffer from a tremendous inferiority complex; Nepal has used the excuse of being land-locked as a veil for its inefficiencies".[21] This expression of a Nepali leader sends a definite message to India and China that Nepal no longer wants to play a subservient role under them. Similarly, Puspa Kamal Dahal, former Prime Minister of Nepal on his visit to India told—"Nepal will keep herself at an equidistant policy from India and China. Nepal has her own obligations and interest with China as a close neighbour in the north as she has with India in the south. It must not be forgotten that the economic relations with China is only one part of much bigger story of Sino-Nepal connection that has existed over the past millenniums. These two countries have a long history of religious intercourse where Buddhism has played a central role in the movement of people, culture and ideas.

It cannot, however, be denied that India's connection with Nepal is far deeper which overwhelmingly outweighs Nepal's relations with China. India's relation with Nepal is grounded on the common history, religion and cultural ethos and not merely on a political bilateral agreement which can be broken-up any time. Religion is one of the most powerful media which promotes emotional and spiritual bond between two peoples and belies all differences. The Pashupatinath temple of Nepal which is worshipped by Indian priests from the south has ever been the most significant spiritual link between India and Nepal for the last few centuries. Thousands of people from India go to Kathmandu every year on the day of *Sivaratri* to offer worship at the temple of Pashupatinath. India's Ministers and top political leaders during their official visits to Nepal never forget to offer *pujas* at the temple of Pashupatinath. Similarly, the famous temple of Viswanath of Benaras, and the temples of Rameswaram, Haridwar, Kamakhya etc. are frequently visited and worshipped by the Nepalese people including the king of Nepal and other leaders. These reciprocal visits at each other's religious places have, undoubtedly deepened the socio-cultural ties between the two countries.

Language as a medium of communication is another source of unification between the two peoples. Both Hindi and Nepali languages being the offshoots from Sanskrit as the common parentage and both being written in *Devanagari* script they are easily readable and understandable to both the peoples. This has afforded a special advantage to the people of India and Nepal while visiting each other's countries. During his visit to Kathmandu Shri Atal Bihari Bajpayi, former Prime Minister of India remarked—"Nepali language is so similar to Hindi that we do not feel we are in foreign country while in Nepal". The Nepali leaders, undoubtedly share the same feeling while they come to India.

In keeping with the tradition of regular exchange of visits the political leaders of the two countries are frequently visiting each other's countries and discussing common problems for mutual help and co-operation. In recent times, the Nepalese Prime Minister, Shri Sushil Koirala, accompanied with high level delegation, attended the swearing-in ceremony of Shri Narendra Modi as a new Prime Minister of India on 26th May, 2014. From Nepal Shri Madhav Prasad Ghimire, Minister of Foreign Affairs visited India on 14-15th January, 2014 while from India Shri Salman Khurshid, External Affairs Minister of India visited Nepal on 9th July, 2013. Other visits from India to Nepal in recent past include visit by Dr. Farooq Abdullah, Minister of Renewable Energy on 20-21st December, 2013, Dr. Karan Singh, Member of Rajya Sabha and President, ICCR, on 14-16th February, 2014, the Chief of Indian Army Staff, General Vikram Singh on 13-14th March, 2014 and Shri Akhilesh Yadav, Chief Minister of Uttar Pradesh on 17-18th February, 2014. The Prime Minister of Nepal, Mr. Puspa Kamal Dahal (Prachanda) visited India on 28-30th April, 2013 and earlier on 24-29th December, 2012, Dr. Ram Baran Yadav, President of Nepal visited India. These occasional visits by the leaders of India and Nepal has kept the two countries ever closer to each other.

With a view to fostering educational, cultural, scientific and technical co-operation between India and Nepal and to promote mutual understanding, an institution named B.P. Koirala, India-Nepal Foundation (BPKF) has been established in December, 1991. This Foundation extends financial support for higher studies, research and other educational activities and in-service training, visits and exchanges of scholars, writers, politicians, media-persons, administrators, businessmen and other professionals in various fields. So far it has organized several cultural programmes, seminars, conferences and has also funded translations and publication of books. The Foundation has been organizing monthly events such as conversations, recitation of poems and cenema shows to engage the local intellectual elites since January 2013.

An Indian Cultural Centre was also opened at Kathmandu in August 2007 to showcase the best of Indian culture not only in the capital city of Kathmandu, but in the rural areas also. It has generated goodwill and knowledge between the peoples of two countries. The socio-cultural bond that exists between the two countries need to be strengthened and further intensified through mutual trust and confidence. Nothing brings two peoples closer to each other than language, culture and literature and it is through the closeness of the people's heart that two Governments can proceed to achieve durable friendship and sustainable co-operation. India must avail full advantage of this relationship and take extra care to boost-up cultural ties between India and Nepal through mutual exchange of Cultural Missions, creation of awareness about historical identity and taking-up schemes for development of Nepali language and literature etc. In this task, the Indian universities can play a significant role by encouraging Indian scholars to take-up research works on the origin and antiquity of Nepal's heterogeneous people, their history, heritage, culture and tradition and the relationship with Indian people.

Long before in 1951, a Library named Nepal-Bharat Library was established in Kathmandu with a view to enhancing and strengthening the cultural relations and exchanging information between India and Nepal. It was the first foreign library in Nepal. It has been one of the biggest and extensively used centres of study and research. It houses books on India and Nepal in the subjects of history, geography, culture, sociology, literature, philosophy, politics, economics, science and technology, medicine, engineering etc. and has catered to the needs of the students and scholars as well as people of all walks of life.

An organization named Indian Citizens' Association of Nepal was formed on 14th September, 1990 in Kathmandu. Presently, it has 462 members and has branches at Pokhara, Damak and Bhairahawa. The aims and objectives of this Association are :

1. To create and foster a spirit of friendship and understanding between the people of Nepal and resident Indians in Nepal.

2. To encourage the members to serve both the countries, India and Nepal.
3. To take an active interest in the cultural and social welfare of the community.
4. To provide a platform to the members for open discussion on all matters pertaining to the legitimate interest of resident. Indians and to work for the protection of such interest, excluding discussions on issues related to partisan politics and sectarian religion.

The association works in consonance with the Embassy of India in Nepal and the Government of Nepal for attaining its objectives.

Notes

1. A.C. Sinha (1990), "The Indian North-East and Nepalese Immigration", in *Himalayan Environment and Culture,* Ed. by N.K. Rustomji and Charles Ramble, New Delhi.
2. M. Hussain (1993), *The Assam Movement*, Delhi: Nanak Publication, p. 255.
3. *Ibid*., p. 260.
4. K.K. Muktan (2002), *The Legendary Gorkhas*, Gauhati: Spectrum Publishers.

* *Op. cit*., Monirul Hussain, p. 262.

5. Monirul Hussain (1993), *Assam Movement*, Delhi: Nanak Publications.
6. A.C. Sinha (1990), "The Indian North East Frontier and Nepali Immigrants", in *Himalayan Environment and Culture,* edited by N.K. Rustomji and Charles Ramble, New Delhi, pp. 217-236.
7. B.L. Upadhyaya (1984), *Assame Nepaliharu* (in Nepali), Tezpur: Sonitpur Comprint, p. 56.
8. *Ibid*.; Monirul Hussain, *op. cit*., p. 141.
9. *Amrit Bazar Patrika*, dated 1st April, 1980.
10. *Assam Tribune,* dated 1st May, 1980.
11. *Shillong Times*, dated 10th, 13th, 14th, 17th, and 18th July, 1987.
12. Assam Gorkha Sammelan, *Bulletin* (1969-1971).
13. *Ibid.*
14. A copy of the Government Notification at Appendix V.
15. Assam Gorkha Sammelan, *Bulletin* (1969-1981), p. 298.

16. *Ibid.*, pp. 239-141, Copy of Memorandum at Appendix III.
17. *Ibid.*
18. T.B. Subba (2003), "Being a Nepali in North-East India" in *The Nepalis in North-East India*, edited by S.C. Sinha and T.B. Subba Indus Publishing Co., Delhi, pp. 205-206.
19. Bisnulal Upadhyaya, (2004), *Khan Mihali*, (in Assamese) Tezpur: Sonitpur Comprint, pp. 22-23.
20. Noorani, A.G. (2009), "Neighbour's Memoir, in *Frontline* Magazine, December 4.
21. Sujeev Shakya (2009), *Unleashing Nepal*, New Delhi: Penguin Books, p. 236.

Appendix I

Treaty of Peace—1815

TREATY OF PEACE between the HONORABLE EAST INDIA COMPANY and MAHARAJAH BIKRAM SAH, Rajah of Nipal, settled between LIEUT.-COLONEL BRADSHAW on the part of the HONORABLE COMPANY, in virtue of the full powers vested in him by His Excellency the Right Honorable Francis, Earl of Moira, Knight of the Most Noble Order of the Garter, one of His Majesty's Most Honorable Privy Council, appointed by the Court of Directors of the said Honorable Company to direct and control all the affairs in the East Indies, and by SREE GOOROO GUJRAJ MISSER AND CHUNDER SEEKUR OPEDEEA on the part of MAHARAJAH GIRMAUN JODE BIKRAM SAH BEHAUDER SHUMSHEER JUNG, in virtue of the powers to that effect vested in them by the said Rajah of Nipal.

Whereas war has arisen between the Honorable East India Company and the Rajah of Nipal, and whereas the parties are mutually disposed to restore the relations of peace and amity which, previously to the occurrence of the late differences, has long subsisted between the two States, the following terms of peace have been agreed upon:

ARTICLE 1st

Threre shall be perpetual peace and friendship between the Honorable East India Company and the Rajah of Nipal.

ARTICLE 2nd

The Rajah of Nipal renounces all claim to the lands which

were the subject of discussion between the two States before the war; and acknowledges the right of the Honorable Company to the sovereignty of those lands.

ARTICLE 3rd

The Rajah of Nipal hereby cedes to the Honorable the East India Company in perpetuity all the undermentioned territories, *viz.*

First—The whole of the low lands between the Rivers Kali and Rapti.

Secondly—The whole of the low lands (with the exception of Bootwul Khass) lying between the Rapti and the Gunduck.

Thirdly—The whole of the low lands between the Gunduck and Coosah, in which the authority of the British Government has been introduced, or is in actual course of introduction.

Fourthly—All the low lands between the Rivers Mitchee and the Teestah.

Fifthly—All the territories within the hills eastward of the River Mitchee, including the fort and lands of Nagree and the Pass of Nagarcote, leading from Morung into the hills, together with the territory lying between that Pass and Nagree. The aforesaid territory shall be evacuated by the Goorkha troops within forty days from this date.

ARTICLE 4th

With a view to indemnify the Chiefs and Barahdars of the State of Nipal, whose interests will suffer by the alienation of the lands ceded by the foregoing Article, the British Government agrees to settle pensions to the aggregate amount of two lakhs of Rupees per annum on such Chiefs as may be selected by the Rajah of Nipal, and in the proportions which the Rajah may fix. As soon as the selection is made, Sunnuds shall be granted under the seal and signature of the Governor-General for the pensions respectively.

ARTICLE 5th

The Rajah of Nipal renounces for himself, his heirs, and

successors, all claim to or connexion with the countries lying to the west of the River Kali, and engages never to have any concern with those countries or the inhabitants thereof.

ARTICLE 6th

The Rajah of Nipal engages never to molest or disturb the Rajah of Sikkim in the possession of the territories; but agrees, if any differences shall arise between the State of Nipal and the Rajah of Sikkim, or the subjects of either, that such differences shall be referred to the arbitration of the British Government, by whose award the Rajah of Nipal engages to abide.

ARTICLE 7th

The Rajah of Nipal hereby engages never to take or retain in his service and British subject, nor the subject of any European or American State, without the consent of the British Government.

ARTICLE 8th

In order to secure and improve the relations of amity and peace hereby established between the two States, it is agreed that accredited Ministers from each shall reside at the Court of the other.

ARTICLE 9th

This Treaty, consisting of nine Articles, shall be ratified by the Rajah of Nipal within fifteen days from this date, and the ratification shall be delivered to Lieut.-Colonel Bradshaw, who engages to obtain and deliver to the Rajah the ratification of the Governor-General within twenty days, or sooner, if practicable.

Seal *Done at Segowlee, on the 2nd day of December 1815.*

PARIS BRADSHAW, *Lt.-Col., P.A.*

Received this Treaty from Chunder Seekur Opedeea, Agent on the part of the Rajah of Nipal, in the Valley of Muckwaunpoor, at half-past two o'clock P.M., on the 4th of March, 1816, and delivered to him the Counterpart Treaty on behalf of the British Government.

(Signed) DD. OCHTERLONY,
Agent, Governor-General

MEMORANDUM for the approval and acceptance of the RAJAH OF NIPAL, presented on the 8th December, 1816.

Adverting to the amity and confidence subsisting with the Rajah of Nipal, the British Government proposes to suppress, as much as is possible, the execution of certain Articles in the Treaty of Segowlee, which bear hard upon the Rajah, as follows:

2. With a view to gratify the Rajah in a point which he has much at heart, the British Government is willing to restore the Terai ceded to it by the Rajah in the Treaty, to wit, the whole Terai lands lying between the Rivers Coosa and Gunduk, such as appertained to the Rajah before the late disagreement; excepting the disputed lands in the Zillahs of Tirhoot and Sarun, and excepting such portions of territory as may occur on both sides for the purpose of settling a frontier, upon investigation by the respective Commissioners; and excepting such lands as may have been given in possession to anyone by the British Government upon ascertainment of his rights subsequent to the cession of Terai to the Government. In case the Rajah is desirous of retaining the lands of such ascertained proprietors, they may be exchanged for others, and let it be clearly understood that, notwithstanding the considerable extent of the lands in the Zillah of Tirhoot, which have for a long time been a subject of dispute, the settlement made in the year 1812 of Christ, corresponding with the year 1869 of Bikramajeet, shall be taken, and everything else relinquished, that is to say, that the settlement and negotiations, such as occurred at that period, shall in the present case hold good and be established.

3. The British Government is willing likewise to restore the Terai lying between the Rivers Gunduk and Rapti, that is to say,

from the River Gunduk to the western limits of the Zillah of Goruckpore, together with Bootwul and Sheoraj, such as appertained to Nipal previous to the disagreements, complete, with the exception of the disputed places in Terai, and such quantity of ground as may be considered mutually to be requisite for the new boundary.

4. As it is impossible to establish desirable limits between the two States without survey, it will be expedient that Commissioners be appointed on both sides for the purpose of arranging in concert a well defined boundary on the basis of the preceding terms, and of establishing a straight line of frontier, with a view to the distinct separation of the respective territories of the British Government to the south and of Nipal to the north; and in case any indentations occur to destroy the even tenor of the line, the Commissioners should effect an exchange of lands so interfering on principles of clear reciprocity.

5. And should it occur that the proprietors of lands situated on the mutual frontier, as it may be rectified, whether holding of the British Government or of the Rajah of Nipal, should be placed in the condition of subjects to both Governments, with a view to prevent continual dispute and discussion between the two Governments, the respective Commissioners should effect in mutual concurrence and co-operation the exchange of such lands, so as to render them subject to one dominion alone.

6. Whensoever the Terai shall be restored, the Rajah of Nipal will cease to require the sum of two lakhs of Rupees per annum, which the British Government agreed to advance for the maintenance of certain Barahdars of his Government.

7. Moreover, the Rajah of Nipal agrees to refrain from prosecuting any inhabitants of the Terai, after its revertance to his rule, on account of having favored the cause of the British Government during the war, and should any of those persons, excepting the cultivators of the soil be desirous of quitting their estates, and of retiring within the Company's territories, he shall not be liable to hindrance.

8. In the event of the Rajah's approving the foregoing terms, the proposed arrangement for the survey and establishment of boundary marks shall be carried into execution, and after the

determination in concert of the boundary linc, Sunnuds conformable to the foregoing stipulations, drawn out and sealed by the two States, shall be delivered and accepted on both sides.

Seal (Signed) EDWARD GARDNER,
Resident.

(Signed) G. Wellesley,
Assistant.

Appendix II

Indo-Nepal Treaty of Peace and Friendship, 1950

The Government of India and the Government of Nepal, recognising the ancient ties which have happily existed between the two countries for centuries, desiring still further to strengthen and develop these ties and to perpetuate peace between the two countries, have resolved therefore to enter into a treaty of peace and friendship with each other, and have, for this purpose, appointed as their plenipotentiaries the following persons, namely,

The Government of India: His Excellency Shri Chandreshwar Prasad Narain Singh, Ambassador of India in Nepal.

The Government of Nepal: Mohun Shamsher Jang Bahadur Rana, Maharaja, Prime Minister and Supreme Commander-in-Chief of Nepal, who have examined each other's credentials and found them good and in due form have agreed as follows:

ARTICLE 1st

There shall be everlasting peace and friendship between the Government of India and the Government of Nepal. The two governments agree mutually to acknowledge and respect the complete sovereignty, territorial integrity and independence of each other.

ARTICLE 2nd

The two governments hereby undertake to inform each other of any serious friction or misunderstanding with any neighbouring state likely to cause any breach in the friendly relations subsisting between the two governments.

ARTICLE 3rd

In order to establish and maintain the relations referred to in Article 1 the two governments agree to continue diplomatic relations with each other by means of representative with such staff as is necessary for the due performance of their functions.

The representatives and such of their staff as may be agreed upon shall enjoy such diplomatic privileges and immunities as are customarily granted by international law on a reciprocal basis, provided that in no case shall, these be less than those granted to persons of a similar status of any other state having diplomatic relations with either governments.

ARTICLE 4th

The two governments agree to appoint consuls-general, vice-consuls and other consular agents, who shall reside in towns, ports and other places in each other's territory as may be agreed to.

Consuls-general, consuls, vice-consuls and consular agents shall be provided with credential or other valid authorisation of their appointment, liable to be withdrawn by the country which issued it, if considered necessary. The reasons for the withdrawal shall be indicated wherever possible.

The persons mentioned above shall enjoy on a reciprocal basis all the rights, privileges, exceptions and immunities that are accorded to persons of corresponding status of any other state.

ARTICLE 5th

The Government of Nepal; shall be free to import, from or through the territory of India, arms, ammunition or warlike material and equipment necessary for the security of Nepal. The procedure for giving effect to this arrangement shall be worked out by the two governments acting in consultation.

ARTICLE 6th

Each government undertakes, in token of the neighbourly friendship between India and Nepal, to give to the nationals of the other, in its territory, national treatment with regard to participation in industrial and economic development of such territory and to the grant of concessions and contracts relating to such development.

ARTICLE 7th

The government of India and Nepal agree to grant, on a reciprocal basis, to the nationals of one country in the territories of the other the same privileges in the matter of residence, ownership of property, participation in trade and commerce, movement and other privileges of a similar nature.

ARTICLE 8th

So far as matters dealt with herein are concerned, this treaty cancels all previous treaties, agreements and engagements entered into on behalf of India between the British Government and the Government of Nepal.

ARTICLE 9th

This treaty shall come into force from the date of signature by both governments.

ARTICLE 10th

This treaty shall remain in force until it is terminated by either party by giving one year's notice.

Done in duplicate at Kathmandu this *31st day of July, 1950.*

(Sd.) Chandreshwar Prasad Narain Singh
for the Government of India
(Sd.) Mohun Shamsher Jang Bahadur Rana for the
Government of Nepal.

Appendix III
Treaty of 1923

TREATY of FRIENDSHIP between Great Britain and Nepal signed at KATMANDU, 21st December 1923 and Note bearing the same date respecting the importation of Arms and Ammunition into NEPAL—1923.

(Exchange of ratifications took place at Katmandu on the 8th April 1925)

TREATY

Whereas peace and friendship have now existed between the British Government and the Government of Nepal since the signing of the Treaty of Segowlie on the 2nd day of December 1815, and whereas since that date the Government of Nepal has ever displayed its true friendship for the British Government and the British Government has as constantly shown its good-will towards the Government of Nepal; and whereas the Governments of both the countries are now desirous of still further strengthening and cementing the good relations and friendship which have subsisted between them for more than a century; the two High Contracting Parties having resolved to conclude a new Treaty of Friendship have agreed upon the following Articles:

ARTICLE 1st

There shall be perpetual peace and friendship between the Governments of Great Britain and Nepal, and the two Governments agree mutually to acknowledge and respect each other's independence, both internal and external.

ARTICLE 2nd

All previous treaties, agreements and engagements, since and including the Treaty of Segowlie of 1815, which have been concluded between the two Governments are hereby confirmed, except so far as they may be altered by the present Treaty.

ARTICLE 3rd

As the preservation of peace and friendly relations with the neighbouring States whose territories adjoin their common frontiers is to the mutual interests of both the High Contracting Parties, they hereby agree to inform each other of any serious friction or misunderstanding with those States likely to rupture such friendly relations, and each to exert its good offices as far as may be possible to remove such friction and misunderstanding.

ARTICLE 4th

Each of the High Contracting Parties will use all such measures as it may deem practicable to prevent its territories being used for purposes inimical to be security of the other.

ARTICLE 5th

In view of the longstanding friendship that has subsisted between the British Government and the Government of Nepal and for the sake of cordial neighbourly relations between them, the British Government agrees that the Nepal Government shall be free to import from or through British India into Nepal whatever arms, ammunition, machinery, warlike material or stores may be required or desired for the strength and welfare of Nepal, and that this arrangement shall hold good for all time as long as the British Government is satisfied that the intentions of the Nepal Government are friendly and that there is no immediate danger to India from such importations. The Nepal Government, on the other hand, agrees that there shall be no export of such arms, ammunition, etc., across the frontier of Nepal either by the Nepal Government or by private individuals.

If, however, any Convention for the regulation of the Arms Traffic, to which the British Government may be a party, shall come into force, the right of importation of arms and ammunition by the Nepal Government shall be subject to the proviso that the Nepal Government shall first become a party to that Convention, and that such importation shall only be made in accordance with the provisions of that Convention.

ARTICLE 6th

No Customs duty shall be levied at British Indian ports on goods imported on behalf of the Nepal Government for immediate transport to that country provided that a certificate from such authority as may from time to time be determined by the two Governments shall be presented at the time of importation to the Chief Customs Officer at the port of import setting forth that the goods are the property of the Nepal Government, are required for the public services of the Nepal Government, are not for the purpose of any state monopoly or State trade, and are being sent to Nepal under orders of the Nepal Government.

ARTICLE 7th

The British Government also agrees to the grant in respect of all trade goods, imported at British Indian ports for immediate transmission to Kathmandu without breaking bulk *en route,* of a rebate of the full duty paid, provided that in accordance with arrangements already agreed to, between the two Governments, such goods may break bulk for repacking at the port of entry under Customs supervision in accordance with such rules as may from time to time be laid down in this behalf. The rebate may be claimed on the authority of a certificate signed by the said authority that the goods have arrived at Kathmandu with the Customs seals unbroken and otherwise untampered with.

ARTICLE 8th

This Treaty signed on the part of the British Government by Lieutenant-Colonel W.F.T. O'Connor, C.I.E., C.V.O., British Envoy at the Court of Nepal, and on the part of the Nepal Government by General His Highness Maharaja Sir Chandra Shumshere Jung Bahadur Rana, G.C.B., G.C.S.I., G.C.M.H., G.C.V.O., D.C.I., Thong-lin Pimma-Kokang-Wang-Syan, Prime Minister and Marshal of Nepal, shall be ratified and the ratification shall be exchanged at Kathmandu as soon as practicable.

Signed and sealed at Kathmandu this the twenty-first day of December in the year one thousand nine hundred and twenty-three *Anno Domini* corresponding with the sixth Paush, Sambat Era one thousand nine hundred and eighty.

W.F.T. O'Connor, Lt. Col.
British Envoy at the
Court of Nepal

(Under Vernacular
translation of Treaty.)
CHANDRA SHAMSHERE,
Prime Minister and
Marshal of Nepal.

Appendix IV
Letter to PM of India : 29-1-1980

To,

The Prime Minister of India,
New Delhi.

Sub: PROBLEMS OF NEPALI SPEAKING INDIAN CITIZENS OF NORTH EASTERN REGION
Dated Gauhati, the 29th January, 1980

Madam,

We, the undersigned on behalf of Assam Gorkha Sammelan beg most respectfully sheweth—

1. That the Nepali speaking people or Assam and other sister states like any other people of this area, are very much concerned about the problems created by the reported large scale influx of foreign nationals in some parts of this region. We maintain that the influx of foreign nationals is not the problem of the Assamese of Khasi speaking people only but also a problem of all other people who are permanent residents here irrespective of their language and religion. This problem has created a fear-phychosis in the minds of the original inhabitants that they are gradually going to be outnumbered by the foreigners. We sincerely feel that the Government of India should take such steps so that they can be assured of adequate safeguard to their

socio-cultural and economic interests. At the same time it should also be carefully observed that not a single Indian is harassed and deprived of his fundamental and political rights.

2. The simple and law-abiding Nepalese have adopted Assam as their home-land. They have been living here in complete amity and harmony with the local people identifying themselves as the children of the soil. As true nationals, they have never failed to respond to the call of the nation at the time of peril. In normal days also they are always active in regular services of the country. With their microscopic population in comparison with others, we believe that they are only the community who has contributed a large number of able bodied sons to the defence of their motherland.
3. But unfortunately, a confusion has been created in the mind of a large number of permanent Nepalese as soon as they were lebelled as foreigners and serve notices to prove their bona fide during the revision of voter's list prepared for the last mid-term Lok Sabha Poll. It was at par with other linguistic and minority communities. The so-called hearing of claims and objections were almost a farce. As a consequence names of a large number of genuine voters were deleted from the voter's list.
4. The recent atrocities committed in North Kamrup is a black chapter in the history of Assam. Mention may be made of similar incidents at Duliajan, Naharkatiya, Shillong, Doomdooma and Dibrugarh also in different occasions. The sad news of arson, looting, murder, physical torture and intimidation must have reached you and we don't like to repeat all these things here. After all a sense of security and peace should be restored in the minds of the minorities including the Nepalese at all costs.
5. We now like to confine mostly to the problems of the Indian Nepalese and forward a few points of your kind consideration.

It is a known fact to all that there is no visa or passport system introduced as yet between India and Nepal. We welcome the Restricted Area Permit which has come into effect recently.

(a) In view of the present situation, we suggest that 30th July, 1976 (the year of introduction of permit system) should be earmarked to distinguish the Indian Nepalese from the nationals of Nepal.
It may be mentioned here that it was on this date that the Ministry of Home Affairs also made an amendment (vide no. 25022/110/76 F-I (i) to the Foreigners (Protected Area) Exemption, 1958 saying that the said order shall not apply to the nationals of Nepal. The original provision had excluded the nationals of Sikkim and Nepal from the purview of the term foreigners.
(b) The passport and visa system may be introduced if Government of India considers it helpful for all practical purposes to check the influx of the Nepali nationals.
(c) In order to avoid harassment to Nepali nationals coming to protected areas without valid permit due to ignorance and also to minimise the extra-burden of the police and unwanted expenditure of the state exchequers in detection, investigation judicial trial and deportation, the Permit Issuing Centre should be opened at the Indo-Nepal border with immediate effect.
(d) National Register of Citizens be entertained to avoid harassment to Indian citizens in the name of foreigners in future.
(e) Prompt measures of rehabilitation of the affected families in the last disturbances be taken up in right earnest under Central Government's initiative.
(f) Your kind invitation to the A.A.S.U. (Assam Students Union) to come over to Delhi for a dialogue on foreigners, issue is highly welcomed. Other organizations, political parties and representatives of minority communities also be consulted in finding out a permanent solution of the problem of foreigners.

We are confident that under your able and dynamic leadership this burning problem will find a solution and normalcy and peace will return and all sections of people can live in mutual harmony in days to come.

Yours faithfully,

1. BISHNULAL UPADHYAYA, M.L.A., President, Assam Gorkha Sammelan.
4. PADAM BAHADUR CHAUHAN, M.L.A., Gen. Secy. Assam Gorkha Sammelan.
3. KHEMRAJ ADHIKARI, ADVOCATE, Member, Assam Gorkha Sammelan and Nagarik Suraksha Samiti.
4. BINOD KHANDAL, M.A., Member, Assam Gorkha Sammelan.

Copy to— The Home Minister,
New Delhi.

APPENDIX V

Office of the Superintendent of Police : Lakhimpur District

ORDER

No.78 Dated the 16-10-79

In exercise of the powers conferred by clauses (a), (b), (c) and (cc) of sub-section (2) of Section 3 of the Foreigners Act, 1946 of 31 read with Government of India, Ministry of Home Affairs Notifications No. 1/7/ 61/ III, dated the 22nd March, 1961 and No. IP, 132/61-(III)-F. III, dated the 15th March, 1961, I, Shri R.N. Mathur, Superintendent of Police, Lakhimpur District, hereby order that the foreigner known as Shri Shrimati Purnamaya Karki son/ wife/Daughter of Ram Krishna and her family, a Foreign national, now residing in Village/ Town Bihpuria Ward No. 11, Police Station Bihpuria, District Lakhimpur, shall leave India within a period of two weeks from the date of this order and shall not thereafter re-enter India.

Suprintendent of Police, Lakhimpur, Dist-North Lakhimpur.

Note — If Shri/Shrimati Purnamaya Karki claims that he/she is not a foreigner, he/she may make a representation, stating therein the reasons for his/ her claim, to Shri R.N. Mathur, P.S. Suprintendent of Police, Lakhimpur, Dist. North Lakhimpur within a period of two weeks from the date of this order.

AGP (I.G. Police) F. 13/64 - 3,00,000 - 26-10-1964

Sd - Illegible
16/10/79
Superintendent of Police
Lakhimpur, North Lakhimpur.

Appendix VI

Notification

Ministry of Home Affairs

New Delhi, the 30th July, 1950

No. 25022/110/76-F.I, (II)—In exercise of the powers conferred by section 3 of the Foreigners Act, 1946 (13 of 1946), the Central Government hereby makes the following order further to amend the Foreigners (Restricted Areas) Order, 1963 namely—

1. (1) This Order may be called the Foreigners (Restricted Areas) Amendment Order, 1976

2. (2) It shall come into force on the date of its publication in the official Gazette.

2. In clouse (a) of the first proviso to paragraph 3 of the Foreigners (Restricted Areas) Order, 1963, "the words for a national of Nepal" shall be omitted.

(R.A.S. MANI)
Deputy Secretary to the Govt. of India.

Appendix VII

Treaty of Trade and Commerce between Nepal and India, 1950

The Government of India and the Government of Nepal, being desirous of facilitating and furthering trade and commerce between their respective territories,

Have resolved therefore to enter into a Treaty of Trade and Commerce with each other and have for this purpose appointed as their plenipotentiaries the following persons:

The Government of India: His Excellency Shri Chandreswar Prasad Narain Singh, Ambassador of India in Nepal,

The Government of Nepal: Maharaja Mohun Shamsher Jang Bahadur Rana, Prime Minister and Supreme Commander-in-Chief of Nepal,

Who, having examined each other's credentials and found them good and in due form, have agreed as follows:

ARTICLE I

The Government of India recognizes in favour of the Government of Nepal full and unrestricted right of commercial transit of all goods and manufactures through the territory and ports of India as provided in Articles II, III and IV below.

ARTICLE II

Subject to such arrangements as may be agreed upon between the two Governments, the Government of India agrees to allow all goods imported at any Indian port and intended for re-export to

Nepal to be transmitted to such place or places in Nepal as may be approved by the two Governments, without breaking bulk *en route* and without payment of any duty at any Indian port.

ARTICLE III

Subject to such arrangements as may be agreed upon between the two Governments the right of passage without payment of excise or import duties shall similarly extend also to goods of Nepalese origin in transit through Indian territory from one approved place to another within the territories of the Kingdom of Nepal.

ARTICLE IV

Subject to such arrangements as may be agreed upon between the two Governments, the Government of Nepal shall enjoy full and unrestricted right of commercial transit, from approved place or places in Nepalese territory, through the territories and ports of India of all goods and manufactures of Nepalese origin for export outside India.

ARTICLE V

The Government of Nepal agrees to levy at rates not lower than those leviable, for the time being, in India customs duties on imports from and exports to countries outside India. The Government of Nepal also agrees to levy on goods produced or manufactured in Nepal, which are exported to India, export duty at rates sufficient to prevent their sale in India at prices more favourable than those of goods produced or manufactured in India which are subject to central excise duty.

ARTICLE VI

The Government of India and the Government of Nepal agree to assist each other by making available, to the maximum extent possible, commodities which are essential to the economy of the other.

ARTICLE VII

The two Governments agree to promote contacts between the trade interests of the two countries and undertake to give every reasonable facility for the import and export of commodities, and in particular to facilitate the use of the routes and methods of transportation, which are most economical and convenient.

ARTICLE VIII

Civil aircraft of either state shall be permitted to fly over the territory of the other in accordance with normal international procedure.

ARTICLE IX

So far as matters dealt with herein are concerned this Treaty cancels all previous treaties, agreements or engagements concluded between the British Government on behalf of India and the Government of Nepal.

ARTICLE X

This Treaty shall come into force three months after the date of signature by both Parties. It shall remain in force for a period of ten (10) years in the first instance, and shall, unless terminated by either Party by giving notice of not less than one year in writing, continue in force for a further period of ten (10) years.

Kathmandu, 31 July, 1950

Appendix VIII

India-Nepal Treaty of Extradition, 1953

The Government of India and the Government of Nepal, being desirous of regulating extradition of criminals as between the two countries, have resolved to enter into a new Treaty of Extradition with each other, and have for this purpose, appointed as their plenipotentiaries the following persons, namely,

The Government of India: His Excellency Shri Bhalchandra Krishna Gokhale, Ambassador of India in Nepal,

The Government of Nepal: Honourable Shri Matrika Prasad Koirala, Prime Minister of Nepal,

Who having examined each other's credentials and found them good and in due form have agreed as follows:

ARTICLE I

The two governments hereby engage on a basis of strict reciprocity to deliver up to each other those persons, who, being accused, or convicted, of a crime committed in the territory of one government shall be found within the territory of the other government, under the circumstances and conditions stated in the present Treaty.

ARTICLE II

Neither Government shall be bound in any case to surrender any person who is not a national of the country by the Government of which the requisition has been made, except where such person is accused of having committed the offence specified in clause (10) of Article III.

ARTICLE III

The offences for which extradition is to be granted in accordance with this Treaty are the following, namely,

(1) Murder or attempt or conspiracy to murder, (2) culpable homicide not amounting to murder, (3) grievous hurt, (4) rape, (5) dacoity, (6) highway robbery, (7) robbery with violence, (8) burglary or house-breaking, (9) arson, (10) desertion from armed forces, (11) offences against the laws prohibiting the export and import of goods, (12) embezzlement by public officers, (13) serious theft, that is to say, cases of theft where violence has been used or where the value of the property stolen exceeds ₹ 500 and cattle stealing, (14) abduction or kidnapping, (15) forgery and the use of what is known to be forged, counterfeiting or altering money; uttering or bringing into circulation counterfeited or altered money, (16) receiving of illegal gratification by a public servant, (17) escaping from custody while undergoing punishment after conviction for any of the offences specified in clauses (1) to (16).

ARTICLE IV

In no case shall either Government be bound to surrender any person accused of an offence except upon a requisition duly made by or under the authority of the government in whose territories the offence is alleged to have been committed and also upon such evidence of criminality as according to the laws of the country in which the accused person shall be found, would justify the apprehension and sustain the charge if the offence had been committed there.

ARTICLE V

Neither Government shall be bound to surrender any person if the offence in respect of which the surrender is demanded be of a political character, or if he proves that the requisition for his surrender has in fact been made with a view to trying or punishing him for an offence of a political character.

ARTICLE VI

Extradition shall not take place if the person whose extradition is claimed by one of the governments has already been tried and discharged or punished or is still under trial in the territory of the other government for the crime for which extradition is demanded.

ARTICLE VII

If the person whose extradition is claimed by one government is under trial for any crime in the territory of the other, his extradition may be deferred until the conclusion of the trial.

ARTICLE VIII

A person surrendered shall in no case be detained or tried in the territory of the government to which the surrender has been made for any other crime or on account of any matter other than those for which extradition has taken place until he has been restored, or had an opportunity of returning, to the territory of the government from which he was surrendered.

ARTICLE IX

If evidence sufficient to justify the extradition is not produced within two months from the date of apprehension of the fugitive or within such further period as may be allowed by the government to which the requisition for extradition has been made or by the Court before which the evidence is to be produced, the fugitive shall be set at liberty.

ARTICLE X

The expenses of any apprehension, detention or surrender made in pursuance of this Treaty shall be borne and defrayed by the government making the requisition.

ARTICLE XI

This Treaty supersedes and cancels all previous treaties, agreements and engagements on the subject.

ARTICLE XII

This Treaty shall come into force without ratification, one month after the date of signature by both parties and may be terminated by either party by giving one month's notice.

Done in duplicate at Kathmandu, this second day of October, 1953.

Appendix IX
List of INA Martyrs

1.	Major Durgamalla Thapa	Hanged to death in Delhi jail on 25th August, 1944.
2.	Capt. Dal Bahadur Thapa	Joined INA in 1942, sentenced to death on 3rd May, 1945, in Delhi Jail.
3.	Lance Naik Bahadur Singh	Soldier in 2/9 GR. Joined INA as L/Naik and killed in action at Pyinmana, Burma.
4.	Naik Man Bahadur Thapa	Joined INA in Singapore in 1942. Served in the Ist Bahadur Group and killed in action.
5.	L/Naik Damar Bahadur	Joined INA in 1942 and killed in action.
6.	Kul Bahadur	Joined INA in Burma in the Body Guard Battalion and died in Burma.
7.	Gyan Bahadur Lama	Joined INA in Malaya as L/Naik. Killed in Action in Burma, on 11 February, 1945.
8.	Man Singh	Soldier in 2/1 GR. Joined INA in 1942 as Havildar in Bahadur Group and got killed.
9.	Mohan Singh Gorkha	Soldier in 2/1 GR. Joined INA in Malaya as Havildar. Killed in action in July 1944.
10.	Prem Bahadur	L/Naik in Indian Army, Medical Corps. Joined INA in Malaya, died in Burma in July 1944.

11. Sital Bahadur	A soldier in GR. Joined INA in Malaya. Served as Havildar in Ist Bahadur Group. Killed in Burma in August 1944.
12. Capt. Bhimsingh Thapa	Joined INA in Malaya in 1943. Served as Captain and killed in action.
13. Hav. Mohansingh Thapa	Havildar Clerk in 2/1 GR. Joined INA in Malaya, Served as S.O. in the Ist Bahadur Group. Killed in action.
14. Ram Bahadur Thapa	Joined INA in Malaya. Killed in action near Chindwin river in Burma in February, 1944.
15. Jamadar Bhimsen Thapa	Soldier of 3/1 GR Joined INA in 1942 in Ist Bahadur Group and killed in action.
16. Capt. Sher Bahadur	2/1 GR. Joined INA in Malaya as Bhandari Captain in Ist Bahadur Group. Died in hospital in Burma in 1944.
17. Bhowan Singh	Havildar Clerk in 2/9 GR Joined INA in 1942 and killed in action in Burma.
18. L/Naik Bhim Singh	From 2/1 GR. Joined INA in 1942 as 2nd Lieutenant. Died in action in Burma.
19. Bhupal Singh Gorkha	From 2/5 GR. Joined INA in 1942 as Intelligence Officer. Shot and killed by Enemy on being detected.
20. Hav. Dhan Bahadur	From 1/3 GR. Joined INA in 1942. Killed in action.
21. Dhan Bahadur Gurung	From 2/2 Garhwal Rifles. Joined INA as Naik. Killed in action.
22. Manilal Gurung	Havildar Clerk in 2/1 GR. Joined INA in Malaya. Served as S.O. in Ist Bahadur Group. Killed in Burma.

23. Kalu Gorkha	Joined INA in Malaya in Ist Bahadur Group. Died by drowning in 1943.
24. Kalusingh Lama	Joined INA in Malaya. Served as S.O. in Training Centre. Killed in action near Chindwin river in 1943.
25. Dhyan Bahadur	From 2/5 GR. Joined INA in 1942 as Havildar in Ist Bahadur Group. Killed during action in Burma.

Source: Dr. P.N. Chopra (1969), *Who is Who of Indian Martyrs*, Vol. 1.

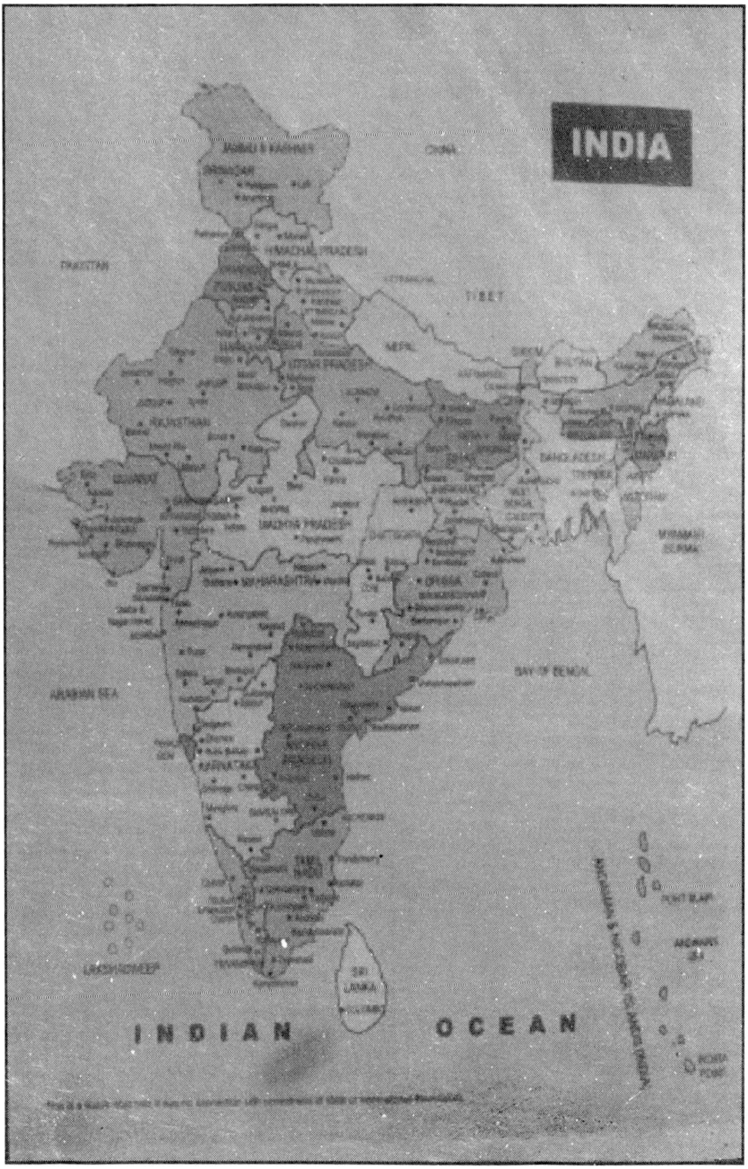
INDIA
INDIAN OCEAN

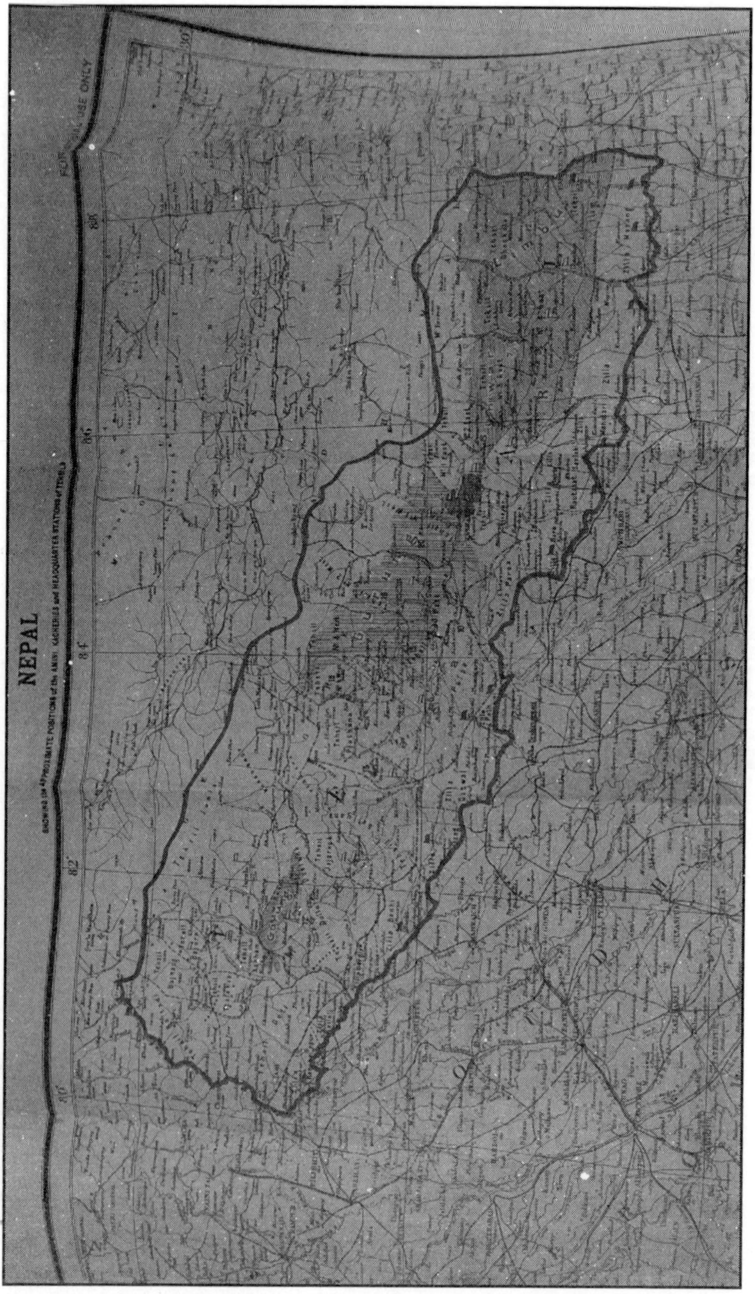
NEPAL

RIVERS OF NORTH-EAST INDIA AND NEPAL

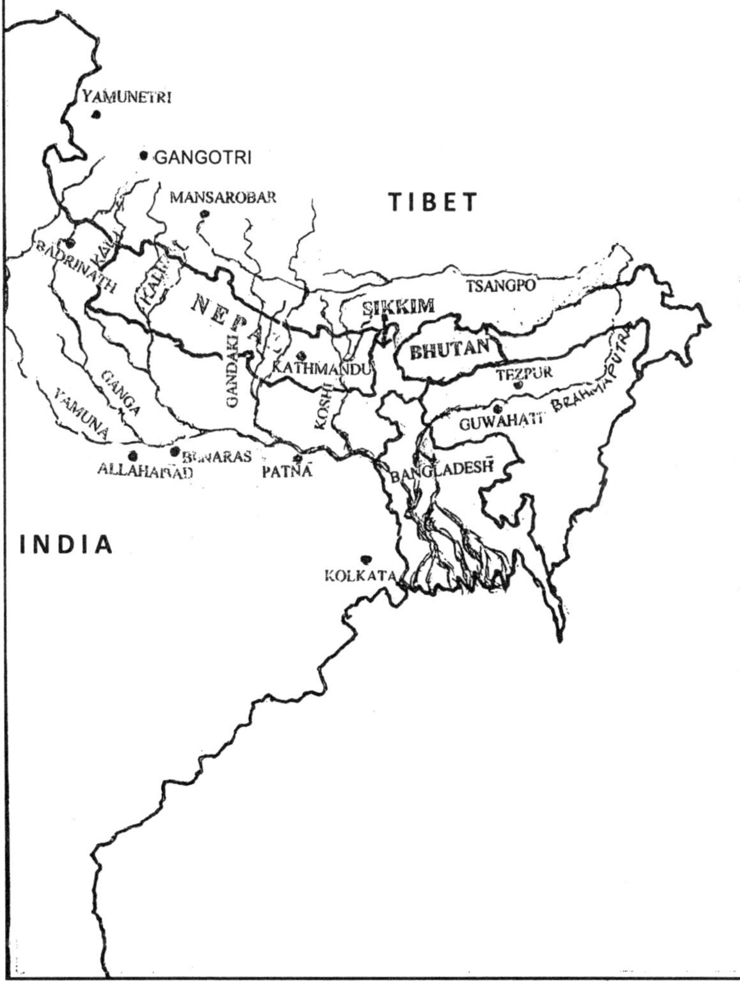

Bibliography

Atkinson, Edwin T. (1973), *The Himalayan Gazetteer*, Vol. II, Part II, Reprint, New Delhi: Cosmo Publication.

Ballantine, Henry (1896), *Nepal: Gurkha's Mysterious Land*, Delhi: Daya Publication House.

Bhatia, H.S. (1957), *Military History of India*.

Bist, D.B. (1991), Fatalism and Development, Calcutta.

Bhanja, K.C. (1948), *The Himalayan Wonders*.

Bhandari, Purushottam (1996), *Freedom Movement and Role of Indian Nepalis*, Guwahati.

Borpujari, H.K. (1998), *Northeast India—Problems, Policies and Prospects*, Guwahati: Spectrum Publications.

Bolt, David (1947), *Gorkhas*, London: Trinity Press.

Chatterjee, S.K (1974), *Kirata Janakrti,* 2nd Ed., Calcutta: Asiatic Society.

Choudhury, J.N. (1988), Pre-Historic and early Tribal migration in *Archaeology of Northeast India*, Ed. Jaiprakash Singh, Department of History, NEHU, Shillong.

Dungel, B.D., *History of the Nepalese Community in Northeast India*, Shillong: Sakhari Samiksha.

Farwell, Byron (1984), *The Gurkhas*, New Delhi: Penguin Books.

Forbes, Duncan (1964), *Johny Gurkha*, New Delhi: Vikas Publishing House.

Gait, E.A. (1926), *A History of Assam*, Calcutta.

Gokhle, B.G. (1952), *Ancient India*, Bombay: Asia Publishing House.

Grierson, G.A. (1967), *A Linguistic Survey of India,* Vols. 1-3, Reprent, Delhi.

Gurung, Harka, "Nepali Nationalism, A matter of Consolidation", in *Magazine Himal*, March 2001.

Guha, Amalendu (1988), *Planters Raj to Swaraj*, reprint, New Delhi.

Gurung, Tejimala (2003), "Human Movement and the Colonial State : The Nepalis of Northeast India under British Empire" in *The Nepalis in Northeast India,* Ed. A.C. Sinha and T.B. Subba, New Delhi: Indus Publishing Co.

Heimendorf, Christov V.F (1947), Status of Interaction among the Hindu Caste and Peasantry, Ed. K.S. Mathur and B.C. Agarwal, Lucknow.

Hodgson, B.H. (1874), *Essays on Language,Literature and Religion of Nepal and Tibet*, London.

Hussain, Asad (1970), *British India's Relations with Kingdom of Nepal*, London: George Allen & Unwin Ltd.

Hussain, Monirul (1993), *The Assam Movement*, Delhi: Nanak Publication.

Hutt, Michael (1993), *Nepal in Nineties*, London: Oxford University Press.

Koirala, M.P., *A Role in Revolution*, Kathmandu, Nepal: Jagadamba Prakashan.

Kant, Roma (1968), *Indo-Nepalese Relations*, New Delhi: S. Chand & Co.

Kirkpatrick, W. (1801), *An Account of the Kingdom of Nepal*, London.

Landon, Percival, *Nepal,* Vol. II, Delhi: Cosmo Publication.

Luniya, B.N. (1998), *Evolution of Indian Culture*, Agra: Lakshminarayan Agarwal.

Majumdar, R.C. and Choudhury, S.C., *Advanced History of India.*

Majumdar, Kanchanmoy (1973), *Anglo-Nepalese Relations in Nineteenth Century*, Calcutta.

Mukherjee, K.L. (1995), *History of India,* Calcutta.

Muktan, K.K. (2002), *The Legendary Gorkhas*, Guahati: Spectrum Publications.

Narayan, Shriman (1971), *India and Nepal*, Delhi: Hind Pocket Books.

Nehru, Jawaharlal (1946), *The Discovery of India*, Calcutta: Jawaharlal Nehru Memorial Fund.

Oldfield, H.A. (1880), *Sketches from Nepal,* Vol. II, New Delhi: Cosmo Publication.

Pant, Y.P. and Jain (1980), *Rural Problems and Rural Development in Nepal*, New Delhi.

Palit, D.K. Maj. General (1984), *Sentinels of Northeast: Assam Rifles*, *New Delhi.*

Rahul, Ram (1978), *Himalaya as a Frontier*, New Delhi: Vikas Publishing House.

Regmi, D.R. (1969), *Ancient Nepal,* Calcutta: Rupbani Press.

Rustomji, N.K. and Ramble, Charles (1990) (Ed.), *Himalayan Environment and Culture*, New Delhi.

Sanwal, B.D. (1965), *Nepal and East India Co.*, Bombay: Asia Publishing House.

Singh, Raghunath, *Jagrat Nepal* (Hindi) Aurangabad, Benaras.

Singh, G.P. (1990), *The Kiratas in Ancient India*, New Delhi: Giayn Books.

Sinha, A.C. (1990), "The Indian Northeast Frontier and Nepalese Immigration" in *Himalayan Environment and Culture,* Ed. N.K. Rustomji and Charles Ramble, New Delhi.

Sinha, A.C. and Subba, T.B. (1993), *The Nepalese in Northeast India,* New Delhi: Indus Publishing Co.

Shakyas, Sujeev (2009), *Unleashing Nepal*, New Delhi: Penguin Books.

Shakespeare, L.W. (1977), *History of Assam Rifles*, Reprint.

Shreshtha, Kusum (1984), *Monarchy in Nepal,* Bombay.

Smith, V.A. (1924), *The Early History of India*, Oxford.

Timsina, Suman Raj (1992), *Nepali Community in India*, Delhi: Nanak Publication.

Thapar, Romila (1966), *History of India*, Part I, London: Penguin Books.

Upadhyaya, Bisnulal (1948), *Asame Nepaliharu* (in Nepali), Tezpur.

———, *Khan Mihali* (in Assamese) (2004), Tezpur: Sonitpur Comprint.

Vansittart, Eden (1915), *Gurkhas,* Calcutta: Government Printing Press.

Woodroff, Dorothy (1969), *Himalayan Frontiers*, London: Barrie & Rockliff.

Government Files and Reports

1. Foreign Department, Simla No. 18, dt. June 15, 1866, Ramsay to Foreign Secretary, Government of India.
2. Parliamentary Report on a scientific expedition to Nepal, Rome 1956, by Tucci, G.
3. Progress Report on Forest Administration, Assam, 1892-93.
4. Report on the Land Revenue Administration of Assam, 1919-20.
5. Report on the Land Revenue Administration of Assam Valley Division, 1939-1940.
6. The Administrative Report of Assam, 1912-13.

Journals and Newspapers

1. *Amrit Bazar Patrika*, dated 1st April, 1980.
2. *Assam Tribune*, dated 1st May, 1980.
3. *Shillong Times*, dated 10th July, 1987.
4. ———, dated 13th July, 1987.
5. ———, dated 14th July, 1987.
6. ———, dated 17th July, 1987.
7. ———, dated 18th July, 1987.
8. *Frontline Magazine*, December 4, 2009.
9. *Bulletin*, Assam Gorkha Sammelan, 1969-81.

Index